REEKING HAVOC

REEKING HAVOC

THE UNAUTHORIZED STORY OF
GIORGIO

STEVE GINSBERG

WARNER BOOKS

A Warner Communications Company

Ⓦ Warner Books, Inc., 666 Fifth Avenue, New York, NY 10103

Printed in the United States of America
First Printing: November 1989
10 9 8 7 6 5 4 3 2 1

Library of Congress Cataloging-in-Publication Data

Ginsberg, Steve.
    Reeking havoc : the unauthorized story of Giorgio / Steve
Ginsberg.
        p.   cm.
    ISBN 0-446-51464-0
    1. Georgio, Inc. 2. Perfumes industry—United States.   I. Title
HD9999.P3934G464   1989
338.7′66854′0973—dc20   89-40044
                                                            CIP

Jacket photo by Jan Jarecki
Book design by H. Roberts

For Mary

ACKNOWLEDGMENTS

In 1979, Michael Coady, then Group Publisher of Fairchild Publications, offered me a position with the Los Angeles bureau of *Women's Wear Daily* and among the many opportunities that move led to was this book. His recognition of the Giorgio story and insistence it be covered closely was a catalyst and I am grateful for his support.

In the course of research I interviewed over 150 people, including many in the cosmetics and retail industries. Gale Hayman was willing to talk about most subjects and generously gave over 20 hours of interviews. Jim Roth and David Horner dug deep into their files and memories and I appreciate their efforts.

Maureen and Eric Lasher, my agents, provided guidance and handholding and I thank Louise Farr for introducing me to them. Jeff Trachtenberg supplied much friendly advice while his sister, Martha Griffith, provided invaluable research. Nancy Wallis's computer expertise helped the transition from typewriter to word processor.

My colleagues at WWD, Jane Lane, Mary Merris, Pete Born, Maureen Sajbel, Glynis Costin and Art Streiber provided information and help.

I would like to thank the following important sources for this book: Jack Axelrod, Lydia Bunka, Robin Burns, Carlo Celoni, Helen Chaplin, Hillel Chodos, Gil Dembo, Steffi Dilworth, Samantha Drake, Carlo Di Giovanna, Luis Estevez, Doris Fields, Herb Fink, Chester Firestein, Joe

Forkish, Kathy Franzen, Susan Fried, Arline Friedman, Freddy Friedman, Michael Gould, George Grant, Marshall Grossman, Barbara Gyde, Halston, Frank Hoffer, Susanna Hoffman, Paul Houdayer, Peter Jaram, Stanley Kohlenberg, Martine Lago, Kenneth Jay Lane, Leonard Lauder, Joe Liguori, Bud Lindsay, Pamela Mason, Allan Mottus, John O'Reilly, Gilbert Paoli, Jim Preston, Allen and Kelli Questrom, Maurice Raviol, Bob Renberg, Margot Rogoff, Rikki Rothman, Bob Ruttenberg, Hank Schubert, Eugene Scanlan, Steve Somers, Igor Stalew, Michael Stern, Sidney Stricker, Katy Sweet, Patrick Terrail, Bertil Unger, Red Weiss, Paulette Weisenfeld, Jean Young.

Finally, *Reeking Havoc* would have been impossible to write without the encouragement and editing of Mary Goodstein Ginsberg, my wife.

Santa Monica, California
April, 1989

REEKING HAVOC

For a man as image and publicity conscious as Fred Hayman, February 28, 1985, was off to a good start. That morning's *Los Angeles Times* social column written by Jody Jacobs mentioned Fred twice. He was spotted at The Bistro, his favorite of Beverly Hills' chic eateries, lunching with Michael Newton of the Music Center. Then, at Jayne and Henry Berger's six-course dinner, Fred was among the "sartorially perfect gentlemen," according to the *Times*'s puffery. The day would end disastrously for Fred, its events eventually yielding the kind of publicity he dreads most.

Gale Hayman, Fred's business partner and ex-wife, had no reason to be in a good mood that day. Her feelings of isolation from their company, Giorgio, Inc., and betrayal by Fred were increasing right along with the mounting success of their Giorgio perfume. That evening a party was scheduled at Giorgio, the boutique at 273 North Rodeo Drive that Gale and Fred had built into Beverly Hills' flashiest store. The boutique had come to epitomize the city's glitzy life-style. Fred and Gale had worked hard to keep their personal differences in check for the last seven years, fearing their animosity could scuttle the astronomically successful businesses. Now Gale could no longer bear to watch Fred act as the main spokesman for the Giorgio fragrance she had created. After all, she considered herself the cosmetics industry's next Estée Lauder.

The party was being hosted by Fred and Michael Gould, the chief executive officer of J. W. Robinson, then the smallest but most fashion-forward of Los Angeles' four department stores. Giorgio had been carried in Robinson's for one year; sales were soaring on their way to an $11 million peak and a Giorgio men's cologne was about to be launched at the store. Smashing all California fragrance volume records with Giorgio, Robinson's deserved a salute. Fred thought a cocktail party for the store's one hundred sales associates and executives would be a gracious gesture and inspire future fragrance sales.

The ambitious Gould also had much to be thankful for. The success of Giorgio had allowed Robinson's to steal market share from Bullock's, the carriage-trade outfit long considered Los Angeles' most upscale store. Gould was eager to dethrone Bullock's, and having Giorgio exclusively in Southern California was an important trump card in his market-share war. As a special thank you to Giorgio, Gould was preparing a surprise: a copy of a three-paragraph letter he had written to Fred was going to be printed in that Sunday's *Los Angeles Times*. The letter was part of a double-page ad introducing the Giorgio men's fragrance at Robinson's. That ad was bad news as far as Gale Hayman was concerned.

Gould brought the framed ad with him to the party, where he engaged in small talk with his employees, sipped champagne, and enjoyed the circulating hors d'oeuvres. Katy Sweet, Giorgio's public-relations director, had him pose for photos with the Haymans and, all in all, the party seemed to be as cheery as the yellow-and-white stripes that dominated the boutique and the Giorgio package.

Fred, silver-haired and natty as always in a double-breasted suit, made the first speech. Ever the perfect host since his hotel banquet manager days, he grandly thanked the Robinson's crew for their enthusiasm and "superb achievement."

Gould then made a short speech and unveiled a Velox of the ad that he was presenting to Fred. As he thanked Fred "not only for the fragrance but more for [his] friendship," Gould hit a sensitive spot in Gale's frayed psyche. Not only had he failed to mention Gale's name in his speech, but he had omitted her name from the ad, as well. The letter praised Fred for starting a special relationship between Giorgio and Robinson's that had "grown into the promise of a lifetime partnership." Gould added, "I look forward to many more years together." Ironically, Gould subsequently would be fired from Robinson's and hired by Fred to run Giorgio at a seven-figure salary. Ultimately they, too, would clash.

It was clear that the evening's pleasantries were coming to a close. Gale's speech was tinged with tension as she attempted to control her anger over the Gould snub. She reminded the group that she was the creative force behind Giorgio and tried to get the saleswomen excited about the new treatment cream she was developing. Cornering Gould after her curt speech, she told him she was deeply hurt by not being included in the ad and wanted to know what he could do to rectify the situation. Humiliated, Gale fled the boutique after demanding that Gould change the ad before it hit the newsstands. She was accompanied by Peter Jaram, manager of the Giorgio men's department, who listened to Gale's complaints on the way to the parking lot.

Back at the store, Gould was perplexed and embarrassed. He would later describe the feeling as that of having been invited to a couple's home for dinner and causing the wife to flee because he had insulted her. David Horner, a Giorgio senior vice president, talked over the situation with Fred and assured Gould that the relationship between Robinson's and Giorgio was secure.

When Gould got home, there was a phone message from Gale, which he did not return. There was another message at 7:20 A.M. the next day. Gould's wife, Karen, called him at his office and asked him to return Gale's calls. Pressured, Gould told Karen to mind her own business. "I'm not going to call her back because I don't want to get into the middle of this." By 11 A.M. a messenger delivered a handwritten note from Gale. It read, "As the Estée Lauder of this company I am dismayed and truly wounded to be overlooked as I am in your forthcoming advertisement." Gould called Horner, told him about the note, and reiterated that he wasn't about to get involved in the escalating feud between Gale and Fred.

The ad was published as planned in Sunday's *Los Angeles Times*. The paper's one million readers had no idea of the turbulence it had caused. Michael Gould and Robinson's had ignored Gale Hayman's request for a published letter thanking her for creating Giorgio.

The episode with Gale was more than just an embarrassment to Fred Hayman. He knew Giorgio was no longer big enough for the two of them and that he would have to remove Gale from day-to-day management. Three nights later Gale was notified by a letter dropped on her doorstep that Giorgio's three-member board of directors had passed a resolution demoting her and exiling her from both the store and the Giorgio perfume company. Although she retained a 49 percent ownership in the company, she in effect had been severed after almost twenty years in the business. More significant, her partnership with Fred was finished.

The firing would trigger a $75 million lawsuit by Gale against Giorgio and Fred in May 1986. Their marital divorce three years earlier had been amicable and civilized compared to the corporate split. The court battle would lead to the all-cash sale of Giorgio, Inc., to Avon in June 1987 for $165 million, making Fred and Gale Hayman richer than most of the celebrities to whom they catered while building the boutique. Giorgio, the best-selling fragrance of the 1980s, and perhaps the scent of the century, was worth fighting over.

CHAPTER ONE

Paris, New York, and Suddenly Beverly Hills

Historically the fragrance industry's battlefield had been set on the opposite coast from a ten-thousand-square-foot Beverly Hills boutique dominated by a pool table, oak bar, and a wall filled with celebrity photos ranging from those of ex-president Lyndon Johnson to Connie Stevens. The war of the noses was waged behind closed mahogany doors and across sleek conference tables belonging to the large cosmetics companies in New York. The industry revolves around a handful of firms that have made the U.S. fragrance market the largest in the world, reaching retail sales of around $4 billion in 1988, according to the Fragrance Foundation, an industry support group.

Overall the cosmetics industry, which includes makeup, skin care, hair care, and toiletries, is a $17 billion business. It spends $1 billion annually in advertising. Growth in the 1980s was modest and few new companies were able to forge substantial sales and profits.

W. J. Fitzgerald, an economist who has tracked the industry since 1979, estimates that in 1987 sales of women's fragrances were $2.1 billion, exclusive of ancillary products (i.e., scented bath and body products). He calculates that department stores have a 50 percent share of the market.

The dominant corporations—Estée Lauder, Cosmair (L'Oréal, Lancôme, Ralph Lauren), Revlon, Chanel, Yves St. Laurent, Calvin Klein Cosmetics (Obsession), and Avon—are tucked into the most visible corporate real estate in mid-Manhattan, in monoliths such as the General Motors Building, Trump Tower, and 9 West 57th Street. All these companies employ teams of marketing mavens, packaging experts, and product developers who spend their careers trying to create a magic elixir and then marry it with a message that sells.

The fragrance industry's goal for the 1980s was to create a blockbuster fragrance, a scent that achieved record volume and captured the mood of the era, transcending time to become a classic. The decade had witnessed the launch of over 150 new women's fragrances, yet the only blockbusters were Giorgio and Calvin Klein's Obsession. The list of failures, however, is long. Most in the industry would be hard pressed to recall what Natchez, Champagne, J'ai Ose, Lutèce, Monogram, and Metal smelled or looked like; yet they will remember all the designers who licensed their names to fragrance houses. Several of the biggest fashion stars were fragrance flops, e.g., Valentino, Bill Blass, Perry Ellis, Bob Mackie, and James Galanos.

Until Giorgio's emergence, no blockbuster fragrance had come from any location other than New York or Paris. Before World War II, the center of the perfume industry was the region around Grasse, in the south of France, where the flowers used to make many perfumes are grown. French perfumeries such as Guerlain and Houbigant were distilling rose, jasmine, and patchouli to create fragrances as far back as the early 1800s. The French were able to control the U.S. market until the 1950s, when advertising-minded American companies started to gain market share. Estée Lauder, Revlon, Elizabeth Arden, Helena Rubinstein, and Charles of the Ritz were among the American firms who changed the rules of the industry and, in so doing, came to rule the business.

A large advertising-and-promotion budget was considered essential to a fragrance company's success. In 1987, the industry spent $126,278,900 on women's fragrance advertising, according to Leading National Advertisers, Inc. The biggest spenders were Revlon, $18,231,500; Cosmair, $13,801,600; and Estée Lauder $12,316,100. Giorgio, the top-selling women's fragrance in department stores, defied convention with an advertising expenditure of only $2,188,000 that did not even rank among the top ten.

Locked into predictable advertising patterns, the major companies plowed their dollars into monthly fashion magazines such as *Vogue, Elle, Glamour, Town and Country*, and *W*, using television during the peak Christmas selling season. Giorgio rewrote the advertising script by extensive use of scent strips inserted in both regional and national magazines, a ploy that caught the industry with its nose either up in the air or out to lunch.

"Hayman snuck up on us because he found a new method of merchandising and sampling," observed Stanley Kohlenberg, a twenty-year industry veteran currently president and CEO of Alfin Fragrances, Inc.

> Nobody ever thought of it. Putting a sample in a magazine? It was a one-of-a-kind idea. The technology was available to the industry but nobody had ever taken the chance. With Charles [Revson] dead, with Madame [Rubinstein] dead, and Elizabeth Arden dead there was only one entrepreneur left, and that's Mrs. Lauder, and she doesn't have to take chances anymore. She owned that class part of the business and what did she care? Gale and Fred were the new entrepreneurs and, what the hell, they gave it a shot. They didn't know enough about the business to know they might fail so they took a chance and it worked. Of course, once it worked everybody else jumped in; and now you can't lift up a magazine without getting a hernia from all the Scentstrips and then you choke to death when you open the book.

The industry has been able to produce just one or two blockbuster fragrances each decade. Chanel No. 5 roared out of Paris in 1924 to become not merely the first great designer fragrance, but the classic scent against which all others are measured. Coco Chanel's fashion look was simple, veering from the frills and furbelows of the 1920s. Perfumer Ernest Beaux mixed jasmine from Grasse with roses and ylang-ylang from Madagascar. The subtle yet compelling combination adhered to Chanel's dictum that, "In perfume, as in fashion, simple understatement is pure elegance," and, "Perfume should complement, never dominate, a woman's personality." Chanel, if she were alive today, no doubt would be horrified to smell the overpowering, everlasting, modern-era scents such as Giorgio, Obsession, and Passion.

Chanel was still a top-selling fragrance in the 1960s, with wholesale shipments around $25 million in the U.S., when it went into a decline caused by excessive distribution. Nothing kills a classy, snob-appeal scent quicker than overavailability. When every corner drugstore, duty-free shop, and K-Mart carries a fragrance, all the advertising hype on Madison Avenue cannot restore its image or mystique. Or so the industry thought until New York–based Chanel used Catherine Deneuve as its spokesperson. Chanel No. 5 had plunged to around $15 million in the early 1970s, but Deneuve's impact was startling and Chanel was reborn, rocketing to $35 million over a two-year span. In the 1980s, Chanel—now under Kitty D'Alessio, a former advertising executive at Norman, Craig & Kummel—has cut back the distribution of Chanel No. 5. This, along with a tightly distributed, sleek cosmetics line, has enabled Chanel to retain its cachet.

Chanel No. 5 remains the only fragrance in the industry that has been able to bridge both the mass (drugstores) and class (department stores) channels of distribution and continue to grow.

The 1920s also produced Guerlain's Shalimar, a powerfully sweet Oriental fragrance that would be a forerunner of the great modern scents such as Opium. Lanvin's Arpège was launched in 1927, followed in 1930 by Jean Patou's Joy. While they became international classics, these fragrances did not continuously produce major volume in the U.S. Arpège was the victim of misguided distribution, ending up in over twenty thousand doors (individual branch stores within a retail chain; e.g., Bullock's department store has 22 "doors," or branches) in the 1970s. Joy, conversely, was distributed so parsimoniously and was so costly (well over one hundred dollars an ounce in the 1970s) that it never had a chance to grow out of its rarefied niche. Joy's U.S. distributor for many years was Borden, the diversified dairy company. Industry quipsters often wondered, "How could Elsie the Cow market a fragrance?" and to a large extent they were justified.

The next blockbuster came in 1947. Nina Ricci's L'Air du Temps helped get the industry purring as it slowly recouped from the shortage of essential oils and packaging materials caused by World War II. L'Air had a light, almost faint topnote; and its magnificent René Lalique–designed, doves-in-flight bottle stopper was practically worth the price of the fragrance. L'Air peaked at $35 million in the U.S. in the mid-1970s, but has survived into the 1980s and is now part of Sanofi. Kohlenberg, then president of Sanofi Beauty Products, noting the success of Chanel No. 5, cut back L'Air's distribution in the hopes of bolstering the scent's image and attracting a new, younger customer. The brand is still a big seller in moderate department stores such as the May Company and The Broadway in Los Angeles and in 1987 accounted for sales of around $15 million in the U.S.

Perhaps the industry's all-time "elevator gagger" came out of the 1950s. Estée Lauder's Youth Dew, a concentrated bath oil, was launched at Bonwit Teller in 1953. After years of wearing light, subtle French fragrances, American women were ready for something heady. Youth Dew, at $8.50, was a fragrance that lasted all day and all night. Anyone sharing an enclosed space with a Youth Dew wearer felt like the prisoner of scent. Giorgio would be the elevator gagger of the 1980s.

Youth Dew also was powerful at the cash register. Many department stores saw sales of $5,000 a week in an era when $500 a week was considered a good take. In the 1950s, fragrances were considered stepchildren to cosmetics. Usage was relatively low and fragrances were usually sold as ancillary items alongside a cosmetics line.

Youth Dew was the original product Estée Lauder used for her gift-with-purchase, the innovative marketing technique that would help build her fledgling company into the prestige category leader. However, the ploy she invented to increase trial of the fragrance ended up costing the industry millions over the next thirty years and causing profit problems for her imitators. The seemingly simple sampling device mushroomed into a gimmicky gift business known as the purchase-with-purchase. The industry began selling everything from garment bags to sweatshirts, umbrellas, and watches—all at significantly reduced rates, e.g., for any twenty-five-dollar fragrance purchase you get a beach bag for only ten dollars. The purchase-with-purchase trained customers to shop the promotions rather than the fragrance, which led to brand disloyalty. Companies with good fragrances but inadequate promotions often were at a disadvantage; yet Giorgio became America's best-selling fragrance without resorting to a single "PWP" or "GWP" during its first three years in department stores. Giorgio finished 1987 with PWPs accounting for just 7 percent of sales, compared to an industry average of around 20 percent.

The success of Youth Dew was Lauder's springboard into the dominant position in department and specialty stores. Lauder avoided mass merchandisers (J. C. Penney, Mervyn's, Sears, etc.) altogether. This primarily upscale focus, along with carefully controlled drugstore distribution, enabled the Lauder family to build a $1.4 billion empire by 1987, with a healthy pretax profit well above 10 percent. In the stores where it does business, the Lauder corporation, with its three divisions—Estée Lauder, Clinique, and Aramis—has been able to represent well over 25 percent of the overall cosmetics business. Youth Dew still commands sizable counter space and contributes 20 percent to Lauder's overall fragrance business. It peaked in the mid-1970s, with volume around $50 million. White Linen and Beautiful, two of the company's contemporary fragrances, have grown steadily and account for more volume than Youth Dew today.

There was no blockbuster women's fragrance in the 1960s; although in 1966 Lauder introduced Aramis, the tortoiseshell-patterned men's line which, until recently, was the volume leader in prestige distribution channels. In 1987, after years of blitzkrieg advertising and promotion, Ralph Lauren's Polo cologne finally managed to topple Aramis from the top rung in many retail outlets.

Political turmoil and an antifashion life-style made the 1960s difficult years for the industry. In 1969, Revlon launched Norell. This first American designer scent would be a catalyst for the fragrance explosion of the 1970s. While sales of Norell never went above $11 million, Norell had the stamp of an American designer and was considered by many to be the first great fragrance made in the U.S. Until Norell, Revlon was known primarily for color (nail enamels, lipstick). Norell's limited success, however, would trigger Charles Revson's interest in the fragrance business and lead to the bold introduction of Charlie in 1973.

Charlie was the first life-style fragrance, the perfect scent and image for the blossoming women's liberation movement. Women were making aggressive strides in the work force, in the bedroom, and on the playing fields; and Charlie was a versatile companion for all these endeavors. Charlie revolutionized the industry, changing the way women used fragrance. Until Charlie, most women wore fragrance occasionally and mostly at night. Charlie was an everyday, daytime fragrance. What's more, it was affordable, which encouraged usage.

Soon almost every fragrance company launched a life-style scent. Madison Avenue sent battalions of young models prancing through magazines and television with the message that women have much more on their minds than marriage and family. Charlie was not meant to replace the heavier, sexier fragrances that were positioned for evening wear. Women were encouraged to have a collection of fragrances rather than one signature scent—the fragrance-wardrobe concept, another strategy designed to help spur the industry's growth.

Young women, especially, were drawn to Charlie, which marked an important turnabout for the industry. During the 1960s, with their accompanying antiestablishment values, high-school- and college-age women had virtually abandoned the industry, preferring earthy, natural musks to the commercially successful, traditional fragrances worn by their mothers and grandmothers.

Marketing executives at Revlon during the creation of Charlie say Charlie was similar in scent to Norell. By 1975, Charlie had racked up $55 million in the U.S. and went on to become the first American fragrance to achieve worldwide acceptance. It reached international sales of well over $100 million five years after it was launched. Ironically, Charlie was Revson's last and most successful product launch. He died in 1975, leaving Estée Lauder alone among the industry's original entrepreneurs.

Part of Revson's legacy was competition among fragrance marketing executives to take credit for Charlie's success. Sid Stricker, a Revlon International senior vice president during Revson's heyday in the 1960s, is now one of the industry's leading executive recruiters. He distastefully observes the self-promotion that occurs during job interviews. "In this business, success has many fathers. By actual count I have interviewed forty-nine people who have told me they were responsible for creating Charlie. I have a big picture of Revson above my chair; what kind of jerk do they think I am? Charlie [Revson] created Charlie. Everybody takes credit for everything but nobody ever said, 'It's my fault.' "

Opium, launched in 1978, went a step further than Charlie. Reflecting the fantasy of the sexual revolution unleashed in the late 1970s, Opium was a bold gamble that paid huge dividends to the Squibb Corporation and its subsidiary, Charles of the Ritz.

The battle to bring Opium to the American consumer was as provoking as Yves St. Laurent's vision. Squibb, a respected drug company, took a quantum risk in financing a fragrance with that name. For six months, Robert Miller, the international president of Ritz, tried to convince the Squibb board that the controversy over Opium would be mitigated by the fragrance's success with American women. St. Laurent, then at the peak of his design career, along with his manager, Pierre Bergé, was finally able to sway Richard Furlaud, Squibb's president.

The French-born Furlaud remained a Francophile, and was won over by St. Laurent's gift of an illustrated poem about mystery and romance. Furlaud told *Women's Wear Daily*, "A pharmaceutical company is not likely to have a perfume called Opium and a French advertising agency called Mafia. It creates a spectacular opportunity to be misunderstood. To explain to me what Opium meant, YSL wrote me a poem which was right out of Baudelaire and Rimbaud."

Opium was an instant success in Paris, so much so that the U.S. launch had to be delayed because the factory could not meet the European demand. When the fragrance was finally launched in the U.S. in 1978, it was a $20 million winner its first year, eventually ringing up worldwide sales of $100 million by 1980. The spicy, Oriental scent peaked at around $65 million in the U.S. Its primary container was a plastic reproduction of an inro, used by the Chinese to store fish hooks and opium. This was breakthrough packaging; the tooling alone required to thread a tassel through the container cost $250,000.

The industry was envious of Opium's innovations and success. Estée Lauder, in a jealous snit, attacked the fragrance in February 1978, in *Women's Wear Daily*, sniffing, "Women today don't want perfume. The era of the really strong perfume is dead. Many of the strong perfumes coming out today are cheaply made with synthetics. And Opium. When I saw St. Laurent's Opium I nearly passed out. Opium is my Youth Dew with a tassel."

Estee was so wrong that she would later pay Opium the ultimate compliment by trying to knock it off with her Cinnabar, a fragrance that thoroughly confused the consumer. Cinnabar was not a new fragrance, but a softer version of Youth Dew with an Oriental theme. Opium was just the start of a powerful collection of heavy scents that would rock the industry in the 1980s. Giorgio would be the heaviest and most successful of the group.

The chances of Fred and Gale Hayman creating the blockbuster fragrance of the 1980s were less than slim. The game was played in New

York and Paris by pros who not only had business degrees from prestigious universities, but also multimillion-dollar budgets to finance their ideas. Fred and Gale were Beverly Hills boutique owners without a college degree between them and without adequate financing. What's more, they had neither experience nor insight into the industry's mechanics.

Giorgio was not the first retail store attempting to trade on its logo in the launch of a fragrance. High-profile retailers such as Bloomingdale's, Wanamaker's, and Neiman-Marcus all tinkered with their own house brands, but the fragrances seldom got a second whiff from their customers and never went further than their own stores.

The Haymans, with their Giorgio perfume, were not selling their store as much as the life-style it had come to symbolize. By 1980, American consumers were on a status craze. "You are where you eat and you are what you drive," seemed to be the credo of an aggressive, upwardly mobile urban work force. Trendy restaurants and flashy cars, preoccupations in Beverly Hills, had hit the rest of the country. Consumers from Sheboygan to Sutton Place had been primed by the media to associate Beverly Hills with hedonistic glamour and the joys of materialism. They soaked up the California life-style on nighttime soaps; they read about it in Judith Krantz's sex-filled *Scruples*, about a Beverly Hills boutique; they voted for Ronald Reagan, the actor-president, in the landslide election of 1980.

The American dream was fast becoming a gated estate in Bel-Air, a cruise down Rodeo Drive in a Rolls-Royce Corniche, and a shopping spree in Giorgio. This California dream was nothing new. The Golden State has long been etched in the nation's psyche as a place to get rich quick. In 1849 gold fever gripped Northern California, triggering the state's growth. In the twentieth century great fortunes were built from the state's once bountiful natural resources: oil, agriculture, and real estate. The movie industry lured aspiring actors, including Gale Hayman's mother, who were seeking instant stardom.

Beverly Hills in the 1980s was proof that the dream could be realized. Busloads of Japanese and American tourists started a steady descent down Rodeo Drive in the late 1970s, wanting to take home a piece of the dream.

Fred and Gale Hayman exploited the fantasy, and in so doing struck it rich. A combination of propitious timing and unquenchable ambition enabled them to create the best-known boutique and fragrance in America during the first half of the 1980s. By following their instincts and ignoring the industry's rules, the Haymans steadfastly pursued the consumer. Their approach was simple and direct: get the powerful Giorgio fragrance under as many noses as possible. They had neither time nor money for the promotional games of the cosmetics industry.

Giorgio was launched in 1981 with an initial investment of $300,000 and an innovative scent-strip magazine advertising campaign. Four years later the $150-an-ounce perfume had become the best-selling fragrance in America, with annual sales over $70 million and an unheard-of 40 percent pretax profit. The volume was achieved despite limited distribution in only 350 department stores. Never in the industry's history had one fragrance done so much volume so quickly and in so few doors.

The Giorgio women's sensation was followed in 1984 by a men's fragrance that also became the top seller in many stores. Back-to-back breakthroughs of both women's and men's fragrances enabled Giorgio, Inc., to hit $100 million in 1985. Giorgio was the first $1 million fragrance at Bloomingdale's in New York, and by 1985 was doing $10 million there. At Robinson's in Los Angeles one out of every two bottles of perfume sold that year was a bottle of Giorgio. In London and Paris, where American fragrances seldom are taken seriously, Giorgio became the top-selling fragrance at Harrod's and Galeries Lafayette. It seemed Giorgio was on its way to becoming a full-fledged cosmetics company, à la Revlon and Estée Lauder, with a complete range of color and treatment products that would someday challenge those titans.

However, unlike Revlon, Lauder, Arden, or Rubinstein—companies founded by one autocratic man or woman—there were two ego-driven people behind the success of Giorgio. Their egos grew in proportion to the success of the fragrance—and so did their greed—leading to an acrimonious showdown befitting the Hollywood setting that spawned it all.

CHAPTER TWO

The Ballerina
and the
Apprentice Chef

The Gale and Fred Hayman story began in conflict during World War II. The German bombers that wreaked havoc in London in 1943 would prevent Gale Gardner from knowing her father. The Haymanns of Zurich, Switzerland, would be forced by spreading Naziism to flee Europe, providing Fred, seventeen, with the opportunity of a lifetime.

Fred Hayman (the n was dropped soon after the family arrived in the U.S.) was born in St. Gallen, a small textile town east of Zurich in the German-speaking part of Switzerland, on May 29, 1925, to Irma (née Levy) and Richard Pollag. On April 10, 1929, Richard Pollag died suddenly, leaving Irma a twenty-seven-year-old widow with two children (Fred's sister, Yvette, had been born in 1921). Pollag's sister, Fanny, died a year later, in May 1930; and Irma soon married Fanny's widower (Irma's brother-in-law), Julius Haymann, a prosperous, short (five-feet-four), and balding textile importer thirteen years her senior.

Originally from Frauenfeld, north of Zurich and near the German border, Haymann had an eight-year-old son, Eugene, the first cousin of Fred and Yvette. Fred and Yvette took Haymann's name, although according to local records they were never officially adopted by him. The three children went through the difficult but thorough Swiss school system. Fred hated it.

Irma was a tiny (five feet tall) aristocratic woman. Along with her petite stature, Fred inherited her dark eyes, dimples, and smooth youthful complexion. Born in 1896 in Morges, on Lake Geneva, close to the French border, Irma wore white gloves and a hat in public and had her dresses made in the small dress shops of Zurich, preferring simple Chanel-like designs.

The Haymanns collected antiques and art as the silk business flourished. However, Julius Haymann feared growing Naziism when, in the late 1930s, he anxiously watched the desperate immigration of Jewish refugees into Switzerland. He sold his business and took his family to Lisbon, Portugal, where they boarded the S.S. *Exeter*, bound for New York. Immigration papers state that the Haymann family arrived in New York on May 28, 1941. They settled in the then-stylish and recently opened Forest Hills South apartment complex at 113th Street and 77th Avenue in Forest Hills, Queens, and became naturalized citizens in May 1948.

According to Gale, Maurice Gardner, a handsome British military officer ("I don't know what branch"), came from Stratford-on-Avon. During 1942 he supposedly visited New York on leave and at a dance club met one of the dancers—auburn-haired, Romanesque-figured Natoma —whose real name was Geraldine La Rosa. It was wartime, and La Rosa instantly fell for this dashing, khaki-clad officer who, Gale says, had once posed for Brylcreem ads.

Gale Elizabeth Gardner, whose birth record reads Natoma Gardner, was born on September 1, 1943, at New York's St. Vincent's Hospital. Gale would later say, "She really didn't want to have me; it was an accident."

Leaving Geraldine in New York, Gardner allegedly returned to England. Gale maintains he was killed in a buzz-bomb attack on London when she was a year old. However, London's St. Catherine's House, where birth and death records of all British subjects are filed, has no death listing for a Maurice Gardner of Stratford-on-Avon during those years and Gale did not pursue her paternal lineage "to a great extent." Although Geraldine had seven brothers and sisters and parents in New York, she was estranged from them and refused to seek their help. She would raise Gale by herself while pursuing a career as an interpretive dancer.

Fred Hayman started work at New York's prestigious Waldorf-Astoria Hotel on October 1, 1942. A family connection had enabled Fred to get into the hotel's two-and-a-half-year apprentice-chef program run by Gabriel Lugot, a cranky Frenchman who previously had allowed only Europeans to enter the program. Eugene Scanlan was the first American Lugot had accepted, and he started the same day as Fred. The two would become lifelong friends. Scanlan recalls, "Lugot spoke very little English and all he did was call me stupid for three years. Freddie was Swiss and spoke fluent French and German and he moved right along."

Scanlan and Hayman were being paid twelve dollars a week and worked in all areas of the kitchen. They did everything from peeling onions and shrimp to cleaning large cast-iron kettles. As they advanced, they worked in the pastry, broiler, and cold-cuts stations. Fred was ambitious, hoping someday to be a restaurateur or hotel owner. He soon realized that the way to get ahead was not through the kitchen, and he began taking night classes in business administration at Columbia University.

Fred enlisted in the Navy in August 1943. He was sent to the Naval Training Station at Sampson, New York, where he was classified as an apprentice seaman. He floated for three years between Portsmouth, Virginia; Norfolk, Virginia; Portsmouth, New Hampshire; and Newport, Rhode Island, going from seaman, second class; to hospital apprentice, second class; to hospital apprentice, first class; to pharmacist's mate. Fred then spent six months on the fuel tanker U.S.S. *Nueces* and was discharged on May 19, 1946, at Lido Beach, Long Island.

While stationed at Norfolk, Fred continued his business courses at the College of William and Mary. He wrote letters to Scanlan and visited New York on weekends. "Fred always had an eye for attractive women and was very dapper. Even in a Navy uniform he looked very sharp. There was a certain classy air about him. He was moving all the time and was ambitious. There were no flies on Freddy."

After the war, Fred's parents returned to Zurich, and for the next seven years they divided their time between Forest Hills and Switzerland. Fred had a job waiting for him at the Waldorf, and he was awarded his diploma from the chef's course. He then toiled in the storeroom, where he learned about wines and food procurement. Next he was assigned to run menus between the banquet office and the kitchen; his language skills and knowledge provided a link between the two departments.

Claudius Charles Philippe, director of the hotel's banquet and catering department, had started his career at the Waldorf in 1931 in the same lowly position as Fred. The son of a French chef father and English mother, Philippe had apprenticed during the Depression under Oscar Tschirky, the Swiss gentleman better known in his prime as Oscar of the Waldorf. According to Scanlan, Philippe must have identified with the ambitious young Hayman. He brought Fred into the catering department around 1949 and subsequently became his stern and somewhat unethical mentor.

In 1948, Geraldine Gardner was diagnosed as having tuberculosis and was sent to a hospital in Saranac Lake, New York. Although the diagnosis was wrong, a lateral X ray showed a twelve-inch tumor on her lung. The tumor was benign, but the surgery cost Gardner four ribs and her dancing career.

During Geraldine's illness, little Gale was shuttled between three orphanages (Catholic, Episcopalian, and Jewish). "The Catholic home was very strict, you had to line up to go to the bathroom and it was just awful. My mother would send me toilet water and I would put it under my pillow, but by the next morning it was gone. I didn't do well and was unhappy there. I was put into the next place," Gale recalls.

While Gale was living at the Jewish orphanage, it appeared her mother might not survive. A young couple came to visit Gale daily and she remembers that the blond wife wore a fur coat Gale stroked when she sat on her lap. The Jewish couple almost adopted little Gale.

Geraldine recovered and she and Gale were reunited in 1949. They were living at 151 West 72nd Street and Gale attended first grade at the Professional Children's School. From second through seventh grades, Gale attended the Lillian Orchard School for Professional Children on Central Park South. Money was tight and Geraldine could not afford the tuition for Professional Children's School again until 1956. By then, Geraldine and Gale had moved into a small fourth-floor apartment in an old townhouse at 25 East 54th Street.

The lights of the flashing RCA sign crept under the curtains of Gale's small bedroom. She watched Geraldine, who took avid care of her body with lotions and creams, and recalls that her mother used only Albolene on her face, never soap, which was too drying. Even before Gale was ten years old, she went to Woolworth's and bought cheap, cardboard-backed, fifteen-cent vials of fragrance and mixed them together. Each night before bed, she would scent her pillow with these inexpensive essences. To Gale, they meant sweet dreams.

Geraldine did not have much time for Gale. Busy pursuing a theatrical career, she came in late at night and slept late the next day. Although Gale can't recall any of her mother's parts, she remembers that Geraldine had many male friends and received a lot of attention when they walked together down the street. Gale spent considerable time alone, roller skating in front of Lever House and ice skating at Rockefeller Center. She wanted to be very feminine, like her mother, and she remembers her first party dress was organza with little butterflies—bought, ironically, at an elegant dress shop in the Waldorf-Astoria.

Inside the regal, twin-towered hotel on Park Avenue, Fred was learning how to sell banquets and cater to the affluent. His teacher was Philippe, who in the late 1930s had managed to convince the Waldorf's president, Lucius Boomer, that Oscar Tschirky was past his prime. One day Oscar of the Waldorf found his desk had been moved out of the executive suite into a bullpen in the banquet department, and Philippe was running the Waldorf's catering operation.

Philippe ruled the banquet and catering departments with a skilled but Draconian hand. There had been no new hotel construction in New York since the war; and the Waldorf, with its twenty-two catering venues—including the Starlight Roof Ballroom, accommodating six hundred, and the elaborately tiered Grand Ballroom with space for sixteen hundred—was the city's preeminent hotel. Philippe knew how to maximize the advantage. Scanlan says, "Every single person that knew Claude thought that he was the greatest or hated his guts. He did a lot of things in those days that were unheard of. He would move a party from one room to another to get a larger party. He would move parties out of the Ballroom days before, even though the committee for the party already had invitations printed up. He was sued a number of times."

Lydia Bunka, Philippe's secretary in the late 1940s, would be Fred Hayman's secretary for three decades. She recalls, "Everyone was an assistant and we only had one boss, Philippe. He was the instructor and made sure everybody understood. He didn't ask; he demanded." Philippe was also vulgar. He had a bathroom adjacent to his office and often would continue dictating letters while urinating with the door open.

Yet Philippe was a genius at party giving, enjoying the minutiae of flower design, table settings, and menus. He understood the power of snob appeal and would argue with guests, refusing to give them the wine they wanted if it wasn't appropriate for the meal they ordered. Philippe was not afraid to belittle a client, since he knew there were others waiting in the wings for cancellations.

The salesmen were instructed always to sell up. If the client wanted to spend only thirty dollars a person, it was the salesman's job to convince the client to choose better wines and fancier entrées in order to boost the price. Philippe often would nag Fred jokingly after a big sale, "What's the matter, you couldn't get another fifty bucks?" John O'Reilly, seventy-three, one of the few assistants who challenged Philippe, continues to bad-mouth him. "Philippe used to say, 'If a customer comes in and leaves with more than carfare, that's a bad sale.'" Fred Hayman would emulate Philippe's perfectionism; Philippe, in turn, was impressed with Fred's manners, intelligence, language skills, and ability to work long hours—a prerequisite for climbing the Waldorf's career tower.

Philippe frequently slept overnight in his office and was at his desk by 8 A.M. Fred commuted from Forest Hills by the Independent subway line. He and the other assistants, O'Reilly, Charles Ohrell, and Joe Liguori, would arrive by 9 A.M. Their days ended around 9 P.M., and they usually put in a half day on Saturday. During the day they wore morning suits, (dark striped trousers with black jackets), changing into tuxedos in the evening to supervise the affairs they had booked.

There was plenty of work for Philippe's team. The hotel was hosting most of New York's important weddings, social events, and corporate dinners. Major social events, such as the April in Paris Ball, which Philippe conceived with Elsa Maxwell in 1951, captured the most space in newspapers. Political dinners also received a lot of press coverage. The Al Smith dinner, for instance, attracted not only the governors of New York and New Jersey, but often the president of the United States. However, the bread and butter for the banquet department were the more parochial weddings and bar mitzvahs. Gene Scanlan (currently general manager of New York's exclusive Union Club, in 1983 he retired as the Waldorf's general manager), who also escaped the kitchen, explains, "Probably sixty-five percent to seventy percent of our business in those days were the Jewish weddings and bar mitzvahs. If you lost the Jewish business and the Archdiocese you might as well lock up the place and throw away the key."

Philippe was responsible for a flourishing $4 million business. Wealthy parents might have to wait five years to book their daughter's wedding on a Saturday night at the Waldorf. Affluent Central Park West businessmen would rather have given their daughters away on a Monday at the Waldorf than risk the social consequences of a Saturday wedding at a less prestigious address.

Fred Hayman stood out among the assistant banquet managers. Although only five-feet-seven, he wore a derby and a dark Chesterfield coat with a velvet collar and by his mid-twenties had developed a reputation for tasteful flamboyance. Joe Liguori remembers Fred starting out in 1950 being assigned to the smaller parties but advancing quickly. "Fred came along nicely and was aggressive. He was tired of the standard menus we were working with. Fred could speak French fluently and this helped with the French menus we had. Lugot [the chef] would do special things for Fred, who was going after fancier starter courses and would use fish as an appetizer."

Fred knew how to motivate Lugot's kitchen. He had worked with many of the cooks and would go into the kitchen and ask them to pay attention to the parties he was responsible for. "Money talks. In those days a twenty-dollar bill meant something and Fred would throw you a twenty if you took care and did a good job on one of his parties," recalls Scanlan of his days in the kitchen during the Hayman era.

The Waldorf specialized in tailoring its parties for prestigious clients. When King Saud signed a contract with Standard Oil of California, a dinner for forty of the king's Saudi Arabian officials and friends was held in the Jade and adjoining Basil rooms on the second floor. O'Reilly and

Hayman worked the affair. The king wanted, in addition to forty dancing girls, a visual reprieve from his desert domain.

O'Reilly remembers, "We created a New England snow scene and we had toy trains on tracks running all over the place. The king controlled all the switches and somebody said to Philippe that I had gotten a large locomotive for my son. Freddy was putting everything together while I went home to get the locomotive so the king could pull his trains."

Every Friday Philippe would hold a meeting at 8 A.M. and criticize the assistants' work. Liguori remembers one meeting when Philippe blasted an assistant for getting up during a dance to lead the band. The assistants were supposed to stay in the background at the parties. Philippe was to be the department's only visible personality. The assistant banquet manager in question was fired and Fred Hayman learned a lesson in strong business leadership. Three decades later the idea of one-company/one-voice would cause a rift at Giorgio, Inc.

Philippe did not go unchallenged. O'Reilly, a gangly, six-foot-three Irishman who refused to accept tips, got into a spat with Philippe on New Year's Eve in 1951. Philippe had been told about O'Reilly's refusal to take a tip from Walter Weisinger, who was responsible for the New York Life Insurance conventions. O'Reilly had swayed Weisinger to hold his 1953 convention at the Waldorf, instead of in Chicago, and refused to take a hundred-dollar tip:

> Philippe on New Year's Eve tells me I had never done a good day's work in my life. When he said that he turned to Liguori and said, "Am I not right, Joe?" and he said yes. He turned to Ohrell and he said yes, also. He turned to Freddy Hayman and he said, "No, you're wrong." Then I knew I was talking to a man in Hayman.
>
> The best thing I remember about Freddy Hayman was that he was ethical, one of the few hotel men I worked with who was. When I retired, I said, "This is a business full of whoremasters, drunks, or thieves," but Hayman wasn't that way. Hayman was a gentleman; he had ethics and class from the beginning. There was no such thing as cheating a guest. I suspect he was that way because of his Swiss background. Those people are so straight.

Working every night until 9 P.M. and commuting back to Queens did not leave much time for Fred's social life. Women, however, were watching the dapper assistant banquet manager in his white-collared blue or striped shirts, patterned after Philippe's. Jean Young, one of Philippe's many secretaries, who also later worked at the Beverly Hilton, said Fred was playing the field and had no trouble meeting young women.

"He was very charming and had a beautiful smile. With his olive skin and straight black hair he reminded us of Sabu, an actor of our day."

The hotel had a reception desk at both the Park and Lexington Avenue entrances. The eye-catching Park Avenue receptionist was a buxom, pretty French Canadian named Thelma. Although the banquet office was upstairs on the fourth floor, Fred made it a point to greet Thelma in French every morning. They started dating, and a brief courtship led in 1951 to the first of Fred's three marriages. The hotel business, with its long hours and easy access to rooms and room service, is conducive to office romances. Fred would meet all three Mrs. Haymans on the job.

Thelma and Fred took an apartment about five blocks from Fred's parents, moving into a six-story building called the Berwick at 72-38 113th Street in Queens. While the building was not as well maintained as his parents', it provided quick access to the footbridge spanning the Grand Central Parkway leading to Willow Lake and the footpaths into the World's Fair grounds. Today rotting cars line the nature trail along the lake, but in the 1950s it was a nice spot for Fred and Thelma to walk on Sundays.

The Haymans dined at the best New York restaurants—Pavillon was one—often with the O'Reillys. Thinking business, the men would order the most complicated dishes on the menu and conjure ways to incorporate these expensive creations into their Waldorf menus.

Fred and Thelma were an affectionate couple, especially in front of other people. According to Joe Liguori's wife, Marti, "Freddy wouldn't go with a girl that didn't have everything, looks and personality. I remember going to New Jersey at Bob Kiehl's home and they were always showing their affections. I said to Joe, 'Why can't we do that?'"

The Liguori's marriage, however, would last forty years, while Fred and Thelma soon would be going to divorce court.

Geraldine Gardner may not have been an overly giving mother, but she did make sure her daughter would get an artistic education. In addition to her regular schooling, Gale was enrolled in the School of American Ballet in October 1951. Although Gale won a scholarship just once in the five years she took ballet training, her mother managed to keep her in private schools until 1958. "We didn't live extravagantly and I had to pay for my toe shoes, ballet shoes, and leotards, and she was able to support that. I didn't consider myself deprived. I was deprived of her time because she was up late at night and up late in the morning because she was leading the theater life."

Geraldine was a stage mother; and by the time Gale was thirteen, she had built an impressive résumé with modeling, television, and screen credits. She got her first modeling job at age eight, at Simplicity Patterns, and she remembers standing in a workroom where "They would fit a pattern on me." In 1952, Geraldine entered Gale in the *New York Mirror*'s Charming Child Contest and she won. In 1955, at age twelve, Gale became Miss New York City, winning a contest sponsored by Mildred of California, a garment company, under the auspices of Gimbels. The award read, "This certificate awarded to Gale Gardner who was selected as the most out-standingly beautiful personality girl, typifying best those qualities of charm and warmth found in the American girl in the CITY OF NEW YORK."

Gale's childhood screen credits included *It Should Happen to You, A Face in the Crowd*, and MGM's *Somebody Up There Likes Me*. Her television credits included small acting and dancing spots on *The Jackie Gleason Show, The Herb Sheldon Show, The Eve Hunter Show*, and four appearances in the *I Remember Mama* CBS production for the Arthritis Telethon.

However, dancing in the Nutcracker at City Center was the most important part for Gale, who was training to become a ballerina. The School of American Ballet is a pressure cooker that weans young girls from their childhood. The school was run primarily to develop dancers for the New York City Ballet Company. If young pupils failed to progress, they had to leave the school. Said Gale, "There was no star system. The ballerinas, the soloists, the corps de ballet, and the students all dressed, showered, and rehearsed together. Mr. B. [George Balanchine] would choreograph and he would train. He didn't do it verbally, but by move-ment, and the dancers would follow behind him. I never thought he spoke English because he never spoke."

Maria Tallchief and Allegra Kent were among the dancers in the troupe. Many of the instructors were stony Russians who pushed the stu-dents to get their insteps higher and improve their expressions and bal-ance. "[Anatole] Oboukhov would come up to you while you were trying to balance with one leg up and stare at you. You couldn't flinch or move. I learned never to be intimidated. I didn't realize it then but I do now."

Muriel Stewart, a British instructor, used to stick her fingers in Gale's back to correct her swayback. There were occasions when Gale had to correct her mistakes in dead silence in front of her peers. "At times you would sit in the locker room and burst into tears, but the next day you were back out there again. I was competitive with myself and only watched myself. I was pushing to get the instep higher and improve my turnout. Everything had to be coordinated."

Backstage at the ballet, Gale watched the prima ballerinas being made up. To her, the whole process was ultimate glamour. She envisioned herself someday sitting in front of the mirror being transformed into the star of the Nutcracker.

Strangely Gale had other dreams: "I would say my prayers before sleep and then start dreaming about having my own store and rummaging around in it. I was in the store all by myself and I could see the shelves of things from all kinds of household goods to wearing apparel to cosmetics. I remember even a ladder going up to the top shelf so I could get up there so I could pick out what I wanted. I never spent much time in stores as a girl. Capezio is where I spent most of my time, buying more leotards."

Wearing a navy-blue skirt, simple gray cardigan sweater, brown oxfords, and white socks, Gale waited for the bus in the doorway of Elizabeth Arden's Red Door salon on Fifth Avenue. She looked old for her age; at twelve Gale had the figure of an eighteen-year-old.

Gale learned early that looking older can be detrimental to getting ahead.

I was thirteen and for the first time the New York City Ballet was doing the Nutcracker. All the students were excited because there are many children's scenes in the beginning, when the kids run out under the tree, and we all thought we would be part of it. Jerome Robbins came in to check out the classes to pick students for that scene. He came in and we all lined up and he walks down the lineup and when he comes to me he says, "This one is too old," and then he picked the ones he liked for the scene. I looked eighteen because my figure had developed and I was devastated. In the locker room I was feeling absolutely terrible and I went home crying.

I went back the next day and was sulking to all my friends who were in that scene. Back in the class, Balanchine was selecting students for the Nutcracker's second act Trepak dance and he needed six dancers to leap through big hoops. He selected me, but the only problem was all the dancers he selected were eighteen and he chose me because he thought I was older. I went to the teacher after the class and asked if it was all right even though I wasn't eighteen. She said, "Don't talk and they won't know," so I danced in the Waltz of the Trepak. So don't ask me my age. When I met Fred I told him I was twenty-eight.

Geraldine was able to get Gale back into the more prestigious Professional Children's School in 1956 for the eighth grade, but money problems led Geraldine to write the school in June 1957 requesting a scholarship for Gale. Her letter to the school said she had been ill (lungs) and couldn't afford the full tuition. Gale wrote a letter as well, saying she learned the most there and would be sad not to be able to return. The school did not have sufficient funds to grant Gale a scholarship, however; and in October 1957 Gale was enrolled at the ADM Lodge School.

The job of assistant banquet manager could be tedious. While parties were going on, the assistants were in their offices making calls, soliciting business from people they couldn't reach during the day. Occasionally the assistants would go up to the Ballroom to make sure the host was satisfied with the service. Fred Hayman tried to make these frequent elevator rides fun. According to Liguori, "The elevator would be full and Fred would say, 'Joe, I'm a little tired; I think I'll take three weeks off and go to Switzerland and visit my friends,' and would start naming names. He could keep a straight face and could have been a good actor, he did it so well. He would say many things on the elevator that made him look like he had a lot of money, which he didn't."

Generosity was another trait that endeared Hayman to his coworkers. Jim Lawlor handled the setting up of the Waldorf's meeting rooms, and he was probably making less than half of an assistant banquet manager's salary. When Lawlor needed to have his teeth capped, Fred came to Liguori and said if they both put up one hundred dollars the dental work could be done. "You develop a great affection for a guy like that, because he was helping one of our people. Jim was a nice fellow, but wasn't aggressive and that's why he wasn't making much money. In those days one hundred dollars was a large amount; but since Fred initiated it, I gave him the money."

Fred had gone as far as he could in the banquet department by 1954. Philippe was still in control and there seemed to be no room for advancement. The Waldorf, however, was part of the Hilton chain and Conrad Hilton was planning to open his West Coast flagship in Beverly Hills in August 1955. He needed a banquet and catering director, and Philippe gave Fred a solid recommendation.

There were no roots to keep Fred in New York. The marriage did not withstand Thelma's jealousy. Fred was spending most of his time at the hotel, not at home with a wife who wanted to have a family. Fred's parents had moved back to Switzerland (they would lose their U.S. citizenship in 1959). Fred took the Hilton position and moved to Beverly Hills eight months before the hotel opened.

Ironically, had Fred stayed at the Waldorf he might have become Philippe's successor. Philippe's twenty-eight-year Waldorf career ended July 1, 1959, when he joined Zeckendorf Hotels as general manager of the Commodore Hotel. He had been indicted for income tax evasion in 1958, when federal prosecutors claimed he had amassed $300,000 in gratuities and kickbacks and failed to report income totaling $144,536. The indictment covered 1952 through 1955. Philippe was allowed to plead guilty to one count of the four-count indictment and was fined $10,000 in September 1960, as reported in *The New York Times*. He did not receive a jail sentence. The federal prosecutor, in a two-hour court hearing, outlined how Philippe had collected the kickbacks and gratuities, mostly from caterers who wanted to work at the Waldorf. The prosecutor also alleged that Philippe had dipped into an employees' fund that contained waiters' tips.

Zeckendorf let Philippe go in 1961. He subsequently was hired by Loew's Hotels to run the Summit Hotel and later the Americana. Philippe's career continued to deteriorate, and by the late 1960s he was mired in La Belle Creole, a Caribbean resort boondoggle in St. Martin that ran out of financing after 160 suites were finished. *Fortune* magazine had a field day with Philippe's fiasco in a May 1972 investigative piece. La Belle Creole is now a Hilton International Hotel. Philippe died on December 25, 1978. Fred Hayman was among those eulogizing him at St. Patrick's Cathedral. John O'Reilly stood outside the cathedral and, in shocking taste, handed laminated prayer cards to those leaving the church. On one side was printed, appropriately, "God grant me the serenity to accept the things I cannot change . . . Courage to change the things I can and wisdom to know the difference." On the other side of the card, O'Reilly had typeset, in bold, Philippe's epitaph:

C. C. Philippe
Died Dec. 25th 1978
Never
Gave
A
Sucker
An
Even
Break

Hayman would never forgive O'Reilly for his joke.

Fred's departure from the Waldorf was noted in the *World Telegram*. Scanlan also was leaving to take the executive chef's post at the new Fontainebleau Hotel in Miami. Ed Hastings, the Waldorf's executive assistant manager, was quitting, too. Columnist Frank Farrell wrote, somewhat dramatically, "How many pillars can you remove from a great edifice before it collapses?"

CHAPTER THREE

Beverly Hills
Rendezvous

There was much fanfare at the highly visible intersection of Santa Monica and Wilshire boulevards in Beverly Hills. It was August 1955, and Conrad Hilton's $16 million Beverly Hilton Hotel was about to open with a week of elegant social events designed to let the city and the West Coast know that the new first-class hotel had arrived.

Conrad Hilton controlled thirty hotels with thirty thousand guest rooms. He had been married to Zsa Zsa Gabor, and his home was not far from the hotel. The Beverly Hilton was to be his West Coast flagship, and also his vehicle for moving through Southern California society.

Unlike his massive hotels in New York and Chicago, which had well over one thousand rooms each, the Beverly Hilton contained only four hundred fifty rooms. The eight-and-a-half-acre site alone had cost $3.1 million. What the hotel lacked in size, it made up for in grandeur—or at least what was considered grand in the mid-fifties. The hotel was built with three slender eight-story wings, and many rooms had private balconies overlooking Beverly Hills. Among the rooms' lavish amenities were private bars, convertible studio beds, and televisions. The Beverly Hilton also had central air-conditioning, a feature that paid off in the hotel's first two months.

An unusual August heat wave during opening week caused many of the wealthy Texans and Arizonans staying at the un-air-conditioned Beverly Wilshire hotel to check out and check into the new hotel. These affluent visitors had fled the summer heat of their home states, and their abrupt departure from the Beverly Wilshire caused a 20 percent drop in that hotel's business.

Even without help from the weather, the Beverly Hilton would have done well. Its showy public-relations campaign included VIP junkets to the opening and gifts of star-shaped cuff links to guests and press. The hotel was being promoted in an era without aggressive hotel sales competition.

Edward Kirkeby was running the Beverly Wilshire at the time and Hernando Courtright was at the fabled Beverly Hills Hotel. Both hotels were solid, trading off fine reputations, but both lacked flair. Kirkeby thought word of mouth was the best way to achieve recognition for his hotels. He told his staffers, "If the customers want to have good food they come here; if they want something special, let them go to Romanoff's or Chasen's [restaurants]."

Such a conservative strategy made it easier for Fred Hayman and the Hilton hypemeisters who were flying in fresh bread, cheese, and turbot from France. Overnight they sought to raise the sophistication level of still provincial Beverly Hills. The Hilton's eighth-floor French restaurant, L'Escoffier, opened without prices on the menus and boasted California's first sommelier. However, there were few takers for his fine French wines, and the restaurant ran in the red for many years.

The Hilton broke other hotel traditions, as well. It offered yellow sheets and towels, as opposed to standard white; and instead of a standard uniform for all the help, staff in different areas of the hotel wore different uniforms. Unfortunately, although it looked impressive, this custom did not give the hotel manager much flexibility in deploying staff and was soon dropped.

The hotel was built by Del Webb who, in addition to a construction company, owned the New York Yankees with Dan Topping. Webb had built the Flamingo and Sahara Hotels in Las Vegas and the Beverly Hilton had a similar commercial feeling, although its stands of palm trees softened the garishness. Las Vegas in the 1950s was a glamorous vacation destination of the Beverly Hills cognoscenti.

A friend of Hilton's, architect Welton Becket, designed the hotel. It was barely functional from an operations point of view. The lobby was confusing and hard to find, the parking structure was inadequate, and the kitchen facilities were too small. In short, Conrad Hilton's $16 million palace was long on marble and glitz but did not flow. When the hotel's catering department suddenly began to exceed sales projections, trucks containing food and extra work space for a kitchen under siege had to be parked in the driveway.

Arthur Elmiger was tabbed by Hilton to orchestrate the kickoff. Elmiger was borrowed from Hilton International, where he had successfully launched Hilton hotels in other resort locales in the Caribbean and Puerto Rico. Elmiger, a Swiss, worked with Hayman on the opening and, after three months, was succeeded as general manager by Robert Groves, who was brought in from the Palmer House in Chicago. Groves would be Hayman's boss for the next nine years and they would clash.

Hayman worked with Elmiger in planning the opening parties and had autonomy in choosing the hotel's silver, linen, and glassware. He had oversized goblets copied from Pavillon in New York and had gold dinner sets custom designed. Fred's primary responsibility was to establish the hotel's food and beverage departments, but he was soon promoted by Groves to director of catering. Selling banquets was his goal; the Hilton's impeccable service, prestige, and snob appeal were the selling tools.

The Hilton was the first hotel in Los Angeles to offer French service at its banquets. Instead of serving individual plates of food, the staff put an empty, warmed plate at each place. Then a bevy of waiters served the guests from platters heaped with hot food. One waiter served the meat, the next the vegetables. There was one waiter for every ten Hilton guests, compared to one for every twenty in most operations. Overstaffing was a lesson Fred had learned at the Waldorf. He carried it with him to Beverly Hills.

The Beverly Hilton had several banquet venues, including the grand Conrad Hilton International Ballroom, the ornate Bali Room, and very French and pretentious L'Escoffier Room. The Bali Room was the hotel's largest dining room, and its wall-of-glass mural in a complex intarsia design raised more than a few curious eyebrows before it was taken down. Created to compete with the Ambassador's famed Cocoanut Grove, the Bali Room offered dinner and big-name entertainment. Although it drew such names as Charles Aznavour during the opening weeks, the room never clicked. The Conrad Hilton International Ballroom was larger than the competition at the Biltmore, Ambassador, and Beverly Hills Hotel, whose much smaller but posh Crystal Room accommodated just four hundred.

Hayman was given one of the hotel's large suites, which he used to entertain prospective banquet customers. His continental charm made it hard for the women who chaired the city's charity parties to say no. Helen Chaplin, who worked for many years as Hernando Courtright's publicist and special-events director at the Beverly Wilshire Hotel, watched Hayman steal her hotel's business in the 1950s.

Fred was giving parties and entertaining in his apartment. Jessie Blackiston was a friend of mine, and was with a lot of charities and was in charge of the Spencer Tracy clinic, and I said, "Why did you take your party from the Beverly Wilshire?" She said, "Oh, Helen, Fred has had us up to so many parties and lunches in his apartment, that we feel obligated." For Fred nothing was too much trouble, and people felt obligated to give him the business.

The hotel's first major corporate sales convention had a major impact on Fred Hayman's career. Rosemarie Reid, with a volume of $20 million, was the dominant swimwear company in the 1950s. Reid's assistant sales manager, Jack Axelrod, was shopping for a new place to hold an annual convention for the company's two-hundred-member sales force.

Axelrod had watched the Hilton being built. He read about the opening and convinced his management that the Hilton would be a sophisticated alternative to the Hotel Del Coronado in San Diego and the Newporter in Newport Beach—resorts with sports facilities that had the event in years past.

Some of my top management questioned me because it was a new hotel. I was very impressed with Fred's presentation and I got the feeling here is a fellow who knows what he is doing. Fred had heard of Reid and he thought our convention would be a feather in his cap. We always had a quality convention and we didn't hold back on money. Fred wanted us to go first class and that's why we hit it off. I wanted the best and we became friends.

Jack and Rita Axelrod were among Hayman's first friends in Beverly Hills. He would be married in their home, would become their partner in Giorgio, and would be sued by them; yet they remain on good terms today.

Back in New York, Gale Gardner was making progress at ballet school. Although her technique was not natural, she had worked hard to improve and her timing was excellent. Gale started to have the look of a ballerina, with her small head and long, although curvy, body. She copied her mother's makeup and skin-care regimens. "My mother was very vain and was very pretty and she knew it. She always wore beautiful makeup and spent time with her makeup and dressing and I would watch her. When you walked down the street with her, you knew the men were looking at her," Gale said.

Geraldine's acting career, however, was not progressing. She had moved with Gale to the Ansonia Hotel, which then was a refuge for artistic people. Opera reverberated throughout the building. There was not enough money for Gale to continue at the School of American Ballet; her training there ended in October 1956. Geraldine in late 1957 decided to uproot her daughter once again. According to Gale, "She said we were moving and I was very upset and I cried. We only had three days to move and I couldn't imagine moving at all, but she wanted to go to Los Angeles for acting opportunities."

Boarding the Twentieth Century Limited in January 1958, Geraldine and Gale spent five nights in upper and lower berths, with Gale crying most of the way. The friends she left behind would continue to pursue the dream she left behind; becoming a prima ballerina was now a fantasy. Southern California was being pounded by a winter storm when the train pulled into Union Station. Morosely, Gale watched the rain drip out of the palm trees. She was prepared for neither the weather nor the cultural shock of Hollywood.

The Gardners took a small, two-bedroom apartment in a building across from the Hollywood Roosevelt Hotel. The building was a short walk from Grauman's Chinese Theater, and many of the tenants were actors and actresses—several past their prime. Mack Sennett was one, and in his seventies regaled Gale with tales of his bathing beauties in the early years of Hollywood. "I was like a sponge, listening. I loved to be around older and wiser people than me," Gale said.

Le Conte Junior High School was a sprawling campus by New York standards, but had the wrong emphasis and curriculum as far as Gale was concerned. Volleyball class was an embarrassment. "It was awful that first day on the volleyball court. We had to serve and when I hit the ball it went straight up. My classmates all looked so hefty and unglamorous. The whole thing was so different I thought I was on Mars. I hated everything about it. I loathed the weather. Where is the snow? Where can you walk to? Where is Little Italy? Where is Chinatown, the library, the museums?"

Gale met Steffi Bekassy at Le Conte Junior High. According to Steffi,

She was an oddball, and definitely from New York. She wore colored tights, plaid skirts, regular shirts. She dressed differently. She was a totally isolated person, a major loner; she did her own thing, extremely individualistic. We became close. I was an oddball, also. I was shy, very shy. She was withdrawn, shy, and she got great grades. She almost had tunnel vision about what she was going to do. She wanted to see the world and to do something big and I always wanted to be a housewife with kids.

To escape Le Conte, Gale convinced the principal that she had completed most of the course work at school in New York. She was allowed to take a test to see if she had been misplaced. She passed and enrolled in Hollywood High School, but was still very much out of place.

Gale had lost her niche. Geraldine had enrolled her daughter in a ballet class in Hollywood soon after arriving, but Gale thought it was a joke. "It was awful and I walked out the first day. The floor was filthy, the teacher was terrible, and the standards were so much beneath what I had been doing. I knew ballet was over and I was trying to find myself."

In the late 1950s, Fred Hayman was building a catering business for the Beverly Hilton. He was also building his own family. Fred married the former Barbara Ann Sziraki, whom he had met in New York on a blind date arranged by Arthur Elmiger. Originally from Mansfield, Ohio, Barbara was a nursing student when she met Fred. He found her dark hair, cat-shaped face, and ample chest hard to resist. She came to Beverly Hills and Fred set her up with a job at Felsmann Florists, the hotel's flower and cigarette shop, in which he had a 50 percent stake. Barbara was twenty-one, had never been married, and was seven months pregnant when she and Fred were married on November 13, 1957, by a Lutheran clergywoman, Jayne Edelweiss. The Haymans' first son, Charles, was born on January 14, 1958. Robert Hayman was born on February 27, 1959, and Nicole Desiree Hayman followed on April 24, 1960.

The Hayman family lived in a three-bedroom suite on the hotel's second floor, complete with Swedish maid; and Barbara accompanied Fred to many of the social events he was either hosting or organizing. Not nearly as polished as Fred, she fit the Eliza Doolittle pattern of Fred's wives and lovers. As did Henry Higgins, Fred attempted to mold his women, and the results caused problems. Barbara would become a successful, UCLA-educated, Beverly Hills psychologist with a penchant for publicity and Eddie Fisher. But it was Gale Gardner Miller who would become Fred's most dramatic transformation. She would help make him a multimillionaire and cause him the most angst.

Fred was building his reputation at the Hilton with the help of his assistant, Paul Houdayer. The two solicited banquet business relentlessly. "Fred made it clear that we had to beat the pavement and get after the account and follow through. Fred's philosophy was he would never give up, but sometimes it was frustrating because many social parties were at the Biltmore or Ambassador hotels for years, and it was hard to bring those people in; but he didn't give up and year after year he would go after those parties."

Fred had learned the value of snob appeal from Philippe, and he always charged a few dollars more for the Hilton banquets. He never used low prices as an incentive to take business away from the competition. Groves said Hayman was the most competent food and beverage man he worked with in his forty-year hotel career. "In many hotels, the catering operation could do a lot of business but lose money; but Fred made it a profitable area for us. He was always watching costs and wouldn't waste money on unnecessary personnel. It wouldn't please Fred to offer a banquet at a dollar less than the Ambassador; he would charge more but promised better service and food."

The Beverly Hilton's facilities were the most modern in town, and Hayman had little trouble convincing Jewish groups, such as the Los Angeles and Beverly Hills Hadassah, to hold events there. Next he won over the prestigious Screen Actors Guild; but the breakthrough parties for Hayman came in 1958 with the Academy Awards Governors Ball and the Golden Globe Awards dinner. Both events brought the hotel international press coverage and allowed Hayman to mix with movie stars who later became his Giorgio clientele.

By 1958, the Hilton's management had realized the Bali Room was a failure and would never compete with the Ambassador's Cocoanut Grove. The room was closed and the space was used to enlarge the International Ballroom's capacity to seventeen hundred, making it the largest ballroom in Los Angeles and the perfect setting for the first Academy of Motion Picture Arts and Sciences Governors Ball. Although there were makeshift carpets on the ballroom floor, the room was more or less ready for the March 25 event.

Houdayer, now the head of Hilton's food and beverage operation in Nevada, recalls the party:

> We got the permission to reproduce the Oscar as a centerpiece for the dessert. We had an ice-cream mold made of Oscar and we served rum raisin ice cream with brandy dates, and we reproduced Oscar in the center. Each dessert platter served ten guests and it was quite spectacular when the parade of one hundred fifty waiters carried the trays in line. The parade was introduced by an eight-foot-tall award that had to be carried on shoulder boards by eight waiters. Fred liked to do some show business along with the food service.

This was the first time since the 1930s that a post-Oscar dinner dance had been organized by the Academy, and on that night in March 1958, most of Hollywood's A list showed up at the Beverly Hilton after watching *Bridge on the River Kwai* garner seven Oscars in the televised presentation at the Pantages Theatre. Spotted at the bash were Clark Gable, Kim Novak, Sophia Loren, Jennifer Jones, Cary Grant, Rock Hudson, and David Niven.

In his coverage of the 1958 Academy Awards and Governors Ball, *Daily Variety*'s Army Archerd noted, "The Bali Room is undergoing renovations and Seaton [Academy President, George] warned, 'Don't put your heels down too heavily or we'll have more footprints here than at Grauman's.' " Ray Anthony's band provided the music and Pearl Bailey sang. On the dance floor, Joanne Woodward held Paul Newman in one hand and in the other clutched the statuette she had won for best actress in *The Three Faces of Eve*.

Not all the stars made it to the party. Marlon Brando arrived at the Bali Room, took one look, and fled to Jay Kanter's, where he munched chicken until 4:30 A.M., according to *Variety*.

The evening's menu was relatively simple: filet mignon with fresh mushroom caps, served with hot hearts of palm amandine and puffed potatoes. But in the race for banquet and catering dollars, the Beverly Hilton became a star that night, making Fred Hayman's job that much easier. The Hilton continued to host the Governors' Ball until 1989 though the event does not command the same lineup of celebrities as Swifty Lazar's private Spago restaurant party.

Compared to the Academy Awards, the Golden Globe dinner was an intimate affair and an easy event for Hayman to capture. Bertil Unger, a lascivious Swede who wears a monocle and writes a column for one hundred European and South African newspapers, was the president of Hollywood's Foreign Press Club and in charge of the 1958 Golden Globe awards. Held at the Cocoanut Grove, the event had never been televised.

Unger felt the Globes deserved as much attention as the Academy Awards. He wanted it on television and realized the Hilton had a much bigger ballroom, more suitable to television than the Grove. Unger thinks the Academy Awards is a dull event:

Have you ever been to the Academy Awards? There are only five awards that you really give a damn about. At the Globes you have a big star turnout for every award and there are no technical awards. We don't give awards for the best set or the best new camera lens. At the Academy Awards you get guys who rent a tuxedo for the night and they show up in white socks and brown shoes. They pick up their award but the general public has never seen them before and will never see them again.

The 1958 Golden Globes were televised and the Press Club made more money on the event and got more headlines than in the previous fifteen years. Unger became friendly with Hayman and would drop Fred's name in his social column, usually alongside that of a star, whose name was mentioned first. Unger was invited to Hayman's suite for dinner and recalls the night when Fred allowed him to take the pretty Swedish maid home with him. "Fred and I think the same way in our personal lives. Every Sunday we would meet at the hotel and would go for walks and talk about business, women, and what is really good to eat, what is really sensational. I'm a gourmet cook and I love to cook for my guests, crab souffleés and other fancy stuff. Fred started his career with this and knows it inside and out."

Unger enjoyed watching Hayman relate to the stars:

He has the right kind of snootiness to impress movie people. He has a little accent and he wasn't impressed with the stars. The worst way to be with the stars is to be impressed with them and you become an ass. He let them come to him; he was very shrewd. A lot of people who make millions in the movies come out of no-where and they are easily impressed with themselves and they believe all the shit that is written about them. They are insecure and will buy status labels, and Fred knew that exactly when he went into the boutique.

When Unger contracted peritonitis in the early 1960s and nearly died, Hayman helped him out with a $500 loan that was never repaid. Fred never asked for the money. His generosity and his ability to radiate power is part of Hayman's attractiveness, Unger says. "I don't think he caters to women's mother instincts at all, like Dudley Moore. Women are impressed with Fred. If a man smells like money, women get horny immediately. They knew he had influence, power, and money; and that is the road to heaven."

Fred Hayman stood out in the unsophisticated Beverly Hills of the late 1950s. Even among the big stars, Hayman was able to make his presence known during social events, and many thought that he was actually running the hotel, not just the banquet and catering department. Pamela Mason, Norma Shearer, and Zsa Zsa Gabor were among those enamored of him. Mason said,

He was a very attractive and charming man, extraordinarily charismatic. He was lighthearted and very easy to be with. In those days I was mixing with Gary Cooper, Cary Grant, and Clark Gable, and Fred was able to stand out. He was the sort of man you assumed would be in charge of everything. At parties he stood out, he could talk to everybody about anything and was never at a loss. As they say, he could paddle his own canoe.

I was married to a terribly attractive man [James Mason], but very unsocial, and so I was envious of Barbara. I thought how lucky Barbara was to be to be married to a man like Fred. Wouldn't it be wonderful to be with a man who speaks to everyone, who seems to be happy, who seems to be having a good time, who knows which brandy to order yet doesn't drink it all. He was a very couth man.

Rodeo Drive in 1960 was just another minor artery in the network of streets running north and south of Beverly Hills' main bloodline, Wilshire Boulevard. The most successful stores in Beverly Hills were I. Magnin and Saks Fifth Avenue. They anchored Wilshire Boulevard along with the less successful Haggerty's Department Store, which would later become Bonwit Teller. These carriage-trade stores attracted the city's most affluent and powerful women, a group that included Nancy Reagan, Mrs. Armand Deutsch, Gloria (Mrs. Jimmy) Stewart, Alice Avery, and Ginny Milner. A flock of smaller stores, including Jax, Matthews, and Harry Cooper, was sprinkled between the flagships, and shoppers easily walked among them. Robinson's, the fourth Wilshire Boulevard anchor, was at the western end of Beverly Hills, adjacent to the Hilton. It would later become a critical outlet for the Haymans' Giorgio fragrance.

The Brown Derby Restaurant, a Beverly Hills landmark, sat on the corner of Rodeo and Wilshire. Just up the street, in the 200 North block of Rodeo, was a series of small shops that wrapped around the corner of Dayton Way. The stores included a shirtmaker, a photographer, a furrier, a tailor, and a small dress shop. The one-story building that housed the stores had been rebuilt in 1952 after a fire destroyed the roof. The fire had been started in the store of Kenneth Hopkins, a noted hatmaker of the era, by one of his young shopgirls.

Of the five businesses, Frank Hoffer's tailor shop and Yvel, a men's custom shirtmaker, were doing well. Ben Levy owned Yvel (Levy spelled backward), but Hoffer was the veteran Rodeo merchant, having been in the building since 1950. He had not seen Rodeo change much in the decade. The street still had gas stations, a toy store (Uncle Bernie's Toy Menagerie, which later was bought by F.A.O. Schwarz), a hardware store, and a stationery store, along with several restaurants frequented by movie people. The Luau, in the spot now taken up by the Rodeo Collection, was owned by Steve Crane, Lana Turner's husband during the scandalous Johnny Stompanato murder in 1958. The stars may have been eating on Rodeo Drive, but they weren't shopping there yet.

George Grant was working Beverly Hills in the late 1950s, peddling expensive Italian raincoats. Born in Russia, Grant knew Rita Axelrod, Jack's wife, from his childhood in Riga, Latvia. Grant had come to the United States when he was eighteen, moving to California in the 1930s to work in Hollywood. He could ride a horse, so central casting had placed him in a few westerns. He also had a bit part in *Bedtime Story*. During World War II, he was stationed at U.S. airbases in the Ukraine and also served at General Eisenhower's headquarters in Europe.

After the war, Grant got involved with Italian knit and rainwear manufacturers in New York and established Giorgio Creations, a company that represented Italian firms in the U.S. The raincoats, manufactured in Milan by Valstar, sold for one hundred dollars at retail. The price was exorbitant, but Grant had his ways of getting merchants to take his product.

Hoffer recalls Grant's sales technique. "He had the most beautiful raincoats and if you gave him a big enough order you could have an exclusive in Beverly Hills, and I bought a lot from him. They were so exclusive that he sold them to everyone, but it didn't hurt me because I had a good clientele and I could sell them. George was an adventurer and entrepreneur, but I didn't trust him from here to across the street."

Grant's road show began to fail after he made a deal to sell Giorgio Creations to Reliance, an apparel manufacturer not known for expensive clothing. But he found a way to sever his arrangement with Reliance, and he walked away with a year's salary. Grant then called the Axelrods to see if they would be interested in opening a retail store with him in Beverly Hills. It would be called Giorgio.

Grant, now seventy-nine, was selling jewelry at Chaumet, the elegant French jeweler on 57th Street, until October 1988, when illness forced him to retire. He recalls, "The Axelrods thought [the store] was a good idea. I was the only one to run it and draw a salary—ten thousand dollars a year, big deal. Our idea was to have only imports and just ladies' apparel."

Rita Axelrod had worked at I. Magnin, and with Jack working at Rosemarie Reid, they had the nucleus for a successful shop. Jack found the location at 9518 Dayton Way, a small shop next to an alley and a good fifty feet off Rodeo Drive. The shop was called Martil's, specializing in afternoon and cocktail dresses, sportswear, accessories, and millinery. The clothing was as stodgy as Martha E. Everett, the woman who ran it. She was retiring, and the Axelrods signed the lease with Harry Kem, who was managing the property for the Anderson sisters of Pasadena.

According to Jack Axelrod, "George had the two crests on the entrance handcarved in Italy and the yellow-and-white striped awnings put up. He brought the chandeliers from Austria and had two fellows from Hollywood, who seemed to have good taste, do the cabinets. With velveteen trim in the windows, the boutique had a European flair and a feeling that nobody else in Beverly Hills had."

Giorgio (the Italian version of George's first name) opened in 1961. It got off to a sluggish start. "The business was fair. It was difficult because the people were very slow in payment, so we ran short of money," Grant said. Needing a capital infusion, Jack Axelrod sought out prospective investors and came up with Fred Hayman.

Hayman was aware of the boutique through his association with the Axelrods. He met with Grant and they struck a deal. Hayman would get into the business for $12,000, the same stake the Axelrods and Grant originally had put up. "We needed him in the business because of all the connections he had. Because he knew everybody in town, every society woman knew him, so it was good business for us to go after him," said Axelrod.

However, with his job at the Hilton, Fred had to be careful about steering business to the little boutique for fear of a conflict of interest. He was already clashing with his boss, Groves, who was more than just a little envious of the niche Hayman had carved for himself in the community. By now Fred had charmed just about every society matron in Los Angeles, with the exception of Buff Chandler (Otis's mother), who refused Fred's invitation to visit his office at the hotel. Forced to play the role of silent partner, Hayman could not do much to help the store, although he checked in on it a few times a week. When people asked why he had invested in Giorgio, he told them it was an investment for his wife.

The store desperately needed help, and Grant was bored and losing patience. Beverly Hills women were not ready for an expensive, all-import boutique. They were loyal to I. Magnin and Saks. Even the larger boutiques on Rodeo, such as Amelia Gray, had built a customer following with primarily American designers.

Fred's wife, Barbara, was spending time in the store watching the books. Grant didn't want her hanging around, according to Hoffer, who had to listen to his frustrated neighbor. "Barbara and Grant didn't get along too well. The reason I know that is because George would spend quite a bit of time kibitzing with me. He would say, 'For a person who doesn't know anything, she is extremely opinionated.' He asked me what he should do and I told him, 'If you can't work together, you either buy them out or sell your interest to Fred.' "

Grant wishes, in retrospect, that he had had more patience and decided to buy Hayman and the Axelrods out. "It was my fault for leaving. I shouldn't have been fed up. I don't remember the volume we were doing, but we were making a profit. It was not as profitable as we would have liked it to be, but if it was that bad, Fred wouldn't have bought it. Fred should be grateful [for] the day he met me. If he hadn't met me, it would have never happened."

About eighteen months after Giorgio opened, Fred Hayman paid George Grant $12,000 for his share of the store, leaving the Axelrods as his only partners. Due to family problems, Jack and Rita Axelrod decided to drop out of the business. They reached a verbal agreement with Fred, allowing him to take sole ownership of the store. The understanding was that Fred would pay the Axelrods $6,500 for their 1.2 shares of capital stock in Giorgio. The Axelrods never got their money, and later they would take Fred to court.

Gale Gardner dropped out of Hollywood High in 1960. Marrying Andrew Miller at age sixteen preempted her graduation and ended her adolescence.

I don't remember how we met; a friend of mine introduced us. I thought of Andy as intellectual and as a bohemian. He worked in construction and was able to fix big caterpillar tractors. He did some work on Chavez Ravine [Dodger Stadium] and I remember one night when he took me out there for a ride on the tractors. When I first knew him, he was working, he drank milk and ate sandwiches. He was tall, blond, and handsome and was from German-American stock. He would play chess at a place called Bit of Europe and was part of a bohemian scene that was reading Nietzsche and was heavy into philosophy.

Four years older than Gale, Miller was her first love. They were married on April 13, 1960, in Los Angeles and were separated by September 13, 1961. Gale filed for divorce five days later. Miller liked to drink. The conflict between his intellectual curiosity and his construction work contributed to his drinking problem, and Gale had little tolerance for someone who lacked discipline. She was not a masochist, either. She claimed "grievous bodily injury and mental suffering" in the divorce filing, stating she was struck on September 10 and that there were many "acts of violence" before that date.

Roy Kurrasch, a Hollywood attorney whom Gale found in the Yellow Pages, represented her in court. Although Kurrasch cannot recall the case now, court papers indicate that the Millers' community property consisted of one 1956 Ford pickup truck valued at $800, personal paraphernalia, and a life insurance policy. In answer to the question, "Cash in possession of wife," Gale filled in "None." Under "Present financial worth," Gale wrote "Nil."

The couple had lived at 1804½ Kingsley, about two miles from Grauman's Chinese Theater in the hub of Hollywood. It was strictly Raymond Chandler turf, a block of dilapidated California bungalows and more recent two-story fifties apartments. After Gale split she took an apartment in the same neighborhood, at 1528 North Serrano Avenue. It was part of a bungalow court of ten tiny, boxy, red-tile-roofed apartments lit with cheap wall sconces. What may have been decent housing in the late 1930s was going to seed by the 1960s. The units are now home to Lebanese refugees.

Gale had taken typing and shorthand classes at Los Angeles Community College, and for a brief time she taught ballroom dancing at an Arthur Murray studio in Glendale. She also claims to have taken night courses to obtain her high-school diploma. At the time of the divorce, she was working as a general office clerk at Petersen Publishing Company (*Teen Magazine*, automotive and sports magazines) where she listed her monthly income at $220. Her annual income for the previous year had been $2,400, while her husband's estimated income was $4,000. Gale's weekly budget was so tight that she was forced to dine nightly on twenty-five-cent chicken potpies.

Miller was ordered to appear before Judge Roger Alton Pfaff on September 25, 1961. He never made a court appearance, and the last time Gale saw him was on October 15, 1962. The divorce was entered on November 5, becoming final on November 22, 1963. Miller was ordered to pay court and legal fees of $175 in seven monthly installments, but Gale ended up paying for Kurrasch's services over a ten-month period.

Gale had never adjusted to California. Her relationship with her mother had become strained, and she wanted to flee. She dreamed of escaping to Europe and took odd jobs to raise money, working briefly as a receptionist/secretary at Lincoln National Life Insurance Company. Gale wasn't bringing in much in the way of pay, but she pooled her money with a girlfriend's and bought a car for one hundred dollars. They took off for Northern California and Lake Tahoe. The car broke down in San Francisco, where at a car dealership they met a man who had just been robbed. He sold them his car cheaply and they made it to Lake Tahoe. "At Harrah's, I got a job as a Keno dealer and I did that for a summer.

I had never gambled a nickel in my life—it's not my style—but I made good money by working nights and weekends and I saved my money. When they needed somebody to work overtime, I would. I'm very focused—that's one of my big attributes."

When the summer ended, Gale and her friend Barbara went to Las Vegas looking for work. At the unemployment agency they met a man who told them there was a hotel outside of town that was looking for young women. Supposedly it paid good money and offered free lodging. They met the man at a gas station at 10 P.M. that night and followed him in their green four-door Buick. "For all my sophistication in the city there was a dichotomy, an area of me that was naïve about hookers and things." After a long drive down a dirt road, they arrived at a resort hotel—or so it appeared.

> He shows us around the hotel lobby and all these girls are wearing shorts and high heels and I still don't get it. He shows us the kitchen area and we sat down and had some soup. He was businesslike and told us we would be serving drinks. We got outside to the pool area and see individual cabanas with girls' names in neon on top of them—Betty, Jane, Susan. I looked at the pool and it was filled with leaves and I realize something is wrong, but I'm still not sure what it is. We were shown to our own room, but it wasn't a bungalow with a name on it. We were inside our room and I was feeling creepy. I said to my friend, "We've got to get out of here," and she said it was a house of prostitution.

Gale's friend decided they should sneak out, and before they left she told Gale she was six months pregnant. At midnight the two sneaked away from the Chicken Ranch, but they got lost and mired in the sand. They somehow managed to extricate themselves by wedging a board under one tire. Arriving back in Los Angeles in the winter of 1962, Barbara went home to her mother and Gale—who had been estranged from her mother since hooking up with Andy Miller—began to scan the *Los Angeles Times* classified section looking for work. She checked off an ad for a cocktail waitress at the Rendezvous Room of the Beverly Hilton Hotel. It offered good wages and benefits. Gale Miller had no idea just what benefits the job eventually would yield.

The Beverly Hilton's banquet and catering department had become the second highest volume producer in the Hilton chain, and Fred Hayman was primarily responsible. By 1961, the hotel was running a $3 million banquet operation, compared to the Waldorf's approximately $9 million. Banquets and catering normally contribute 40 percent of a major hotel's volume; but at both the Waldorf and the Beverly Hilton, the banquet departments accounted for over 50 percent of the business. The food and beverage business is a major profit center for a hotel—the profit margin is 25 percent.

Hayman's success led to a promotion. As the new resident manager, he had hands-on responsibility for the day-and-night operations of the hotel, in addition to overseeing the banquet and catering operation. His salary at the time was estimated by those who worked at the hotel to be around $50,000 annually. The more successful the hotel became, the more arrogant Fred was becoming, and he gained a reputation among staffers as being a "little Napoleon." Many guests and banquet customers assumed Fred was the general manager, running the entire hotel. Robert Groves may have been Fred's boss, but to the general public he was a faceless bureaucrat.

When dignitaries stayed at the hotel, Fred greeted them and made sure their needs were taken care of. The Democrats held their national convention in Los Angeles in 1960 and John F. Kennedy stayed at the hotel. The Axelrods recall being invited by Fred to the hotel to watch Kennedy land in a helicopter. Hayman met John Kennedy on several occasions. Photographs of the late president were displayed in the Giorgio boutique and at the Giorgio fragrance launch party, and a bust of Kennedy has a prominent spot in the den of Fred's Charleville Boulevard apartment in Beverly Hills. Fred would attend the January 1965 inauguration of Lyndon Johnson.

Upon his promotion to resident manager, Fred Hayman changed his wardrobe. Don Loper, a fanciful, fashionable clothing designer with a shop on South Rodeo Drive, next to the old Romanoff's, had become Hayman's friend. Loper walked into the Hilton's tailor shop and asked tailor Gunnar Talstead, a tall Norwegian, to see some fabrics and styles. Talstead had taken over the shop from Bud Watson, who had a drinking problem and had been in the business because of a connection with Del Webb. The shop had attracted a movie-star clientele, with Lorne Greene, Randolph Scott, Fred MacMurray, Robert Taylor, and Louie Prima among the regulars.

"Loper said he would get back to me, and then in a few days he came back with Fred and he wanted to build a new wardrobe for him," Talstead recollects:

I had to go down to the Ambassador Hotel to pick up a special gold button in the hotel's gold shop that Loper insisted on. The style of the suits at the time was wide but Loper said, "No, no, no, I want to cut this off at the shoulder," and we had to make it just the way Mr. Loper wanted. He wanted the suit tailored and narrow—a beautiful, modern-looking suit. We made a beautiful vest coat with a ribbon to show he was really dressed and formal. The suits were all dark and gray and he was the best dressed man you have ever seen.

Talstead estimates Hayman paid $200 to $300 per suit. He did not ask for any special discounts.

The job of resident hotel manager was custom-made for a perfectionist and workaholic like Fred Hayman. Paul Houdayer observed,

Fred was very demanding about grooming and all of us had to dress well. He was concerned about the food, the service, and the accommodations. A hotel takes wear and tear, but if something were torn or damaged it would get repaired right away. There are some hotels that don't do it right away, but he kept the Hilton in top condition. He was also a diplomat and would listen to complaints and could reach a sound solution. He wasn't confrontational.

Fred also was trying to be innovative and to keep the hotel, which was now almost ten years old, contemporary and classy. Some of the changes were successful, but some did not pan out. Hayman was responsible for the building of a new bar off the main lobby, called The Library. The bar had floor-to-ceiling bookshelves and was quiet, the way a posh bar in a first-class hotel should be. The bar, one of Hayman's successes, still exists today; and Fred put a miniature version of it in his Rodeo Drive boutique. However, his attempt to breathe some business life into the Rendezvous Room was less noteworthy.

In 1962, Hayman tried to give the Rendezvous a cultural lift and instituted an opera program. The experiment ended after six months. *Los Angeles Times* columnist Art Seidenbaum wrote on December 27, 1962, "The six month stay of grand opera singing in the Hilton Rendezvous Room has ended with many bows and with a distinct catch in the throat. The problem was that people who wanted opera also wanted dinner; you can't digest all that magnificent music on an empty stomach. And the Rendezvous Room, alas, is not set up to feed the fans." Hayman was quoted in the article as saying, "The people loved the music. If a mistake was made, it was mine in not worrying about both kinds of appetite at the same time."

For the next Rendezvous Room act, Hayman tried to bring in talented unknowns to perform for union scale wages. Auditions were held three afternoons each week as Hayman tried to find a backlog of singers and comedians. A steady stream of aspiring nobodies paraded before Hayman. They included Dvaughn Pershing Plus One, a guitar-and-piano team, and Ronald Kardashian, a singer who wore a bold checked jacket and was accompanied by a scratchy record player. Dan Moore told Hayman he was from Idaho and proceeded to sing a "Negro" work song, a love ballad, and an Israeli folk song. Moore was hired.

Several weeks later the Rendezvous Room had an opening for a cocktail waitress. The Hilton ran an ad that attracted Gale Miller. Fred Hayman was about to make the most important personnel decision of his life.

CHAPTER FOUR

Divorce
and Marriage,
Beverly Hills Style

Gale Miller needed a job. Getting to Europe was still a goal and she had to rebuild her finances. Her credit rating was nonexistent and she was buying her clothing at seedy thrift shops on Western Avenue and Hollywood Boulevard. The labels in these used clothes meant nothing to her; she did not follow fashion. Her tiny apartment at 2025 Grace Avenue in Hollywood was in the back of a private house. Rent was coming due, but Gale had a prospect.

The ad in the *Los Angeles Times* asked that "only the most experienced" apply for the Hilton job, which also required that applicants be twenty-one years of age. Gale was ready to lie about her cocktail-waitressing skills and her age. She walked into Fred Hayman's office in a bat-wing dress of moss-green wool. It was the kind of sexy dress Marilyn Monroe might have worn, tight in the bust with jeweled sleeves and tulip skirt. It also was the type of dress Christian Lacroix would update twenty-five years later. Gale's vampy, high-heeled black leather pumps and sheer stockings completed the nineteen-year-old's interview outfit.

"I walked into the office and Fred was sitting there. He was an attractive man, slightly graying and wearing a suit too large for him. He was slumping down in his chair and, having been in ballet, I noticed his posture. I noticed his dimples right away. He was extremely sophisticated and very worldly, and he smiled a great smile."

An employee had to be twenty-one years of age to serve liquor in California and Gale Miller said she was twenty-six. Her get-up made her look the part. Fred hired her after Gilbert Paoli, the manager of the Rendezvous Room, also screened her. Said Gale, "I was attracted to Fred that first day, but I wasn't going to do anything about it. I needed a job; I was very hungry for a job. It's easier to find a boyfriend. I could have gone that route easily, but that was not my choice. I wanted to be independent. I wasn't looking for a rich boyfriend, but a job. I didn't want to get involved, because I wanted to go to Europe." Her career as a cocktail waitress would be brief.

Fred's initial impression of Gale, according to Gilbert Paoli, was not flattering. Paoli recalls an evening at the Rendezvous Room, soon after Gale was hired. "Gale was sitting in a corner of the room, she was smoking and had a run in her stocking. Fred said to me, 'Why don't you fire her?' He wanted to fire her, but after that incident they started dating."

Barbara and Fred separated on February 27, 1963. Sziraki, who declined to discuss any portion of her relationship with Hayman, filed for divorce on June 18, 1963. She moved their three children, aged three, four, and five, into an apartment at 140 South Swall Drive in Beverly Hills.

Prior to the divorce filing, a full property settlement had been drawn up. Fred agreed to pay a property division sum of $10,000, plus a payment of $50,416.37 in quarterly installments of $1,250 over a ten-year period. In addition, Fred agreed to pay annual alimony of "not more than $12,600 and not less than $6,300" per calendar year, payable until the remarriage of the wife. The payment was based on Hayman's gross-income estimate of $36,000. If his income were to drop below $36,000, alimony would also be reduced; but it would still require 35 percent of his gross income, or $6,300, depending on which was greater.

The settlement also stipulated a child-support payment of $150 per month per child. In addition, Fred was to pick up all the expenses if the children went to private schools. Medical bills over fifty dollars were Fred's responsibility, as were Barbara's legal fees of $1,500. Finally, Fred was to assume all the couple's existing debts.

Considering these heavy obligations, Fred's net worth as of February 28, 1963, was not much. His property consisted of his checking account balance of $7,500 at City National Bank and savings of $11,000 in an account at Long Beach Federal Savings. There were two loans receivable to him, a $10,500 loan to Giorgio, Inc., and the $500 loan to Bertil Unger for his medical problem. Fred's stock portfolio included various holdings in twelve non-blue-chip firms ranging from two shares in Pillsbury Company to 3,067 shares in the Massachusetts Investor Growth Fund. He held five hundred shares of Metropolitan Development Corporation and

Equitable Savings & Loan. He also owned fifty shares of Felsmann Florists, in the Beverly Hilton, and five shares of Giorgio, Inc. In addition, Fred owned a small lot in Tamarisk Park Estates in Palm Springs.

On July 18, 1963, the court approved the settlement agreement and granted Barbara the divorce. The grounds were listed as "extreme cruelty" in the seventy-seven-page divorce filing, but did not give specifics.

Gale remembers seeing Barbara around the hotel just prior to the separation. "She would come into the Rendezvous Room with Fred and groups of people drinking and I would be serving drinks. When I met Fred he was very successful at the hotel, and his wife was wearing Don Loper clothes and fine jewelry. I worked every night until two A.M. and I didn't like it."

During the day Gale was taking courses in an attempt to find a career direction. She was interested in psychology and philosophy and went to foreign films on her day off. One night after the Haymans' separation, Gale got an invitation to have breakfast with Fred after work. They went to an all-night diner called Ollie Hammond on La Cienega Boulevard. "During this period, Fred would tell me how deeply hurt he was when Barbara left with the kids without any notice. We talked about it, and I believe I was a great source of comfort for Fred."

Gale's stint at the Rendezvous Room ended embarrassingly. On her twentieth birthday, she was stopped by the Beverly Hills police for a traffic violation after celebrating with a girlfriend at the Luau Restaurant on Rodeo Drive. Gale's driver's license listed her true age, and when she told the police she was a cocktail waitress, they became suspicious. That night two plainclothes men arrived at the Rendezvous Room and took Gale to police headquarters. After getting a lecture about the law in California, Gale promised she would not serve drinks again until she was twenty-one. That meant she was out of a job. She confessed her real age to Fred the next day. He was "shocked," thinking she was at least twenty-five.

Fred Hayman would shortly join Gale in the unemployment ranks. First, however, they would fall in love. "It took about three months. I was mad for him. There was great chemistry between us, and I really loved him. He was very physical and every morning he would be up running at six A.M."

Bob Groves, the general manager of the Hilton, did not share Gale's affections for Fred. Although he had built a tremendously successful catering business for the hotel, Fred also had built himself a little empire, and it was obvious to those working in the hotel that Groves thought Fred had overstepped his bounds.

Lydia Bunka, Fred's secretary, watched the situation deteriorate. "Fred clashed with Mr. Groves. He was a corporate man—very bureaucratic—and as dry as he was, Fred was flamboyant. They weren't seeing eye to eye. He was constraining Fred, who wanted to improve the quality and the service in the hotel."

Charles Bolla, who later became the hotel's general manager until his retirement in 1987, said Fred was ambitious, which fueled the clash. Groves had the job many in Beverly Hills thought belonged to Fred.

Groves, now retired and living outside Palm Springs, denies that he fired Fred. "All those people are really wrong. Fred had a nice offer from the Schines [owners of the Ambassador Hotel] and I couldn't blame him for taking a step up. I had no complaints about Fred. I stayed in the background, and he did enjoy the limelight; but it didn't bother me as long as the hotel was showing a profit." Groves said he did not approve of Fred's 50 percent interest in the hotel's flower shop, which Hayman was going to sell; but once Fred left the hotel the shop was subsequently closed as part of a remodeling. Hayman's investment in Giorgio was known and approved, Groves said.

Fred's successful years with the Hilton organization ended on a sour note when he was locked out of his office and then notified he was being let go. Paoli, who went to the Ambassador with Fred, said, "When a banquet director builds a clientele, he has a file that belongs to the hotel and they are afraid if he takes the file he will have the records of people who booked parties for years. They don't tell him he is being fired, they secure his office and then they tell him. That's the hotel business."

Not only was Fred without a job and a wife, he was also without a home, as he had been living at the Beverly Hilton. Fortunately he knew Ben Silberstein, who owned the Beverly Hills Hotel, and was offered a guest room there. Gale visited Fred during his several months in limbo. "He was going through a difficult time. He was feeling very isolated because no one was in contact with him. I was with him every night and he had a small room at the Beverly Hills Hotel—not the kind he was used to at the Beverly Hilton."

Hayman had been wooed in his final months at the Hilton by the management of the Ambassador Hotel. The Ambassador had been a great hotel when it opened in 1922; and its popular nightclub, the Cocoanut Grove, achieved international recognition as a Hollywood haunt. However, by the time Fred Hayman was named vice president and manager on January 11, 1964, the hotel needed an infusion of both capital and adrenaline.

A three-paragraph story in the *Los Angeles Times* on January 12 noted Hayman's twenty-one years with the Hilton organization, but erroneously reported that he had resigned as "president manager" of the Beverly Hilton. Philip Weber, Hayman's new boss, was quoted as saying Hayman would be responsible for all phases of the operation, including carrying out plans for a new twelve-hundred-room hotel on the present site on Wilshire Boulevard near Hancock Park and a banquet facility to accommodate twenty-five hundred. Welton Becket, the Beverly Hilton's mastermind, was in charge of the project, which was to include two office towers on Wilshire Boulevard.

The *Times* story did not hint at the family feud that was building within the Schine clan, who had owned the hotel since 1945. J. Myer Schine, the company's founder, then in his mid-seventies, entrusted his son, G. David Schine, with the family's diverse holdings. The Schine empire included eleven hotels, sixty movie theaters, and lucrative real estate. In addition to the twenty-three and a half acres on which the Ambassador sat, the Schines owned three thousand acres of oceanfront property in Palm Beach and Boca Raton, Florida, including the Boca Raton Hotel and Club. While J. Myer was wheeling and dealing in the 1950s, G. David gained notoriety while only in his twenties as an unpaid consultant to Senator Joseph McCarthy's committee investigating communists. Schine's attempts to get an Army commission were reported on television, where Schine was described as McCarthy's "controversial aide."

In January 1963, a management sweep was made at eight Schine hotels by G. David. Bill Ebersol, the vice president and general manager of the Pierre Hotel, was put in charge of the Ambassador. Ebersol's job was shortlived and his ouster provided a new job for Hayman. Ebersol recalls, "I went to work for David Schine and after four months his father came back in the picture and he didn't like what David had done and started undoing things that David did."

Hayman had built a solid team at the Hilton and, once in place at the Ambassador, he started reassembling the same players. He brought in over forty people. Paoli was put in charge of the Cocoanut Grove, Houdayer was named to head up food and beverage, and Irene Fuhrmann was put into the accounting department. Fuhrmann later became controller of Giorgio, Inc.

Hayman attempted to make the Ambassador competitive with the Beverly Hilton and Beverly Wilshire hotels by redecorating the Embassy Room and fixing up several other smaller rooms. The odds were against him. Not only were the Ambassador's facilities faded and its management divided, but the demographics of the city were shifting. Where once the mid-Wilshire district attracted businesses and tourists alike, Beverly Hills had become the coveted destination of the affluent traveler. Businesses, too, were moving west, in the direction of then new Century City. Though it would have taken a small miracle for Hayman to take market share away from the Beverly Hills hotels, he did begin making inroads, especially in the catering business.

"We doubled the [banquet] business in one year to around two and a half million dollars," said Houdayer, adding,

> We redid the restaurant; we fixed up the showroom [Cocoanut Grove], and this allowed us to take quite a bit of business away from the Beverly Hilton. We stole many of Fred's old accounts and we had many new-car-announcement parties, fashion shows, and luncheons. When we went there, there were a number of local and regional conventions with exhibits and we replaced them with the good social events. Conventions require many meeting rooms and you use up your space and you don't produce any food and beverage revenue, and so we brought some profitable business there.

Although the Ambassador was more than a full-time job, Hayman had concerns about Giorgio. His little investment on Dayton Way was becoming troublesome. The murky circumstances surrounding Fred's buyout of the Axelrods in 1963 were the cause of a lawsuit filed by Jack and Rita Axelrod on January 30, 1964. The breach-of-contract complaint accused Fred of reneging on an oral agreement with Rita Axelrod. The agreement, according to court documents, stipulated that Fred had verbally agreed to pay Rita $6,500 for her 1.2 shares of capital stock in Giorgio, Inc.

The suit dragged on for a year. Fred was supposed to make a court appearance on January 15, 1965, but he was granted a continuance because he was in Washington, D.C. (with Gale) at President Johnson's inauguration. Fred's attorney, Ernest Braun, wrote in his defense that the "alleged oral agreement for sale of shares of stock is invalid and unenforceable under the statute of frauds," and added that no agreement had been reached with Rita Axelrod. Rita's attorney argued that Rita delivered her stock and resigned as a Giorgio director. Horace Kalik wrote the court, "The defendant has refused and still refuses to pay the plaintiff all or any portion of the aforesaid sum of $6,500 despite plaintiff's written demands for such payment."

The case was dropped by March 1965, leaving Fred the sole owner of Giorgio for just the $12,000 he had paid George Grant. The Axelrods remain friends with Hayman today. Jack Axelrod said, "We decided the friendship meant more to us than the money." This little legal imbroglio foreshadowed the storm that Fred and Gale would generate twenty years later in their battle for control of Giorgio.

Gale Miller may have had a new boyfriend, but she had not made a good first impression on his friends and acquaintances. Fred's men friends thought Gale was sexy, but the women found her a little tacky. Some thought Gale was Mexican because of her dark complexion. Lydia Bunka, Fred's protective secretary, saw Gale working in the Hilton and said, "I thought she wasn't his type and it was a mistake. I didn't think she was in his league."

As he had transformed Barbara into a conservatively stylish woman, Fred sought to make over Gale. Rita Axelrod, who had watched Fred remake Barbara, said, "He does something to women and they become beautiful. He does a Pygmalion on them. Barbara was a little country girl, but Gale—she didn't look like anything. Fred can bring out the looks. He sees something that nobody else will see."

The outlandish thrift-shop wardrobe Gale had collected had to go.

When I met Fred, he hated my clothes; and we gave them all to Frank Maxwell [a houseman at the Hilton], even the dress that I bought from Jax that I had seen in *Vogue* and saved up to buy. It was a white, high-necked poetic cotton dress and it was thirty-six dollars. It was a cute dress, but he thought it was horrendous. From a girl who wore thrift-shop clothes to a girl who was wearing expensive clothes—that to me was elevation, that was going forward. I wasn't complaining at all. I thought it was fun to wear a whole new style. It was glen plaid suits, black patent leather shoes. As I look back, it was too old for me then. His taste was older, more formal and classic. It appears he was shaping me—he has that tendency—but he didn't shape my personality. In no way did he shape my creativity, my strength, or my ambition. Maybe I'm the only woman in his life that he didn't do that to.

The nagging question of Gale's career came up and Fred asked what her strong interests were. When she answered beauty and fashion, Fred sent her off to Comer and Drane, a beauty trade school that offered a two-year course in subjects ranging from electrolysis to hair coloring and skin care. After completing a manicuring course, Gale dropped out of the school because she wanted to work and help Fred with his heavy payments. Although not yet married, they lived together in a small, noisy apartment on Harper Avenue in West Hollywood.

Jerry Rothschild's barbershop on Beverly Drive in Beverly Hills hired Gale and she manicured some of the richest nails in the city. It was the kind of job that could have been a way out from Fred and his problems, but Gale was committed. "I was very thorough and made good money. There were a lot of opportunities to meet successful men and I could have easily diverted to an easier life. I was cute and young, but I didn't choose that route. I was loyal to Fred."

Fred's hotel career was coming to an inauspicious end. The Ambassador had perked up under Hayman. Several high-profile visitors, including the Beatles, stayed at the hotel. The Cocoanut Grove was booking Barbra Streisand for $3,000 a week, filling the room with a thousand people and making money; but the Schines' internal squabbling led to an attempted sale of the family holdings to Realty Equities Corporation of New York. Although an earlier attempt to sell the company to New York real-estate king Harry Helmsley had fallen through, a contract to sell to Realty Equities was signed and it appeared the Schines would walk away with slightly under $75 million. Realty Equities was planning to sell off most of the assets valued at over $150 million, but it intended to keep the Ambassador and build a Rockefeller Center–type complex, including a large underground retail center.

The deal was never consummated and the Schine family feud worsened. G. David's brother, C. Richard, had been running the family's Florida real-estate operation and, after their father's retirement, took on G. David in a battle for control of the company. The executive office at the Ambassador Hotel had the state-of-siege look of a Third World presidential palace during a bloodless coup. Fred Hayman had resigned just prior to C. Richard's sudden ousting of the entire Hayman team. Bunka was in Hayman's office when the coup was being attempted. "Richard came in with security guards and said he was taking over the hotel from his father, and we couldn't get into our offices. They were sealed. We were allowed to be free and do whatever we wanted, but, oh boy, it was a mess."

G. David would retaliate with his own goon squad of a dozen security men and retake the hotel. G. David reinstated the Hayman team. The bickering abated when Lester Crown, J. Myer's son-in-law, interceded and restored a semblance of calm; but the hotel's momentum was crushed and the master plan was never enacted. By 1967, G. David Schine had become a Hollywood producer. He produced *The French Connection*, and currently operates a technology company in Hollywood. He says his brother was never involved and does not recall the power struggle.

The hotel's chances of staging a comeback were ended the nightmarish June night in 1968 when Robert F. Kennedy was gunned down in its pantry. The five-hundred-room hotel was closed in January 1989 and has been for sale since May 1987.

His failure and frustration at the Ambassador led Fred Hayman to become entrepreneurial. He was miscast in the corporate world, dreading meetings and having little patience with back-office politics. Owning a restaurant seemed like the perfect solution.

Joe Drown, the affluent owner of the Bel-Air Hotel, had watched Hayman's success at the Hilton. In his later years, Drown's idea of a good time was going into the study of his Bel-Air home at 801 Stone Canyon Road and poring over the financial statements of the various businesses in which he had invested. He anonymously donated large sums to charities and was very much a recluse when he decided to take the majority interest in Mike Lyman's Restaurant in downtown Los Angeles. Fred Hayman was to be the front man who would run it. Hayman also invested $30,000 of his own money in the restaurant. According to Gale, that was all the money Fred had in 1966.

If Hayman's timing was bad at the Ambassador, it was worse at Mike Lyman's. There had been six Mike Lyman's around the city during the restaurant chain's heyday in the 1940s. The location at 8th and Hill in downtown Los Angeles did a substantial lunch business catering to garment manufacturers. By the mid-sixties, though, downtown Los Angeles was on the decline, which was hastened by race riots in nearby Watts. The restaurant was acquired for less than $50,000, according to Gene Baker, who was the controller for Lyman's Grill. He said Hayman completely changed the restaurant's menu and décor from English tavern to French bistro. A gourmet liquor store was opened adjacent to the restaurant.

Renamed Fred Hayman's Downtown, the restaurant never caught on, despite the efforts of Fred and Gale. Gale dropped Fred off at work every day at 8 A.M. and then drove their Lincoln back to their one-bedroom apartment at 153 South Camden Drive in Beverly Hills. Gale was acting as Fred's assistant in the restaurant and also working as a manicurist in Beverly Hills.

On November 21, 1966, Fred and Gale took two hours off in the afternoon, walked up Hill Street to the county courthouse, and got married. Lydia Bunka and Irene Fuhrmann trudged up the hill with them and Judge William Rosenthal performed the civil ceremony. Gale wore a black-and-white Chanel-like suit she had bought at Giorgio. The outfit made her look considerably older than her twenty-three years. Although graying, Fred was a youthful-looking forty-one. The Haymans went back to work that afternoon. There was no money or time for a honeymoon.

No amount of Fred's attractive maître d' techniques could save the failing restaurant. Hayman formed an honorary club called the Bull and Bear for select customers, mostly garment manufacturers, and would often send them free drinks. Herb Fink, who later opened several boutiques on Rodeo Drive and in 1988 launched a fragrance called Spoiled, ate in the restaurant daily and remembers Fred sending over free drinks to his table. Fink thought the freebie was "sporty."

George Foos, the chief executive of the May Company, also came into the restaurant frequently:

I got to know Fred quite well and one day he said he wanted to come over to my office. He and his wife came over and told me they were thinking about opening an apparel shop in Beverly Hills and asked if I thought it was a good idea. I said, "Fred, there are a zillion apparel shops and unless you have something different I can't see it would make any sense." I did everything to discourage them and the next thing I can remember Fred was standing in his empty Beverly Hills store and saying the business was "tough, but we are going to make it," and they made it work.

Just before Fred closed the downtown restaurant, Gale started working at Giorgio. The boutique, which was being managed by Marian Waxman, was losing money and Fred had taken a loan from his mother to keep it open, according to Gale. The store carried apparel made by Los Angeles–based manufacturers and lines sold by representatives based in Southern California. Waxman had retail experience working at Harry Finer's in the Fairfax district, and her husband, Sam, was the manager of Eddie Harth's men's store on Wilshire Boulevard in Beverly Hills. Marian understood store operations and how to buy. Gale was an eager student.

"When I went into the store, I worked for nothing. I was the errand girl. I would receive merchandise and I learned how to mark it and ship it. I would sweep the floor, clean off the street before we opened, and Windex the windows and make the store look neat. If any typing needed to be done, I would do that," Gale recalls.

Waxman took Gale on her buying trips downtown and together they bought off-the-shoulder Marilyn Monroe–style cocktail dresses. Not satisfied with the standard 50 percent markup, Waxman made deals with the manufacturers, buying groups of ten styles at a reduced wholesale price and taking a higher markup. Manufacturers were willing to unload overstocked inventories to a small store like Giorgio that did not compete with their major accounts. Waxman and Gale would load piles of the manufacturers' outcasts into the Lincoln, mark them up, and then put them out on the Giorgio sales floor. The store was barely breaking even, but Waxman was encouraging Gale, telling her she had a good eye for the merchandise.

"Marian was a good teacher. She taught me the mechanics of the business, the way you mark things up. I was learning what it was like and I was enjoying it. She was very clever with the money and made sure every piece that came into the store had a good markup." Gale was excited about the store's potential and talked about it with Fred every night. He began to listen as his restaurant career became more frustrating.

While struggling with the downtown restaurant, Drown and Hayman opened another restaurant called Hamburger Tavern in Beverly Hills. Hayman's concept was a menu of twenty-one unusual variations of hamburgers. It might have worked had not Marilyn and Harry Lewis conceived their Hamburger Hamlet restaurant a few years earlier. Hamburger Tavern did not do well, despite a visible location on Wilshire Boulevard, and Fred did not get along well with David Price, Drown's attorney. Fred dropped out and started looking for another restaurant project. He was negotiating to take over Romanoff's location on South Rodeo Drive, but he was not making much progress.

Gale recalls, "I was telling Fred how the merchandise in the store could be a lot better, and I would talk about the store. Fred said to me, 'This deal at Romanoff's is not going through. I think I would like to spend a few months at the store with you. Let's see if the two of us can do something with it. If it doesn't work, we will sell Giorgio.' "

Fred Hayman was finished with the hotel and restaurant businesses. He applied the skills he had honed there to the Giorgio boutique, becoming the richest one-store retailer in Beverly Hills and perhaps America.

CHAPTER FIVE

A Store
Is Born

In May 1967, Fred Hayman joined Gale in the store full time and they immediately started doing things right. First they fired Waxman; then they brought in a jobber and cleaned out all the old merchandise. The clothes had never fit properly, nor had there had been any originality in them since the store's inception. Receiving little money for the old inventory, the Haymans sought investors to help replenish the stock. After failing to find anyone willing to risk his money, they took out a small-business loan.

Sales volume was under $100,000 and the store was not profitable. Its major assets were the eye-catching yellow-and-white stripes, the energy of Fred and Gale, and Marian Waxman's card file, which contained a list of manufacturers and sales representatives.

That summer the Haymans took their first buying trip together. They drove ten miles down Wilshire Boulevard to the Sheraton Town House Hotel near MacArthur Park. They pretended to know what they were doing.

Neither of us had ever placed an order. Fred said to the salesman, "We would like to buy these dresses." The salesman says, "Fine," and takes out an order book and gives it to Fred and he passes it to me. Marian had written all the orders before and I had not seen the form with all these terms and stuff. Instead of writing the quantities next to the sizes (six-eight-ten-twelve, etc.), I started making X's. He looked at us like, "Who are these people?" and asked us, "Where did you say your store was?" He was rather kind and said, "Here, let me do it," and he wrote those first orders for Victoria Royal's beaded chiffon dresses and evening clothes.

George Grant had set up a buying service in Italy and Fred agreed to pay him a monthly fee to supply Giorgio with quality imports that could take a healthy markup. The relationship did not last long because Gale and Grant clashed. Grant said,

Fred was very lucky he met Gale. Barbara gave him three kids and the other one gave him millions. Gale had a good sense of style but she was a bitch to the first degree. I was supposed to do the buying from Rome for three hundred dollars a month but Gale wanted me to work practically full time for them. So I told her, "This is what I'll do for you, and if you don't like it, you know what you can do." She was unreasonable I thought, so I quit.

Rodeo Drive in 1967 was still a seed awaiting cultivation in the high-fashion turf. The three blocks from Wilshire Boulevard north to Santa Monica Boulevard were dominated by restaurants, gas stations, and service-oriented shops. Gene Shacove, a hairdresser, had his salon on Rodeo Drive and would later inspire Warren Beatty's lusty lead character in *Shampoo*. There were a few high-fashion stores. Marvin Chanin's Paraphernalia featured Rudi Gernreich, and Amelia Gray sold expensive American designer clothing. There were no boutiques on the street specializing in European designer clothing, nor were there hordes of tourists. Beverly Hills was still a small town where Danny Kaye and his softball team played at Roxbury Park and ate postgame pastrami sandwiches at Nate 'n Al's delicatessen.

George Grant had furnished Giorgio with a heavy brass étagère on which small items were displayed. In straightening out the store, Fred decided to use the clunky piece of furniture as a miniature bar. He brought in bottles of liquor and had Gale serve drinks. Every day, Fred manicured the shiny-leafed ligustrums in their white pots outside the shop. When a customer came in, it was he who did the schmoozing while Gale observed. Fred had sold expensive weddings and bar mitzvahs for fifteen years; now he merely was asking rich women to buy dresses.

A customer would walk in and Fred would start to chitchat, "How is your husband, how is your son?" He is very subtle. While he was doing this I would size her up and try and figure out what she would like to buy. I would be the one to say, "Oh, Mrs. Grant, we just got this dress in. How do you like it? I think you would look terrific in it." We worked well together and when they were ready to go into the fitting room I would take over.

Business was slow the first eighteen months and the store lost $40,000 in 1968. Fred started a direct-mail campaign to try to hype the business in a gracious manner. Personal notes inviting the women to come in, have a free drink, and see his new venture were part of the soft-sell come-on. Although Fred had known many stars and socialites at the Hilton and Ambassador, there was some uneasiness between them now. From a powerful hotelier Fred had become a shopkeeper, and some people snubbed him. Fred considered this a challenge rather than a comedown. After almost twenty years in the hotel business, he had grown to dislike corporate life and was determined to build his own business. At this point his staff consisted of himself and Gale. Lydia Bunka helped out, doing secretarial work on weekends, but that soon changed.

Several women who had known Fred at the hotel finally started shopping at Giorgio and began to enjoy the little boutique. Director Vincente Minnelli's then-wife, Denise, had given a surprise birthday party for him at the Beverly Hilton in the early sixties and remembered how efficient and obsessive Fred was about details. She became an early Giorgio customer because of the personal attention she knew she could expect from Fred. Naja Gardiner, whose late husband, British actor Reginald Gardiner, had appeared in thirty-seven films, said the shop had a personality and a new point of view:

> Most of the stores in Beverly Hills, such as I. Magnin and Saks, carried the same things. When Fred came into Giorgio he said, "Come in, my lady, have a little drink." I thought it was original and relaxing to come in, sit down, talk with the proprietor, and have a few laughs. When I went to Giorgio, I had the feeling I was going to Paris or Milan to buy something. It was the beginning of the resurrection of Beverly Hills.

The merchandising breakthrough that established Giorgio as a fashion store occurred about eighteen months after Fred and Gale had teamed up. Leon Block, the owner of Dunhill of London's U.S. franchise, had produced a man-tailored sports jacket for Jacqueline Onassis and was seeking a West Coast outlet for the design. Block approached the Haymans at the suggestion of George Grant. He presented the jacket to them in the boutique and had Gale try it on. "The jacket was double-breasted and came in a navy hopsack fabric. While Fred and Leon were negotiating, a customer came in and I sold the blazer. Leon turned to Fred, not realizing we were married, and said, 'This girl is a terrific saleswoman. Don't let her go.' We ordered five pieces—one in each size—and that item was one of the things that got us going in the beginning," Gale recalls.

The blazer, priced at $125, caught on; over the next ten years it would become a staple in the Giorgio stock. The jacket was lightweight, perfect for the California climate, and the not-so-mere fact that Jackie O wore the jacket made Beverly Hills women take notice. Actress Norma Shearer bought the jacket in a multitude of colors. Wallis Annenberg, daughter of media tycoon Walter Annenberg, not only bought it in several colors, but ordered it in different lengths and wanted the pants to match. Janet Leigh and Ginny Mancini also purchased it.

Realizing they had a hot item, Fred and Gale pushed Block to make the jacket in assorted colors and fabrications, ranging from vicuña to wool. The store offered variations of the jacket in a coat dress and full-length coat. Now retired and living in the Ritz Towers in New York, Block recalls that Giorgio had the California exclusive on the jacket and that the tiny boutique soon became a $100,000 account for Dunhill of London. Block, who later shipped suits and ties to Giorgio, sold his franchise back to Dunhill's parent company in 1984 for $3.5 million.

The Dunhill jacket success gave the Haymans needed cash flow, but they still could not afford to go on buying trips to New York and Paris. Carefully managing their limited finances, Fred was eager to expand the store. Irene Fuhrmann, Fred's loyal controller, said,

> Hayman was always astute with the figures. He developed his own format for reviewing numbers. He loves percentages . . . could always see problems in statements quickly. From the outset the business was very carefully planned; otherwise the store could never have grown so quickly and profitably. I think his European sensibilities show up in his business style. Spend as much as you have and not more. He has always believed in growing from within from profits. We never spent more than we could afford. He was never a believer in taking big loans.

While Fred was handling the financial side, Gale was studiously trying to learn the fashion business. Staying up late at night to clip every fashion magazine she could get her hands on, Gale absorbed the international trends and tried to blend them with her own fashion point of view. Color was important to her and the boutique stocked nothing murky or drab. To the contrary, Fred and Gale tried vibrant—and often successful—experiments with turquoise, yellow, and purple.

Whenever a movie star or socialite entered the store, Gale's fashion antennae zeroed in. "I studied Denise Minnelli [now Denise Hale], the way she would be in the fitting room with a fitter and take a very inexpensive dress and remodel it completely. She would remove the collar; she would raise the waistband and take off the belt and it would start looking like a Courrèges. She would put a sapphire pin on it and then I would see her photographed in the social columns."

Norma Shearer had numerous fittings for a single pair of pants, and Gale learned the nuances of tailoring. "Our customers were not avant-garde; but they knew fashion, quality, and fit. I learned that you could have a fabulous dress, but if it didn't fit you would lose the sale. I was a stickler on quality control. It was a big issue with me and I had to fight with manufacturers in the beginning when I had no clout. They didn't want to take the clothes back." Gale fought with several manufacturers and designers and lost important lines because of it.

Gale's emotional and confrontational approach to the business was balanced by Fred's calming diplomacy. If Gale worked with a cautious customer for two hours and no sale resulted, she came home at night and cried. Fred, on the other hand, preached the often forgotten dictum "The customer is always right," and encouraged Gale to keep showing women a variety of styles and accessories to maximize a sale. Once they said no or showed impatience, it was time to pull away without forcing the sale.

The sales training soon took effect and Gale developed a coterie of women who considered her their fashion guru. Fred provided Gale with a stage; now she was starting to pirouette on her way to becoming a prima retailer. Her costumes reflected the latest trends. A customer could walk in and find Gale dressed like a tarty little French schoolgirl in a beret, black stockings, and ballet slippers. Other times she was a coiffed, cosmopolitan New York sophisticate. Gale was the store's interactive mannequin, while Fred was its punctilious maître d'.

The circle of star customers grew and they began to spend more of their wardrobe budgets and allowances in the store. Although Janet Leigh had Edith Head making her gowns for the Oscars, she bought almost her entire wardrobe at Giorgio because she did not enjoy browsing in many stores and she trusted Gale:

> I really don't like to go to ten stores to find one thing; I don't have
> the time. It was wonderful to go to Giorgio and get whatever I

needed unless it was tennis clothes. Gale would always wait on me. If I didn't like something, she wouldn't push it on me. Some stores will insist, "This is wonderful," but she didn't linger on something that wasn't right. If I said the price was too much, she would find me something within the price I wanted to pay and I liked that. I didn't get hassled."

Gale was more aggressive with some women and did try to shape them. Ellen Graham, a photographer who specializes in celebrity portraits for the top fashion magazines, had shopped mostly in New York. She found the Beverly Hills stores too provincial until she discovered Giorgio in the late 1960s. "I thought Gale was a hard sell. She usually turned me toward bright things that I would never look at, clothes that were a little more flamboyant, flashy, and feminine. Gale was an expert at selling and she could talk me into anything, whether I liked it or not, and I liked it. I respected her. I thought she knew what she was doing and she had style."

Although the Haymans had established a liberal return policy at Giorgio, when an affluent customer returned a dress after wearing it for a special occasion Gale would become indignant, not wanting to take it back. Fred, however, encouraged loans to customers and coached Gale not to fight over such incidents because trust is critical in building a loyal patron. Over the years, the Haymans found the majority of their customers were honest and did not try to take advantage of their lenient policy.

Giorgio was an eclectic little store. It combined Fred's continental formality with Gale's funkiness. Fred never addressed a customer by her first name, an officious touch that, in casual Beverly Hills, impressed some people. From the start, the Giorgio look was flamboyant and sexy, the way Gale enjoyed dressing. Although Fred took a conservative approach to his own wardrobe and grooming (he never wore fragrance), he grasped the commercial potential of appealing to Beverly Hills' growing nouveau riche population and Hollywood's new crop of stars. These new stars wanted glitz and Giorgio provided it in beads, sequins, and fur-trimmed coats.

There is a saying in the apparel industry, "You can never get poor by catering to poor taste," and Giorgio's detractors attribute the store's early success to its ability to corral fashion victims. As the store became more successful in the early 1970s, it carried a wider spectrum of merchandise, catering to more classic tastes with dark suits and conservative silk dresses. However, the store did not gain its notoriety by playing it safe.

Designer Luiz Estevez won the Coty Award in the late 1960s and moved to Los Angeles in 1968 because it reminded him of his native Cuba. He had entrée into the highest Hollywood social circles and witnessed the changing of the social guard, a change that helped Fred and Gale build their business.

I remember going to a party for Barbra Streisand at the Ray Starks' when he brought her out to do *Funny Girl,* and he had a big tent and there were all the stars there. Streisand sat in the corner and never moved. By then most of the famous Hollywood stars had either died or peaked. There was a whole new group such as Ryan O'Neal coming along. The days of Mayer and Goetz had its peak. When Fred and Gale opened their store the new element was coming along.

Miss Stella had the couture salon at I. Magnin, and Mary Benny and Edie Goetz and a whole clique was shopping there and buying the couture copies Magnin made for them. When that ended, Fred and Gale moved in. Their success was the timing. It was the right idea for the right place and for the right people. Their merchandise was Hollywood glamour, a little bit glitzy, but quality. It was on the borderline of chic.

During the 1930s, 1940s, and into the early 1950s, the big studios owned Hollywood and dictated what their stars wore. The studios had costume designers, hairdressers, and wardrobers and made sure their properties were always well dressed and manicured. Howard W. Koch, a director in the 1950s who would later produce eight Academy Awards presentations in the 1970s and 1980s, recalls,

When a star went to a press conference or went to lunch at the Brown Derby, they [sic] looked smashing. I can remember seeing Betty Grable getting out of a car to go into the Brown Derby and she had on the right stockings, the right dress, and the perfect little hat. The studio made sure they looked that way, and the only time they were able to let down was in Malibu, which was their escape. Even in Palm Springs, where the dress is less formal, they were stylish and casually chic because of the gambling joints out there and the big contingent of people Darryl F. Zanuck had out there. They never looked like they just came out of bed or had rats in their hair. It was a different era, but the whole world changed and became more casual.

Left to their own fashion predilections, actresses and actors frequently failed to look the glamorous part. Many of those who had begun to shop on Rodeo Drive had no sense of style and were not that interested in clothing. The Marlene Dietrichs and Gloria Swansons were the exception rather than the rule. Herb Fink opened his Theodore boutique on Rodeo in 1969, and to this day says the movie crowd is the worst dressed, not only in Beverly Hills, but the world.

> The movie crowd is pretty, or studied and arty and not necessarily well dressed. It's not one of the things that is of keen interest to them—although dressy clothes are important because they go to premieres—but they don't know how to wear daytime clothes. Most people don't. In the old days you bought a skirt from one company and you didn't have to have a great mentality for putting something together. The biggest decision was what jewelry to wear with it. When we opened we tried to create images, we wanted to give them the freedom to express themselves. Giorgio in those days was pretty much Las Vegas to me, glitzy.

Giorgio's glitzy reputation was partially due to the adventurous designers Fred and Gale were discovering in New York. Following their success with Dunhill's blazer, Fred and Gale maximized the design talents of Victor Joris, Thea Porter, Halston, Giorgio di Sant'Angelo, and Diane Von Furstenberg, who were in their most creative periods when Giorgio was starting to build its name.

Victor Joris designed for Cuddlecoat, a New York coat and suit manufacturer founded in 1916. Justin Lipman, then the firm's president, met Fred and Gale in 1967 when they were struggling, and he decided to take a chance with them by offering them a line of credit and dating. It was standard to give a retailer thirty days to pay his bills; but, according to Josh Lipman, Justin's son and Cuddlecoat's current president, Justin had faith in Giorgio and gave the Haymans sixty and ninety days to pay their bills. Joris won the Coty Award twice, for his peacoat in the mid-sixties and for his floor-length maxi-coat in 1970, and Cuddlecoat became a $7 million company. Designer jeans and the sportswear explosion of the early 1970s subsequently ended Cuddlecoat's high visibility.

Mary Lou Luther, the new fashion editor at the *Los Angeles Times*, walked into Giorgio in 1969. Her first impression was, "I thought I had just walked into an outlet for Cuddlecoat. I never saw so many Cuddlecoats in my life. It was their single biggest resource and I was interested in how could this boutique be this manufacturer's number-one account, especially for a suit and coat manufacturer, in this climate?"

The reason was simple. The Haymans were starting to cater to jet-setters who wanted more than just one Cuddlecoat. One day Mrs. Lloyd Hand, the wife of the White House chief of protocol, phoned the store and said Imelda Marcos was going to visit the store. After the security guards and cars arrived, Imelda got down to action, plundering the Filipino treasury. Gale showed her the store and she seized on a Joris Nehru suit and started ordering it in myriad colors and fabrics, many of which Gale and Fred did not stock. Further, they had no idea whether Cuddlecoat could produce. Fred wrote up the large order and called Lipman, who made the effort to meet the unusual request.

Giorgio was more than just an account for the Lipman family. The Haymans and Lipmans became friends and Fred found a job at the Waldorf for Justin Lipman's nephew. When the Lipmans visited Los Angeles, Fred and Gale took them to Chasen's for dinner and picked up the tab. In the garment business, the retailer seldom, if ever, picks up the check. "My father agreed to anything Freddy wanted," Josh Lipman says.

> Giorgio was catering to a special kind of woman who likes doing things differently. We made crepe evening pants with the crepe side on the back with a satin finish. Freddy liked the way the pants looked on the reverse and we made a special order for him with the satin side out and he sold a ton of those. He requested we sew a Giorgio label into the coats and he wanted that label sewn in upside down. When a woman threw that coat over a chair in a restaurant the woman next to her could read that label.

By the fall of 1969, many Giorgio labels were turning up all over Beverly Hills. Fred and Gale were out of the red forever, thanks to a 300 percent sales increase that December. They expanded the boutique from eight hundred square feet to six thousand square feet and the store's main entrance was now at the corner of Rodeo Drive and Dayton Way. Yvel, the custom shirtmaker shop operated by Ben Levy, had the coveted large location next door to Giorgio but his lease was expiring. According to Frank Hoffer, Levy was elderly and didn't want to retire. "Fred was generous and felt sorry for Yvel and made a deal with him. He took over his store but kept him on as the haberdasher and gave him a contract for about two years. Fred absorbed all the costs of combining the two stores. He would pay some of the profits to Fred, but the money he gave to Fred never amounted to more than the light bill." Fred was now paying $10,000 a month in rent, but he had a showcase store that could generate major volume.

The enlarged and remodeled store was unlike any other store in

Beverly Hills—and probably America. Fred positioned a large pool table in the middle of the gold carpet and, nearby, behind an Old World oak bar, Frank Maxwell served cappuccino, tea, wine, and spirits. Maxwell had been the houseman at the Beverly Hilton and worked as a bartender at private parties in Beverly Hills. Seeing the pool table and gracious, liveried Maxwell in front of the gleaming brass-and-cooper espresso machine made visitors feel they were entering the home of a wealthy man. A small den with a fireplace, bookshelves, and photo-filled wall behind the bar was another touch designed to make men, as well as women, comfortable. The clothing and accessories were almost incidental. Jammed in tight wooden cabinets and on round racks, the clothes were not elegantly displayed. Many dresses were stored in plastic bags and rummaging through the cabinets was almost like trying to find something in a dry-cleaning store. The dressing rooms were cramped and uncomfortable.

Movie stars used the store as a meeting place. David Janssen enjoyed going to the store to shoot pool when he wasn't working, and his then-girlfriend Dani used to meet him there. She had the perfect figure for Halston and Gale immediately gained Dani Janssen as a loyal Giorgio customer and friend. Dani introduced Gale to the Church of Religious Science in North Hollywood, attended by Valerie Perrine, Marisa Berenson, and Linda Evans. They were "interested in finding out a little more about life than shopping in Beverly Hills," according to Janssen. Dr. Carlo Di Giovanna, the church's minister, would become Gale's guru through her travails with Fred in 1983.

Jill St. John found Giorgio to be the perfect sanctuary from shopping tedium:

> Giorgio took the bite out of shopping. You could sit down, relax, have a cup of cappuccino, and they brought things to you. The salespeople wouldn't waste your time by showing you things that you didn't like. Shopping is not my favorite pastime; I would rather be outdoors. I find the price of clothes obscene, and it really goes against my grain to pay a fortune for them; but if you are forced to pay those prices, you might as well go to Giorgio where there are nice salespeople and a cappuccino.

Most of St. John's wardrobe for television shows and Bob Hope specials she appeared in during the 1970s and 1980s came from Giorgio. Sequined dresses, cashmere blazers, and black silk suits were among St. John's frequent purchases.

New Yorkers in the fashion business who visited the boutique thought it was comical, something conceived by a Hollywood set designer.

However, as a Beverly Hills store it achieved coveted stardom, its first $10,000 sales day occurring on October 6, 1970. Giorgio finished that year by going over $1 million in sales, according to Irene Fuhrmann. The store was also starting to attract media attention. *Women's Wear Daily* ran two photos and a seventeen-paragraph story on January 7, 1970, liberally quoting Fred, and dropping the names of twelve of their star clients. "Giorgio's who-who [sic] customers are a coveted list . . . from Mrs. Howard Keck, the 20th customer to buy Victor Joris' $1,000 fox trimmed maxi coat . . . to Lucille Ball. Lucy dropped in holding the hand of Candy, her pet chimp dressed like a tyke," wrote *WWD*'s June Livinghouse. Gale was not quoted and her name was misspelled (Gayle) in the body of the story.

Fred's quotes were boastful, "The greatest designer in the world is Victor Joris. If he were in Europe, St. Laurent would be number two. We went to New York especially for his Coty Award not just for friendship, but out of respect and admiration." Fred added that the store sold four hundred Joris linen maxis in a five-month period and predicted the store would move eight hundred maxi-coats, ranging up to $1,000 each, by the time the season ended. The store's sale policy also made interesting reading: no clearance sales. If a garment doesn't move over a reasonable length of time it is exiled to a six-foot rack at half price. From there the "mistakes" are given to charity. The policy still exists today.

The big stores on Wilshire Boulevard began to notice Giorgio. Doris Fields, the manager of I. Magnin's Beverly Hills store, had a $30 million sales volume to protect. Her main competition for many years had been Saks, although at fifty-one thousand square feet, Saks had less selling space. Magnin had a vast cosmetics department staffed by twenty-two women; and its merchandise manager, Van Venneri, based in San Francisco, was known throughout the industry. Fields had moved to Beverly Hills in 1943. A member of the Chamber of Commerce, she wanted Wilshire Boulevard to remain the main shopping venue. However, she couldn't stop the Rodeo Drive publicity and resulting tourist avalanche that was orchestrated by Hayman a few years later.

Fields, now retired, remembers the first day she saw Giorgio:

If there was a counterpart to Madame Defarge it was Fred Hayman. Behind the pool table he had a desk, and as you walked in you saw Fred behind the desk. Every sale that went by, Fred was recording, counting every receipt, he was there watching everything. He was very cognizant of every customer, making her important to the store. I think he catered to a different group than we did, mostly movie people and a lot of women who weren't sure of themselves. They could walk in there and feel comfortable. The store was warm and friendly. Even if they weren't convinced of their status and taste level, they would have salespersons who would guide them and they weren't fearful of making a mistake.

The Haymans started traveling to Europe to buy in February 1971. Their appointments often followed the Magnin team. If the Magnin buyer ordered a dress in black, Giorgio ordered white. If it came in silver, the Haymans wanted gold. Whatever conservative standard Magnin set, Giorgio had a flamboyant adaptation. Fields said, "Fred was the first Beverly Hills merchant to go to Europe and really buy in depth. He went to Sonia Rykiel and bought it like Magnin was buying Anne Klein. He put a lot of money into the business because there were people in Beverly Hills who wanted to be different and not wear the classic looks we were catering to."

Gale and Fred took risks with young designers who were not carried in Beverly Hills or, in some cases, on the entire West Coast. By sheer bullying, Gale got Halston before anyone else in Los Angeles. Fred and Gale had gone to the Coty Awards in New York when Joris was being honored. During the fashion show, Halston's tie-dyed chiffons billowed across the stage, mesmerizing Gale with their vibrant colors. After the show, Gale approached Halston and told him how strongly she felt about the clothes. The next day she searched through the New York phone book and found Halston's atelier on 68th Street:

Ed Austin, Halston's assistant, picked up the phone and I said, "We have a store in Beverly Hills and we would like to buy your clothes." Austin said they didn't have production and were just making clothes for the ladies, like Jackie O. This was before he went to Seventh Avenue. I said we were in the neighborhood and we would like to stop by. I was being very pushy, because I fought for designers that really excited me. Fred was listening to the conversation and was saying, "Oh God, Gale, get off the phone."

We went up there and Austin said, "I don't know why you came up here, we are not set up to sell boutiques." Halston came out and asked what was going on. I reminded him that we had seen him last night and told him the women in California would love his clothes, the colors are right. I asked if we could have a few pieces and Halston said to Ed, "Let's make them a few pieces," and they did. We sold them instantly and then went back for more.

Halston's tie-dyed pajamas were tailor-made for the casual Beverly Hills life-style. They were comfortable and women could dress them up with jewelry at night. Gale compares the colors to Monet paintings. The stars—Jill St. John, Ali MacGraw, Liza Minnelli, and Totie Fields—came to Giorgio for Halston. Judith Krantz had just moved to Beverly Hills and discovered the store because she liked Halston. Later she would give the store a boost in her first novel, *Scruples*. The chiffons were expensive (around $2,000), but with an exclusive, the store couldn't get enough. In April 1971, Giorgio sold one hundred Halston tie-dyes at $315 each. Of the 150 different manufacturers carried in the store that year, the best-selling items were Halston's silk jersey shirt dress and his halter dress, both at $280.

With large orders of $50,000, Halston came to visit the boutique. "I thought it was very casual, and not the stuffy approach like in Bergdorf, which was quiet. They had a new, modern approach where people would hang around for three or four hours and try things on. It had a salon feeling, where the superrich Hollywood and Beverly Hills women would spend and sometimes buy fifteen or twenty things. I was amazed." When buying his line, Gale would often try on the clothes to see how she felt in them. She was her own best model and Halston considered her avant-garde. "They always wanted the latest and had a great sense of humor and enthusiasm to promote a fashion as well as sell it. With Fred's business skills, they were a good balance."

The first European designer to score at Giorgio was Thea Porter. On the Haymans' first European buying trip they bought Porter's caftans and brocaded fabrics. Porter had been brought up in Lebanon and had a flair for luxury resort wear and Giorgio bought every gypsy dress she could produce. Fashion was entering the rich-hippie era and Porter designs were perfect for the rich Beverly Hills hippie. Porter was invited to Beverly Hills and the Haymans hosted parties where she met the press and their star customers. Giorgio became Porter's top-volume United States account, surpassing Saks Fifth Avenue, with wholesale shipments reaching over $300,000 annually. She describes Fred as rational, extremely sweet and kind. Her relationship with Gale was not as harmonious. Porter says:

> Gale is completely mad, the way she dressed—from her hair to her earrings to the clothes—she was just amazing, over the top. She was extremely arrogant and had the feeling that she had the absolute perfect taste. She would have me remake things because she said they would never sell. It was absolutely endless, the demands, but it was fun because we did a lot of business.

Despite the volume Porter was able to generate, a predictable clash with Gale led to the demise of their business relationship after seven years. Porter says that Gale sent sketches of American designer clothes and asked her to copy them using her special fabrics. When Porter refused to copy someone else's designs, Gale called her a temperamental designer and severed the relationship, according to Porter. Gale sees it differently:

> That story is unbelievable. Oh, my God, you know I made her. She was a lady with a great fabric sense but knew nothing about making a dress. She lived in Lebanon and was able to pick up wonderful brocaded fabrics, and she made a caftan. I told her to make a slip to go under the caftan. If I sent her sketches of another designer, it wasn't to knock them off, but to direct her. I was angry with her because she didn't check her fit before she shipped. These dresses were expensive, and why should we eat a dress that she didn't make properly. I refused to accept that shipment and she said she would never talk to me again, and I said, "That's fine."

The rich-hippie period was made for Gale, who considered herself bohemian before it became stylish. She eagerly abandoned the Chanel suits she had worn out of deference to Fred in favor of the more outlandish Giorgio di Sant'Angelo rag dresses, American Indian antelope fringe outfits, and peasant skirts. Sant'Angelo's sheer antique dress with a silk chiffon bottom sold for $2,000 at Giorgio and he built a $200,000 business with the store in the early 1970s. Looking back on his positive relationship with the store, Sant'Angelo has just one regret: "I didn't like the fragrance part of Giorgio because I didn't like the use of my name. It made it impossible to do my own Giorgio fragrance. I did a Giorgio Sant'Angelo fragrance, but I always wanted to call it Giorgio. I am the original Giorgio, and then all the others show up."

The Haymans broke the rules of high-fashion retailing by not limiting themselves to high-priced garments. When they saw Diane Von Furstenberg's first collection at the Gotham Hotel in New York in 1971 they bought her long silk jersey dresses even though they were priced substantially lower than the rest of their stock. The Haymans used new designers such as Von Furstenberg, mixing their $200 dresses with $2,000 imports from Paris. This gave the customer many options and heightened her curiosity when she fanned through the racks and wooden cabinets. A woman who couldn't afford a $2,000 Sant'Angelo got a psychological boost when she found a $200 Diane Von Furstenberg, in much the same way a woman buys a designer fragrance although she can't afford his apparel. The bulk of Giorgio's business by the mid-1970s had settled in the $400-to-$500 range. Sales volume went from $1.2 million in 1970 to $1.7 million in 1971, to over $2 million in 1972. By 1976, volume had doubled to $4 million.

Von Furstenberg remembers Gale as young and cute, while Fred was older and "bossy." After her huge success with her wrap dress in the early 1970s, Von Furstenberg went mass and sold to many department stores, becoming less important to Giorgio. Von Furstenberg's fragrance, Tatiana, in 1976 became a leading brand in the industry. Von Furstenberg was poised to become one of the industry's great personalities but fell short. "I wanted to be the next Estée Lauder and I did everything to get there, but I grew too fast and I sold to the wrong company [Beecham]. I am disappointed, but perhaps it's not a lost cause. Gale has asked me for advice and we talked about the cosmetics industry. It is very difficult to do it twice, to have two successful products in this industry."

Accessories, especially Kenneth Jay Lane's large-millimeter pearl ropes and Adolfo hats, had become an important part of the Giorgio business. Gale considered fragrance another accessory and told Fred it would make a nice addition to the back of the jewelry case. Joy was Gale's favorite among her collection of heady floral scents, and she lavished herself with the spray cologne. Fred and Gale arrived at International Flavors and Fragrances, one of the largest fragrance supply houses in the world, asking for a similar scent. (IFF has produced many of Estée Lauder's scents, including Youth Dew.)

Said Gale, "They brought out twelve copies of Joy and lined them all up. They asked me to smell them and then say which one I liked. I looked at them and said, 'These are all copies of Joy?' They said, 'Each is a little different,' and I said, 'Okay,' and just picked one right then. It was just a half-hour meeting."

The first Giorgio fragrance was introduced in 1973. It was a blatant knockoff of Joy. The plan, according to Fred in *WWD*'s "Eye" column on February 5, 1973, was to market a forty-dollar-an-ounce fragrance, along with three other sizes, sold only in the boutique and through mail order. If it became a success, it would be distributed to other outlets, a scenario that would unfold a decade later.

The Haymans made a minimum purchase of one thousand stock bottles from Pochet of America and had IFF do the filling. The fragrance was packed in a yellow-and-white striped box and displayed on the jewelry shelf. There was no promotion or advertising behind it—not exactly an important introduction during a year when Charlie was capturing the nation's attention. The Giorgio/Joy knockoff gradually sold out and was never reordered. At the time Gale was not interested in competing with the fragrance industry, but was intent on discovering exciting new designers to solidify Giorgio's fashion image in Beverly Hills. By 1979, fragrance would become Gale's passion.

CHAPTER SIX

Rodeo Drive:
True Glitz

Fred and Gale had more than just an exciting business and marriage. Despite working six days a week and remaining on call for their customers after store hours, they were in the grip of entrepreneurial euphoria, in this case a more potent intoxicant than love or hate. Gale for the first time in her life was sniffing success and enjoying it; but she was still deferring to Fred, especially in the management of the company's assets. Fred was the company's spokesman and, to outsiders, appeared to be the dominant force in Giorgio.

The store volume was approaching $3 million in 1973, with monthly increases in the 40 to 70 percent range. Giorgio enjoyed this astronomical growth despite over twenty new stores in Beverly Hills, including Bonwit Teller.

Contracts were signed on July 26, 1973, establishing the Haymans' compensation packages. Fred's base salary was $80,000 plus 5 percent of Giorgio's pretax net income, to a maximum of $160,000. Gale was earning $60,000 plus 3 percent of the pretax net income, to a maximum of $120,000. Those salaries would more than triple by 1980; and by 1985, thanks to the success of the fragrance, the Haymans would divvy up over $20 million in profits. By 1986 Fred's base salary would be $5 million, the highest in the fragrance industry.

Although $60,000 was a relatively hefty salary, especially compared to what she made during her manicuring and odd-job days, Gale claims the money did not represent success or security.

> I never looked at that money. It went directly into Fred's account or the corporate account. The money was turned back into the business to make it grow. I had a checking account for small expenses, but I signed over my checks twice a month. Ask Irene [the controller] where the checks went. I trusted Fred implicitly and we both put back money to make the business grow. I'm not materialistic. I wasn't driven by the money and I'm not today. I never bought anything; I told Fred what I needed. I was not into real jewelry then and I'm still not.

They merchandised the store by consensus. If either of them didn't like a particular item or designer, they would pass no matter how passionate one or the other felt. Occasionally they debated about the clothes in front of the manufacturers, but for the most part the Haymans were in sync despite their age and stylistic differences. "There was a very strong communication between us. I would look at the clothes and we could talk to each other without speaking. He would give me a high eyebrow and could tell what I was thinking and we would walk out. Fred and I worked like fuel and energy."

The Haymans also were building a strong staff. Fuhrmann was more than just an auditor. She served as a modern-era executive vice president/chief financial officer and was tough enough to stand up to Fred, who regarded her as a confidante. No major decisions were made without Fuhrmann's approval. On the sales floor, Toni LoCicero, a former Helft's saleswoman, was the first person hired to work the floor with Gale, and she remains at the boutique today. Marguerite Schaefer had moved to Beverly Hills from Pennsylvania for health reasons and was hired as a stock girl. Toni and Marguerite were talented and servile enough to master the soft-sell, service-oriented principles Fred established. The saleswomen were taught first to find the customer's price range rather than waste time trying to sell a thousand-dollar gown to a woman who wants to spend only one hundred dollars. Fred was quoted in a 1976 feature in *WWD*: "If she's a loyal customer take her to the sales rack when you know there's a bargain she'd like. The place must be warm and human. I tell them to think of themselves walking into the lobby of Claridge's or Côte Basque, being presented with a French menu that they can't understand."

The Haymans were not content simply to work out of their store to build its reputation. They started entertaining and showing up at any and all fashion events in Los Angeles. Their heavy socializing in the 1970s brought truth to Woody Allen's line, "Fifty percent of succeeding is just showing up." It seemed no event was too minor. Even the mundane fashion shows and parties given by the Los Angeles Apparel Mart attracted Fred and Gale. The Haymans were not just increasing their visibility by showing up at industry functions, they also were learning about the business. In addition, these events enabled the Haymans to court the press, which would pay major dividends when the fragrance was introduced.

Giorgio was the only small Beverly Hills store to woo Mary Lou Luther, the *Los Angeles Times* fashion editor. Herb Fink of Theodore and Charles Gallay were the other two Beverly Hills shopkeepers who were seriously pursuing European high-fashion designers at that time. However, Fink and Gallay believed the press should do its homework and discover their stores without a personal invitation. Mistakenly, they did not believe a high-fashion retailer needed to curry favor with a powerful editor.

The big stores, such as Saks and I. Magnin, advertised in the *Times* and occasionally tried to bully the paper. Jack Matthess, the store manager of Saks, once called Luther complaining about a reporter, Beth Ann Krier, who wore blue jeans while covering Saks' staid Adolfo fashion show. Luther recalls, "I said, 'Jack, how dare you be critical when there are a lot of women shopping in your store and wearing blue jeans?' The lovely Ms. Krier did call and apologize; but Fred and Gale, on the other hand, invited her to The Bistro for dinner in her blue jeans. They were so smart to do that."

When the new fifty-five-thousand-square-foot Bonwit Teller at the corner of Rodeo Drive and Wilshire Boulevard did $60,000 on its opening day in November 1972, the Haymans showed their competitive flair by hosting a dinner party for twenty-two at The Bistro. *Women's Wear Daily* dispatched Karin Winner to cover the party, giving it more coverage than it probably merited, given Bonwit's New York reputation. The story, entitled "Upsmanship," included eight photos and said Fred was not to be outdone by Bonwit.

This type of coverage was an early reflection of the press's correct intuition that the exciting retailers emerging in Los Angeles were not major department stores but smaller Rodeo Drive boutiques. Bonwit never made an impact in Beverly Hills and closed in 1986. Unlike New York, which was and is dominated by the large stores, such as Bloomingdale's, Macy's and Saks, the smaller shops such as Giorgio on Rodeo Drive would become the fashion leaders in Beverly Hills during the 1970s and 1980s.

Fred's candidness and his ability to come up with amusing one-liners made him good copy. When the recession of 1973 hit and many of his customers were unable to obtain gasoline, he described his clientele as the "nouveau poor." Mary Lou Luther recalls meeting a miffed Fred Hayman on the street in Paris in the mid-seventies. "He told me he had just spent four hours at Chloe and spent $40,000 and they didn't even offer him a glass of water. This is what made Fred believable to the press. He wasn't afraid to knock the icons of the industry. I used that in my column and I always felt what he was telling me was what he believed and felt."

Timing and luck are essential to successful fashion retailing, and the Haymans had plenty of both. Just when the rich-hippie trend was at its peak, Halston sent the Haymans his full-length black shirt dress as a test item. Gale hung it in the store to compare it to the other merchandise. The change from hippie to classic—and the "Mr. Clean" clothes of Halston—was right up there on the wall in front of Gale. Suddenly everything else looked dated. Instead of putting the black dress on the floor for sale, Gale hid it for several months so the rich-hippie inventory could be sold off. She then aggressively went after the new look without being stuck with unfashionable inventory.

The Haymans were still living in their small apartment on South Camden Drive. They walked the two blocks to the store and had a glamorous, albeit hard-working, life-style. They went to Europe and New York for the collections and hosted dinner parties at The Bistro for visiting designers and editors while building a name for Giorgio and themselves. However, on May 22, 1973, their life-style changed when Fred and Gale became full-time parents of three teenagers.

Divorced from Barbara for almost ten years, Fred went back into court in February 1972, concerned about his children's welfare. In the court filing, Fred claimed that Barbara, who had not remarried, had "frequently absented herself from California for long periods of time and has indicated she will continue to do so. During her continual travels she rarely, if ever, takes the children and the children are left in the care of a maid."

After divorcing Fred, Barbara had obtained her master's degree in psychology from UCLA and at a New Year's Eve party in 1970 she saw Eddie Fisher, whom she had met at the Hilton in the early sixties while he was married to Debbie Reynolds. A love affair ensued, wrote Fisher's unauthorized biographer, Myrna Greene, in *The Eddie Fisher Story*, published in 1978. Barbara did everything she could to help Fisher break his drug habit and revive his singing career. Supposedly Barbara lent Fisher money, but she also couldn't resist talking to reporters about how she had helped him overcome his dependency. According to Greene,

Fisher feared she was in the relationship because she was planning to write about him, and their love affair ended. Fisher, in his later autobiography, fails to mention Barbara Hayman.

Barbara had her own health problems and was in and out of hospitals. Although Fred did not seek a custody change in early 1972, he asked the court to force Barbara to have a governess take care of the children when she traveled. Countering, Barbara's attorney, Maurice Levy, Jr., asked the court to increase child-support payments from $150 to $650 per month for each child, partially because Barbara did not have the financial ability to contribute to the children's support. Fred then attempted to terminate spousal support and stopped payments.

Their feud was reflected in the increasing problems the children were having. Barbara stated in the court papers that the children were emotionally disturbed because of the friction between the parents and the differing dress, manners, school grades, and religious expectations that were applied by each parent. "The children have been rebellious and refuse to obey petitioner and the children often quoted their father." The children's school grades and conduct at school had "substantially deteriorated." Barbara's solution was to place the three children in a private boarding school, but Fred rejected that court proposal. He wanted Nicole placed in the Bishop School in La Jolla, to which Barbara did not agree.

The court ruled that Barbara must not be away on vacation trips for more than four weeks and that she could not have "adult males" staying overnight while the children were present. Child support was increased to $250, but the court ordered Barbara to move the children from the Happy Valley School in Ojai (about sixty miles north of Beverly Hills), to Beverly Hills, where she was ordered to find a new residence. Barbara's ability to cope with the rebellious children had completely deteriorated by May 1973, and Fred won custody.

The children had been spending time with Fred and Gale on weekends. Gale maintains that having them full time ended a stressful period. "They were relieved to be living with us and they were all very happy. Finally all the negativity was over and they came under our roof. We hired a housekeeper who was there to give them lunch and dinner, and it was a positive time. We weren't worrying about them all the time. It was terrific. I loved the kids as if they were my own and I still do," Gale says now, fighting off a tear.

Needing more space, the Hayman family moved into a large, two-story apartment at 9679 Charleville Boulevard, south of Wilshire and just three blocks from Rodeo Drive. The property, which the Haymans bought from actor MacDonald Carey's ex-wife and where Fred still resides, would be assessed at just over $500,000 in 1979.

Fred's flair for entertaining soon made the Charleville apartment, although not grand by Beverly Hills standards, part of the Beverly Hills social landscape. Fred and Gale held frequent dinner parties, impressing everyone with abundant caviar and unusual touches. "Fred has a taste level that can be intimidating, but in a nice sense; and people look up to Fred for that," Luther recalls. "At those early dinner parties he served baked potato with caviar, and in those days I didn't know any living human being serving baked potatoes and caviar. Just before Christmas he had a dinner party and he had carolers singing for us. Who would hire carolers to sing for ten people?"

At another Christmas dinner the Haymans gave the women guests diamond pins from Laykin, the prominent I. Magnin jeweler. The pins, which spelled LOVE, were not boxed, but were placed on white linen. "These special gifts were presented in good taste. It wasn't showy or pretentious. It would have been pretentious to put that pin in a box," recalls Doris Fields, one of the guests.

The dinner parties mixed society names with personalities from the fashion and entertainment industries. The guest lists included Pamela Mason, Jacqueline Bisset, Helen Reddy, Peter Yarrow (of Peter, Paul and Mary), John and Maureen Dean, *WWD* editor Michael Coady, Henry and Ginny Mancini, and Hollywood film designer Adrian. According to Mason,

> The people were well mixed, with some you knew and a couple you didn't know. I met Michael Coady there for the first time and Jody Jacobs [then the L.A. *Times* society columnist]. Fred is a genius at public relations and was running a dress store and wasn't afraid to exploit that fact. He gave a perfect dinner—usually five to six courses—starting with prosciutto and melon, soup, a little fish dish, a meat dish with several vegetables, and dessert. He had different wines with each dish and everything was always correct. With the caviar was always the aquavit. After dinner he would have the chef come in and take a bow. Fred then made a little speech toasting his guest of honor.

Social climbing was an important part of building the premier fashion boutique on Rodeo Drive. The store's volume had reached $4 million by 1976, averaging $13,000 in daily sales, with a customer list that included Nancy Reagan, Doris Duke, Greta Garbo, and Ali MacGraw. The staff had grown to ten saleswomen, ten stockkeepers, and ten alteration people. A men's department had been established in a 1,250-square-foot corner of the store and was beginning to catch on after a slow start in 1975.

Initially the Haymans tried to run a flamboyant men's operation to complement the women's, but it failed. Frank Hoffer, the expert tailor next door, watched the couple struggle with men's apparel.

> They had just come back from Paris with a line of men's clothes and Fred came to show me, asking what I thought. I told him, "I look at it with different eyes than you. You look at it with the eyes of a Beverly Hills merchant and I look at it with the eye of a fine custom tailor. To me these clothes look like shit." The only people who could have worn those clothes were rock stars. There was no American built who could wear such small skimpy suits that they bought.

After dumping the rock-star getups, the Haymans started buying the finest and most expensive Italian men's wear from Brioni. The conservative suits and sports jackets appealed to wealthy men whose wives and girlfriends shopped in the store. The dichotomy of a conservative men's store married to a glitzy women's boutique made as much sense as the marriage of Fred and Gale's diverse personalities and talents. At this point Gale lost interest in the men's side of the business because it lacked fantasy and theatrics.

Fred built a $1.9 million men's business over the next five years with Brioni accounting for around 75 percent of the volume. In 1982, when Fred canceled Brioni, he and his men's store manager, Peter Jaram, were able to leverage the Giorgio logo and replaced Brioni with Giorgio private-label blazers, suits, and shirts. In the ten years Jaram has worked for Giorgio, fewer than a hundred dress shirts have been put on sale and only forty suits annually. The boutique may have been famous for its glittery women's clothes and later the fragrance, but the men's business was also successful. In the 1980s, the men's growth outpaced the women's.

Television and movie stars had discovered the store, and now their agents and producers were wardrobing productions with Gale. If a game show's ratings or a soap opera siren's image were declining, Giorgio was recognized as the store that could provide the instant sex appeal that might reverse the ratings.

Wheel of Fortune producer Nancy Jones, a pretty blonde, had approached other retailers and had been turned down. Jones knew Fred from his hotel days; and in 1974 when the show was struggling with Vanna White's predecessor, Susan Stafford, Jones asked Fred to supply the show with clothes from Giorgio. *Wheel of Fortune* needed Giorgio at the time more than Giorgio needed the show, but Fred agreed to make the Merv Griffin production its exclusive game-show client.

Fred and Griffin had become buddies when the latter sang at the

Cocoanut Grove, and Fred's hunch that *Wheel of Fortune* would someday be important was fortuitous. "Things evened out when we went into our nighttime show," Jones says. "When he had his perfume, we had forty-two million viewers and then everyone—every perfume company in the world—wanted to be on *Wheel of Fortune*. But we had a relationship established with Giorgio and we had to say no. It would have been a conflict with someone who had been good to us early on." Paid advertising in high-fashion magazines could not possibly have provided the type of free exposure Giorgio received with Vanna White in the 1980s.

The Young and the Restless was among the soap operas on which Giorgio was getting a credit in the mid-seventies, giving the store's name some national visibility. In addition, a new generation of television stars gravitated to Giorgio. Loretta Swit was one. She moved to Los Angeles in the early 1970s after a sixth-month run of *Mame* in Las Vegas. Her big television break came with the role of Hot Lips Houlihan in *M*A*S*H*. Swit had lived in New York and thought Beverly Hills people were caught up with being physically beautiful, noting the city's many yoga institutes, tanning and beauty salons. Giorgio was the fashion oasis in the midst of this narcissistic treadmill. Swit was outfitted at Giorgio for her television specials with Perry Como, Tony Orlando, Mack Davis, and Sonny Bono. She became smitten with Gale's fashion sense, and she was influenced by Gale's choice of risk-taking colors and sexy cuts.

On the CBS television movie, *Games Mother Never Taught You*, Swit starred as a mother who becomes a business executive. The studio bought ten outfits and spent several thousand dollars at Giorgio on business suits and dresses for Swit to wear.

> I thought all the clothes worked for me and were so terrific I would wind up buying them from the studio after the production. I would describe the character to Gale and, along with the wardrobe people, we developed the clothes. Gale was good at putting a character's look together. Gale knew how to make a character look younger or older. The clothing is critical to a movie. It's like the lighting in a horror or murder movie.

The ranks of Beverly Hills nouveau riche were exploding in the 1970s. Real-estate, television, and music-industry moguls were making quick fortunes and spending them at the same pace. Beverly Hills became a proving ground for the axiom that money often has nothing to do with taste, intelligence, or class. The Rolls-Royces of the nouveau riche were docked and loaded daily outside of Giorgio.

Alice Cohn is the widow of Dan Cohn, who made it big in real estate and construction. As hard as he worked earning it, Mrs. Cohn worked equally hard spending it and carving a niche for herself in Beverly Hills society. Not content with her mundane given name, Alice threw a coming-out party at which she proclaimed herself Contessa Cohn. Following Dan's death, the Contessa was squired about town by her Arthur Murray dance instructor. In 1987, larger-than-life-size likenesses of the two dancing bodies—the Contessa's swathed in a white gown—smiled down at passing motorists from a shocking-pink billboard on Sunset Boulevard in West Hollywood. Contessa Cohn was one of Giorgio's biggest customers.

Candy Spelling, wife of television producer Aaron Spelling, was another major Giorgio customer. (Spelling-Goldberg Productions was responsible for such television hits as *Dynasty, Charlie's Angels, Love Boat*, and *Hotel*.) The new Spelling residence at 594 South Mapleton Drive in Holmby Hills (between Bel-Air and Beverly Hills) is built on the old six-acre Bing Crosby estate. The late crooner no doubt would be horrified to see what has been done to his property. The Spellings constructed a fifty-six-thousand-five-hundred-square-foot French chateau–style mansion, dubbed Spelling Castle by the Los Angeles newspapers. It includes a bowling alley, screening room, gym, doll museum, and four two-car garages along with the requisite Olympic-size pool, tennis courts, fountains, and formal gardens. Approval from a building-and-safety commissioner was required to build two oversize closets (about twenty-eight feet and forty-two feet long respectively and both eight feet wide) to hold Candy's clothes.

Giorgio was not the only store on Rodeo Drive where the nouveau riche were being outfitted. There were savvy local merchants on the three shopping blocks of North Rodeo Drive—including Herb Fink, Richard Carroll (men's wear), David Orgell (crystal, china, gifts) and Jerry Magnin, who opened Ralph Lauren's first Polo shop in America in 1971. However, it wasn't until the European status retailers arrived that Rodeo started attracting tourists from the Far East, Middle East, and Europe. Gucci opened in 1969 and, though its success curtailed the era of affordable rent on Rodeo Drive, it was the catalyst that turned a once-provincial street where shopkeepers met in the morning over coffee at Walter's Pastry Shop (now on Cañon Drive) into an international shopping mecca.

The opening of Gucci was almost a religious experience as far as Beverly Hills' increasingly status-crazed consumers were concerned. Carlo Celoni, who started as a salesman there before directing the store in the early 1980s, recalls, "People came into Gucci as if they were going to the temple or church. They would whisper. They were afraid to speak out. They felt it was a reverent place. It was so quiet, one day I told Dr. Gucci [Aldo], we should have some music." The music in Gucci was the cash register humming.

Starting out with a small store in the middle of the 300 North block,

Gucci expanded, gobbling up the leases of the three stores on its walls to become a fifteen-thousand-square-foot anchor store. The store was averaging $1,000 a square foot by the late 1970s for an annual volume in the $15 million range. Gucci's rent has gone from $7,000 a month to $24,000 a month to $100,000 a month over the course of its twenty-year Rodeo run. Dr. Gucci often complained about the rent, threatening to move to Cañon Drive where he acquired a warehouse building, but the store has never left Rodeo.

Combining European snob appeal with quality leather goods and clothing, Gucci quickly became the top-volume shop on Rodeo, a crown it held until Jerry Magnin satisfied his ambition in 1988, when his new Ralph Lauren store became the street's biggest volume retailer. In a town where visible status symbols were de rigueur, Gucci had come to the right place at the perfect time. Labels were becoming more important than the quality of the garments; and the more expensive the item, the more the customer wanted it—provided, of course, that it came from Gucci and had the ubiquitous intertwined G logo. The store's biggest customers included Carol Burnett, Nancy Reagan, and Frank Sinatra, but when the tourist influx hit in the late 1970s many of the stars were scared away. Before Mexico's economic collapse in the 1980s, that country's wealthy travelers thought nothing of buying jewels and several dozen pairs of Gucci loafers in a single shopping spree.

The wild spending did not go unnoticed by other leading European fashion and accessories companies, who soon boarded the gravy train to Conspicuous Consumption, California, hoping to duplicate Gucci's success. None did. The first wave of the European invasion of the mid-seventies included Van Cleef & Arpel, Hermès, Celine, and Ted Lapidus, all clustered in the 300 North Rodeo block. They were at an immediate competitive disadvantage. Stores such as Gucci, Giorgio, and Theodore, who were already established on the street, had signed favorable long-term leases in the 1960s when rent was either a dollar or less per square foot per month. Jerry Magnin was paying seventy cents a square foot for his fifteen-year lease when he opened his Polo shop in September 1971. He would later buy the property.

The landlords of Rodeo Drive quickly recognized the European herd instinct, and they knew they had leasable space worth a lot more than the rents they were charging. By doubling the going rent rate, the stakes of operating a shop on Rodeo Drive became higher almost overnight. Rent should be kept to 6 percent of sales for a retailer to be profitable, but as rents escalated on Rodeo the arithmetic changed. Rodeo Drive rents were at least 8 to 10 percent of a store's annual sales, which meant less leeway for inventory mistakes.

Another European retail phenomenon hit Rodeo Drive during this period—key money. Quite simply, if a merchant with fifteen years left on his prime Rodeo Drive lease at one dollar a square foot is approached by another ambitious retailer who wants to open a store badly enough in the prime Rodeo location, the original merchant has something much more valuable than merchandise to sell. Subleasing arrangements went to the highest bidder, with the keys to the store turning over for as much as $300,000. The new tenant still has to pay rent after buying out the original lease holder. The Europeans saw Rodeo as a beacon and felt that even if they didn't shine profitably in Beverly Hills, the limelight would rub off and allow them to operate in the black in less costly locations such as Houston and Kansas City.

The first big Rodeo Drive key money deal helped make Bud Lifpitz rich. Lifpitz had operated the Mayfair Riding Shop for over ten years at 329 North Rodeo Drive, and was somewhat successful selling riding boots and breeches. Then along came the proverbial offer he couldn't refuse. According to an August 1979 article in *Women's Wear Daily*, "One day a real estate broker came into my store and asked me if I would like to sell my lease. He said his client was Ted Lapidus. I went home that night and picked a number out of the hat," Lifpitz recalls. That number was $250,000, and the Lapidus franchise holder, Mier Teper, took several years to make the key money payment. Lifpitz stayed in business, moving up the street to a less desirable location at 459 North Rodeo. However, eighteen months later, Lina Lee, the wife of a rich Beverly Hills businessman, came asking to buy his lease. Again he sold out; but this time he decided to get out of retailing and make real estate a full-time occupation before retiring to Malibu.

The newcomers had seemingly bottomless pockets and were eager to build retail palaces once they acquired the leases. The Europeans were joined by the Iranians, who were moving to Beverly Hills and inflating the housing market by paying over $1 million for homes.

Bijan Pakzad and his partner Daryoush Mahboubi Fardi opened Bijan, a men's store, on Rodeo in 1976. They built a $400,000 brass-and-glass staircase and a $75,000 chandelier to light it. The Mahboubi family in Teheran was the equivalent to Chicago's Wrigley clan, operating that country's largest chewing-gum company. Dar, as he became known, was UCLA educated. He had started buying up Wilshire Boulevard property before going after Rodeo Drive. Bijan had apprenticed in the men's business in Beverly Hills and almost overnight became the most arrogant and expensive retailer on the street. The general public was not allowed in the store. Entry was gained only by appointment. Ties started at sixty-five dollars in 1979; a fox bedspread was $42,000; and six ounces of his first fragrance, a men's cologne, went for a mere $1,500. Bijan boasted he saw only five customers daily and put down American consumers.

"Taste is very difficult for Americans to understand," Bijan told *WWD* in August 1979. He said his volume was $6 million annually, a figure his competitors doubted and divided in half.

Bijan disliked Fred Hayman. The feeling was mutual, but Bijan always had the first and last word; Fred didn't want to acknowledge him publicly. Bijan did not hesitate to call Giorgio "that Italian bazaar" to anyone who would quote him. It irked him that Giorgio was getting so much publicity. Bijan's tirade against Giorgio included:

> His doors are open to everyone, my doors are closed. He has clothing from seventeen dollars to, God knows, five thousand dollars. I start at two thousand five hundred and go to ninety-five thousand. I don't give Coca-Cola or champagne, because I think that is Hollywood. If someone can afford a two-thousand-dollar sports jacket they don't need a free glass of champagne. The most important difference between us is, I design every piece of my items and he is buying. He is driving and I am flying but we both reach the same place [success].

The rivalry between Rodeo's most flamboyant merchants continues today. Bijan has backed up his numbing braggadocio by becoming a force in the perfume business. His fragrances accounted for $12 million their first year, 1987, when his women's fragrance was the top seller at Saks Fifth Avenue and Bullocks Wilshire.

Fred was not looking for a confrontation with Bijan, nor did he want one between the merchants on the burgeoning street. Rather, he wanted to make a concerted effort to develop the image of Rodeo. He watched the arrival of the new status stores and knew the local nucleus (Carroll, Magnin, Orgell, Fink) was solid. He recognized Rodeo's international marketing potential. Fred had seen the great shopping streets of Europe in his travels—Bond Street in London, the Via Condotti in Rome, and the Faubourg St. Honoré in Paris—and was convinced Rodeo was the West Coast's answer to these elitist shopping venues. If the merchants banded together instead of fighting, the street could be promoted and turned into a tourist attraction. Fred started organizing the Rodeo Drive Committee along with David Orgell and by July 27, 1977, the committee was collecting annual dues of up to $6,000 from each member merchant. The committee's first-year budget was $250,000. It was no easy task to herd and steer the group in the same direction. Fred was the committee's chairman and also its forceful wrangler, trying to rope in the many maverick merchants who failed to see the benefits of joining.

The early meetings were strained and Fred was at his most persuasive in cajoling merchants to join. Said Jerry Magnin, "He called me one day and said we are forming this committee. I said, 'I'm against things like this,' but Fred is very persuasive and charming and he said, 'Jerry, it wouldn't be complete without you, you have to be on it,' so I joined."

The entrepreneurial merchants by nature distrusted their competitors, and some feared Fred's intentions were self-serving. International hair stylist Vidal Sassoon operated a salon in the 400 North block of Rodeo; and his image-makers, George Shaw and Laurance Taylor, were dubious about the committee, dubbing it the "Fred Hayman Memorial." Shaw said Sassoon would not have joined had it not been for Helen Chaplin of the Beverly Wilshire talking them into it. "It was obvious Fred had ideas for Fred and he was going to benefit and we would get lost in the shuffle. We would pay dues for him to emerge. We sent a few bucks, but never joined with our hearts; and then we started sending our secretaries to the meetings."

Hayman convinced many of the merchants that by pooling their dollars and energies they could hype the street and all would benefit from the increased tourist traffic. Magnin and Fink had doubts about the strategy, fearing that if it succeeded their local customers would be run off by the tourists.

Fink was as maverick as any Rodeo merchant, questioning the necessity of forming a committee and suspect of its intentions. Eschewing the safe brand of merchandise purveyed by most of the stores, Theodore was the first store on the street to carry European designers Gianni Versace, Sonia Rykiel, Krizia, and Claude Montana. Fink's clothes could be worn by only the sveltest women in town. "We sold clothes to anorexics. If you weren't an anorexic, you became one. It wasn't for the masses, but to be in business you have to do something that creates a mood. Nobody needed another suit. Who needed another girdle?"

Fink was avant-garde with his own store, but conservative in promoting the street. However, he was mesmerized by a fire-and-brimstone speech given by Fred Hayman at one of the early committee meetings:

He got up on the podium and started trying to get the people enthused about the street and was saying what we could do with the street if we really got behind it. Before he was finished he started yelling, "Money! Money! Money!" and I thought this guy was crazy. But he was trying to say, "You're in business to make money and here is a good place to do it." He wanted us to get behind the idea of a press and advertising campaign for the street, to work as a unit—not against each other—and if we do, we will make a lot of money. And it's true, everybody made a lot of money.

Hayman had never used a publicist because he was a master of this dubious craft, but the committee needed a public-relations agency. Max Baril, a committee member, suggested Maslansky Koenigsberg, the firm he had used to promote his store, Fred Joaillier. Michael Maslansky, along with his partner, Neil Koenigsberg, had been successful entertainment publicists. After winning the Rodeo Drive Committee account, Maslansky Koenigsberg tabbed Katy Sweet, a tall, blond, UCLA theater arts major, to handle it. Sweet became Giorgio's in-house publicist in 1982.

The thrust of the committee's public-relations and advertising campaign played to America's hunger for glitter, glamour, and extravagance, featuring Rolls-Royce cars (Katy Sweet herself today drives a vintage one) and diamonds. The campaign's slogan was, "Rodeo Drive Makes You a Star—Even If You Are." During the 1977 Christmas season, the committee ran sixteen full-page ads in national and local magazines, including *Los Angeles Magazine, Playbill, Vogue, Palm Springs Life*, and *San Francisco Magazine*. Forty-five merchants participated and traffic on the street increased noticeably.

Maslansky, in order to stir press interest, came up with Rodeo Drive quotes from famous people. Some of the quotes are worth recalling. Andy Warhol was quoted, "Rodeo is like a giant butterscotch sundae—even the nuts are delicious." Diana Vreeland supposedly said, "Rodeo is marvelous; one day I walked out of my hotel and saw a multiple collision involving two Rolls, a Stutz, and a Ford! My son, who lives in Los Angeles, brushed it aside as just another afternoon on Rodeo . . . !" Last, and perhaps least, was Suzy Knickerbocker's, "Rodeo is the ultimate cure for existential boredom."

The press bought the hype and immediately seized on the committee's contention that Rodeo was the playground for the rich and famous. Within a year, Rodeo was the subject of a *New West Magazine* cover story and received major editorial space in *Time, Town & Country, Cosmopolitan, Bazaar*, and *The New York Times*.

The journalistic bandwagon helped make the words *Rodeo Drive* synonymous with opulence and ostentation. "When Johnny Carson mentioned Rodeo Drive on the Academy Awards broadcast, we knew we had become generic for wealth and stardom. If he could say Rodeo Drive and not mention Beverly Hills or California on an Oscar broadcast, we knew we had arrived," Sweet said.

Rodeo was becoming the retail version of television's *Lifestyles of the Rich and Famous*. Merv Griffin did a ninety-minute television salute to Rodeo on May 29, 1978, which closed the street for a day to allow five Rolls-Royces to be lined up across the street as a backdrop for the models. Although the Beverly Hills City Council debated waiving the $10,000 user fee for allowing Griffin to film there, in the end it voted four to one to charge the fee. At Fred Hayman's urging, the Rodeo Drive Committee picked up the tab.

Town & Country's twelve-page spread on Beverly Hills retailing, in August 1977, was an expensive and puffy piece that included a strange photo of the Haymans outside Giorgio. Gale's name was misspelled in the caption and, in heavy makeup and black lace, she was a wild contrast to Fred in his conservative checked blazer.

Time magazine and *The New York Times* both did business stories on Rodeo in 1978, but gave readers a sense they were writing about two different places. *Time* more accurately estimated retail sales of $200 million on Rodeo, while *The New York Times*, in Pamela Hollie's December 1978 piece, inflated the street's strength, claiming the street "should gross a billion dollars this year." The Beverly Hills Chamber of Commerce, in a 1979 *WWD* article, attributed 20 percent of the city's overall $527,320,000 1978 retail sales to Rodeo Drive.

Accurate or not, the word was out. Rodeo had become the world-class shopping street that Fred had envisioned. Tourists were now anywhere from 40 to 60 percent of Rodeo's business, and the better merchants, including Giorgio, were trying to keep their local clients in the face of the invasion.

The stores that relied on the tourist trade were vulnerable to international currency fluctuations. When the American dollar was weak, their business was strong because foreign tourists came here and American tourists couldn't afford Europe. Rodeo became a barometer for the entire California economy with its increasing dependence on foreign money.

While Fred was playing Mr. Rodeo Drive, Gale was in the store fretting. She had no interest in the committee, never attended a meeting, and was growing increasingly fearful of the competition. The Haymans had built a $4 million business in ten years; but now, with new competitors spreading on the block, Gale saw symptoms of a fashion plague that could put a pox on the house of Giorgio. Lina Lee, owner of a fashionable boutique up the street, was clearly the enemy. Her millionaire husband's deep pockets allowed her to go to Italy, where she was stealing Giorgio's resources. By writing larger orders than Giorgio, Lee was able to take away several of Giorgio's important lines, including Gianfranco Ferre, Muriel Grateau, and Krizia. Manufacturers are reluctant to sell to two stores in a condensed market and will go with the store with the largest order. The apparel industry's business ethic does not include loyalty to the store that helped build and promote a line in its early days. Gale said,

> I started to notice Lina had very young clothes and we had young clothes. I didn't want to see her advance and become more important than us. It's very simple: the day you stop growing, you

die. All these new stores were opening, and the pie is only so big, and we were starting to lose our share and we were plateauing. We just couldn't cram any more merchandise into our store and were getting the maximum out of it. I discussed this with Fred, but he said I was overreacting and he was prepared to fight it out [with Lina Lee]. I saw a bigger problem; down the line we would be preempted by other retailers.

On a Hawaiian vacation in 1977, Gale started pestering Fred and gave him three possible ways of safeguarding and expanding the business. A Giorgio catalogue, a second Giorgio store, or a fragrance were the three alternatives. Another store would mean a new layer of management and Fred was reluctant to expand the ranks. The fragrance idea also drew a cool reception, but Fred was lukewarm to the catalogue.

Gale badgered Fred for a year about a fragrance. Fred reminded her of the unsuccessful Joy knockoff fragrance they had tinkered with in 1973, but she argued that copies never make an impact and she was ready to do something original now. She said,

I was getting revved about the fragrance and saw a need for a new fragrance that was really different from what was out there, something modern. I told Fred, "I see the need for a fragrance for the woman of today. Women are assertive now and are making their own decisions and not dictated to by designers anymore. I see a parallel between the fashion and fragrance industries." Fashion was changing, but the fragrance companies were marketing mostly classical scents with a few exceptions. I saw a chance to tap into that niche to find something really unusual and modern.

When Fred finally relented in 1978 and allowed Gale to start testing fragrances, she immediately began to call perfume suppliers. Among them was Roure Bertrand Dupont, a top fragrance supplier that had produced Opium and the successful Halston men's scent in the late 1970s. Gale asked the Teaneck, New Jersey–based company for submissions. Bud Lindsay, Roure's urbane president at the time, now retired and living in Miami, is one of the deans of the industry. He arrived at Roure in 1969 after twenty-four years as a star salesman at IFF. He had worked with Estée Lauder on her early fragrances and saw a similarity in Gale. "She had that burning desire, that enthusiasm of a child, the enthusiasm it takes to be successful in this business. If you are scared about the magnitude of your corporation and your position, then you don't take the first step. She had the pizzazz of an early Estée Lauder in that she knew what she wanted and, goddamn it, wasn't going to settle for anything else. We were giving her very nice fragrances, but she wanted a powerful fragrance that came on strong and she finally found it with Florasynth."

Lindsay's perfumers watched Gale reject submission after submission, usually after a cursory whiff, and they questioned her ability to judge their work, given her inexperience in the field. Tom Virtue, then Roure's aggressive senior vice president of sales and now Lindsay's successor, describes Gale as a "difficult" client to whom Roure made at least fifty submissions. "We were chasing a phantom. Her concept changed; initially she went from wanting a heavy, sexy fragrance, but then she wound up with the floral. We had to interpret her emotions and she had a keen sense in her own mind, but it didn't translate to us. I stayed longer than I thought we should on the project. By the end of the second month you knew this was a very driven person with a premonition of what she had to do. She was a very dominant personality."

Companies such as Roure are armed with marketing studies to convince clients of the marketability of a fragrance. Such studies meant nothing to Gale, and when Roure asked Gale for her customer profile she told them the profile was her Giorgio customer. This is not exactly how perfume companies and suppliers such as Roure normally communicate. Gale said,

> After one year with Roure I was becoming very frustrated. They listened to me, but I didn't make a lot of sense to them. I wasn't doing it the industry way with a marketing plan with surveys and all that. In those days I didn't know what the industry was doing. I wasn't reading about the industry. I was only customer driven. What did my customers want to buy in fashion and fragrance? I saw a need for a powerful fragrance.

Gale, at thirty-four, was reaching a crossroads in her professional and personal lives. Her philosophical differences with Fred over the direction of Giorgio were reflected at home. The roles of stepmother, submissive wife, and junior business partner no longer fit comfortably. Gale was beginning to step out on her own at Giorgio, initiating the fragrance and looking for ways to expand the company's volume and market share. She was also ready to be less dependent on Fred. Their nineteen-year age difference was becoming more apparent. Living with the three teenagers was not easy, and a rift between Nicole and Gale was worsening; although her relationship with the boys, especially Robert, was better.

Fred had always been been emotionally calm and in control. He conveyed an image of decorum and order, and the antique-filled Charleville apartment reflected his conservative tastes. Rising early every day, he jogged unaccompanied through Beverly Hills; while Gale, a night person by her own admission, often stayed up late studying fashion magazines and reading.

Gale and Fred separated on June 30, 1978. The separation was surprising to most of the Haymans' friends and business associates, but not all. Author and former University of San Francisco anthropology professor Susanna Hoffman had become friendly with Gale in 1977 and had been to dinner at the Haymans' home. She saw a familiar older man/younger woman pattern in Fred and Gale and felt their separation was predictable:

> I found Fred to be a man of wealth and status and he played on his elegance. As an older man to a younger woman he was selling his sophistication, not his warmth. For cocktails at Fred's, there was caviar in a huge ice-filled bucket and the impression was always important. Gale was charming and lovely—I felt comfortable with her—and it was evident that she wanted more from Fred.
>
> Gale knew she was the creative element and she wanted it to be known. She had the intelligence to know that beauty is not enough, that her beauty was a false high card and other qualities such as creativity are much more satisfying. We were exchanging books and she was a ceaseless reader.
>
> Their relationship was not uncommon and it often backfires for the older man when the younger woman grows up. The rebellion that should have taken place against her parents takes place in the relationship, and walking into that house is like walking into a minefield. A lot of illusion is involved from the beginning, and the man can't understand why there is rebellion.

Gale moved into the Beverly Comstock Hotel with a few suitcases, leaving her personal life with Fred at the apartment. "I felt it was his house. It was his personality. He loved it very much and the kids were there. It was easier for me to move out, and I didn't ask for anything from the house except for three Thea Porter pillows." They agreed, however, to remain close in business and kept the separation a secret from their employees for six months. Together they had built a well-known Beverly Hills store that was acknowledged in the fashion industry as having more influence than its relatively small size should dictate. Gale's fledgling fragrance venture was about to propel it a lot further.

CHAPTER SEVEN

Where Have All the Entrepreneurs Gone?

While Gale and Fred were building Giorgio in Beverly Hills, the fragrance industry in New York was going through an upheaval. Control of the industry began to shift in the early 1970s from fiery entrepreneurs to conservative conglomerates. Although the Haymans were completely unaware of this industry change and shakeout, it would provide them with a marketing niche and talent for their new venture. Not only was there a need in the industry for a bold and daring new fragrance, but at this time there was a surplus of cosmetics marketers on the street due to corporate acquisition fallout. Jim Roth and David Horner were two such animals, fresh out of Max Factor, a company ravaged during the turbulent 1970s.

When Charles Revson died in 1975, the industry lost more than the contentious genius who ran Revlon. The era of the founding entrepreneurs died along with him, and the intense personal rivalries that pitted Revson against Rubinstein, Arden, and finally Lauder were over. The competitive passions and obsessions of the founders were catalysts for the cosmetics and fragrance industry and led to a no-holds-barred creative philosophy. Volume and profit grew in proportion to America's ever-growing appetite for product. Then Wall Street's deal makers discovered the industry.

Between 1971 and 1974, Elizabeth Arden, Helena Rubinstein, Max Factor, and Charles of the Ritz all were acquired by companies who had never been in the cosmetics business. Ethical pharmaceutical giant Eli Lilly acquired Elizabeth Arden for $37 million in 1971 when the company was doing $67 million in sales. This acquisition triggered others, with Norton Simon, Inc., gobbling up Max Factor, Colgate-Palmolive taking Rubinstein, and the Squibb Corporation getting Charles of the Ritz and its Yves St. Laurent fragrance subsidiary.

For big drug companies such as Lilly and Squibb, with extensive research-and-development departments, the cosmetics fit seemed natural. They soon discovered cosmetics companies could operate with substantially lower profit margins than their existing businesses. Marketing a fragrance requires vastly different advertising, sales, and marketing strategies than marketing a drug. Although drugstore distribution channels overlap to an extent, the upscale department stores were foreign and unproductive turf for these cosmetics-industry novices.

The cosmetics industry also appeared to be a compatible environment for the packaged-goods companies, Norton Simon and Colgate. These companies understood advertising, packaging, and new product development, but they relied heavily on quantitative market research, seeking a formula for success. There are no formulas for success in the prestige fragrance business. It takes just one great nose to say, "This is the scent," but when the decision is made by committee, it is often an unsuccessful compromise. The business remains a giant crapshoot in which it takes a recognizable name, superb packaging, and a healthy advertising budget just to get to the table. Still, the bottles must be filled; and there is no way of ensuring the public is going to try the fragrance, much less come back and buy it again.

"This is a very strange business, it's a mixture of packaged goods and fashion," says Stanley Kohlenberg, who started out his career as a pharmacist then switched to sales and then into advertising. He learned the fragrance business from Rubinstein and Revson and jokingly says someday he will call his autobiography *Ashes and Slush* in deference to Revson's biography *Fire and Ice*, written by Andrew Tobias in 1976.

To be successful you have to have fashion-oriented people who understand tempo, who can also put things in little boxes and make them profitable. We have the people who can put the things in the little boxes, but we don't have the fashion-oriented crazies. You have to be in two places, Seventh Avenue and the Plaza district [Plaza Hotel, midtown Manhattan].

You have to understand how women think about beauty and how the magazines think about beauty. The relationship between the great editors and the entrepreneurs was very tight, but now the P.R. departments handle it. Madame [Rubinstein] would invite the beauty editors to her apartment whenever she could. Charles [Revson] would count credits in Vogue just to see how many times Revlon was mentioned against Lauder. Today's execs are uncomfortable with the beauty editors, and how can you spend two hours talking fashion with them if you're a guy in a gray suit worrying about profit-and-loss statements?

Soon after the conglomerates bought into the industry there was plenty to worry about. Profits at all four acquired companies started dwindling in the mid-1970s, especially in the U.S., and the squeeze by the conglomerates choked the creative juices of their fragrance managements. The pressure to launch blockbuster fragrances intensified after Revson scored with Charlie in 1973, but there was no other Charlie on the horizon.

Max Factor was almost a textbook case of how a big conglomerate (NSI) botched and, some say, ruined what was a successful company. The first mistake NSI made when it bought Factor was the acquisition price. The stock value of the February 1973 deal was around $480 million, well over twenty times the company's earnings. Factor's volume was around $165 million and the company had consistent profits in the 10–12 percent pretax range prior to the merger.

Alfred and Chester Firestein, the Factor family members running the business, sold out after their successful Japanese business developed an inventory crisis in the spring of 1972, affecting the entire company's profit and triggering the sale. Chester Firestein, a grandson of founder Max Factor, agreed to stay to manage the business and, although it grew substantially from a volume standpoint, profit problems loomed.

England, in addition to Japan, was a major profit center for Factor, but the oil crisis in 1974 practically shut down the operation. Firestein recalls,

In 1973 we had a banner year, but in 1974 the oil shock shut down our English plant and it was a heavy profit producer. There was no fuel and everyone in England was on allocated fuel and we were on a ten-hour work week. Our people did remarkable things to keep going. They were jerryrigging hand-and-foot-operated equipment and they were working by kerosene lamp. Here were people in a major company working by candlelight and wearing snow hats and winter overcoats on a production line. Obviously we couldn't keep up with production.

Factor's sales grew dramatically between 1973 and 1976 to over $300 million, partially because of the better exchange of promotional concepts between the U.S. and overseas markets. However, profits were eroding during the oil crisis and Factor's autonomy in NSI's decentralized patchwork system of companies was ebbing. Firestein said the external pressure being applied to Factor was a growing albatross.

When NSI sold *McCall's* magazine, part of the deal was we were required to take a certain amount of full-page advertising. Max Factor had to take twenty-four pages at a certain amount per page and we had used three or four before. How can you effectively run your marketing program with twenty percent of the advertising budget in a [magazine] with an audience that you are not trying to reach?

NSI's other businesses included Hunt-Wesson foods, Johnnie Walker Scotch, Avis Rent-A-Car, and Halston Enterprises. When the other divisions had problems, a 10 percent payroll cut was mandated that had a different impact on Factor than it did on the other companies. Said Firestein, "A cosmetics company has fractionated sales and we're not selling by the carloads. We sell many individual pieces [of a line]. It's not an item business. It's much more difficult to manage when you are cutting expenses because you have to abandon certain lines."

The profit pressure on Firestein intensified. NSI wanted 15 percent more pretax profit each year and if it meant cutting budgets to get the profit, they didn't care. "Which baby do you want me to kill?" Firestein asked the NSI treasurer who had flown to Los Angeles for a profit powwow.

I said, "Do you really want us to kill one of the countries we are in? You want to emasculate it so you can produce the profit? What will happen next year? Do you want me to cut a second and third one?" He said, "Those were the orders and that is what we will have to do." Their answer to all of it was, Which baby were you going to kill? They didn't care. The bottom line was all important and I don't fault the objective. That objective is absolutely reasonable. They have a right to ask for the profit, but I objected to the way they went about it. I felt I had lost control of the business and I felt it was going to come down around my ears if I stayed. They were smart guys, but they didn't understand the cosmetics business and they didn't care to.

Firestein later would go into the banking business and open the first bank on Rodeo Drive. Fred Hayman and Firestein would tangle in 1979.

Following Firestein's resignation in December 1975, there was a six-month search for a president until NSI chief executive officer David Mahoney raided Revlon International, naming Sam Kalish as Factor's president. Kalish came out of Revlon with the reputation of being a "gorilla in a $1,900 suit." As president of Revlon International, Kalish had helped forge Revlon's international business along with chairman Robert Armstrong, a gentleman who provided balance with calming diplomacy. Kalish had many enemies at Revlon, and when he departed Sid Stricker hung a dart board in his office with Kalish's photo on it and took target practice.

Kalish was untethered at Factor, and his reign terrorized the company. What had been a paternalistic, almost laid-back firm was now being shaken by frequent firings. After many years of family management there was a certain amount of dead wood. Kalish took it apart but never built a solid organization, and his era was punctuated with the industry's biggest fragrance disaster of the 1970s.

The Max Factor fragrance business was one of the best-kept secrets in the industry. Under the Firesteins the company never attempted to market a blockbuster. Instead, every Christmas it gift packaged existing fragrances, Toujours Moi, Hypnotique, Primitif, and Geminesse. Although none individually was significant, together they placed Factor among the top ten vendors in department stores. Compared to other major companies in which fragrance contributes about one-third of sales, the category was underdeveloped at Factor, accounting for just 10 percent of overall sales. Cosmetics and treatments represented the balance. Mahoney wanted Factor to go after the fragrance market aggressively and they did.

The Factor sales force was not geared to getting behind one big fragrance to convince retailers they had another Charlie. Despite this, NSI told Kalish to do what Revlon had done with Charlie and to a lesser extent with Jontue, launched in 1975 as a follow-up to Charlie.

NSI was buoyed by the success of its Halston introduction in 1975 and thought Kalish could duplicate Halston's sensational start in the prestige market with a similar thrust in the mass market. The Halston launch cost only $972,000 and the designer's fashion and social clout allowed Factor to leverage the brand in better stores such as Bergdorf Goodman and Bloomingdale's.

The Halston division was a separate group within Factor, headed by Joe Forkish. The women's fragrance was a luxurious blend of floral, fruity, and amberwood notes that Halston and Forkish had selected at the eleventh hour. Elsa Peretti had designed the sexy curved bottle. The scent, after doing $1 million the first year, rocketed to $17 million the second year, showing a 22 percent pretax profit. It hit $35 million in the third year, eventually topping out at around $50 million by 1980.

Sampling was a key part of the strategy and, at Bloomingdale's alone during the first six weeks of the launch, two hundred fifty thousand samples at a cost of $100,000 were given away free. Forkish later would apply these same principles to establish the business plan for Giorgio; but he would not execute the plan.

As successful as Halston was, the other new Max Factor fragrance of 1975 hit the other end of the spectrum. Stephen B. was black designer Stephen Burrows's first and last fragrance. The eager Factor sales force oversold it in what was at the time one of the industry's largest wholesale sell-ins, filling the pipeline with $7 million worth of inventory. Unfortunately for Factor, a year later between $3 million and $4 million worth was still on the shelf. Retailers lost confidence in the brand, and Factor's unwillingness to spend the many millions in advertising needed to support such a large sell-in further doomed the fragrance, which had neither a good scent nor a well-known designer's name. Retailers said their customers thought they were buying a Stevie Wonder fragrance. After taking over, Kalish acknowledged the Stephen B. disaster and plotted a new fragrance to resurrect Factor's reputation in the drug chains.

Max Factor launched Just Call Me Maxi in September 1977. Although those brave enough to stand up to Kalish expressed their doubts about the concept, the scent, and the name, Kalish bullied the scent into the mass outlets. Again the Factor sales force went out and oversold, this time cramming $10 million into the pipeline. Retailers bought the fragrance knowing they could return it, as the industry operates on a consignment basis, and they were impressed by Kalish's multimillion-dollar television campaign to support the product.

Maxi bombed during the Christmas 1977 season, with approximately 70 percent coming back to Factor as returns. Rumors of Kalish's impending firing were swirling early in 1978, prompting Mahoney to issue denials and praise Kalish in the press. Kalish, however, was not liked by his own staff, Halston couldn't tolerate his rudeness, and retailers were calling Mahoney and complaining about Kalish. The inevitable firing that ended Kalish's two-year debacle came in June 1978. Firestein was quoted in WWD upon Kalish's ouster: "The character and methods of the business that made the company successful were seriously altered and in some cases were reduced to ashes. Unfortunately at this point, the phoenix hasn't risen from the ashes."

It never did. The healing process at Factor ended tragically when Kalish's successor, Dale Ratliff, died suddenly. Mahoney had again robbed Revlon, tabbing Ratliff, a superb sales executive, to be the new Factor president. Ratliff was out jogging in Beverly Hills in early 1979, after only a few months on the job, when he suddenly died of a heart attack. Factor was snakebitten and its employees shell-shocked. The company's momentum was lost and Linda Wachner's unsuccessful attempts to revive it in the early 1980s led to NSI's dumping the company to Beatrice. It was then sold to Esmark and was relocated to Stamford, Connecticut, where International Playtex ran it. Finally, in 1987 Revlon acquired Factor and moved what was left of the company back to Los Angeles in March 1988. Under Allan Kurtzman, a cosmetics-industry veteran, Factor is making a comeback and launched a Jaclyn Smith fragrance at Bloomingdale's in April 1989.

Lost temporarily in the ashes of the Factor volcano were two out-of-work executives, David Horner and Jim Roth. If any phoenix were to rise from Factor's ashes, it would be Giorgio, and Roth and Horner would help lift it off the ground.

Horner and Roth spent six mostly miserable years together working in the international divisions of Revlon and Max Factor. Horner's turbulent career was reflective of the changes going on in the cosmetics industry. Although he had enough financial savvy and ambition to run a company he was much too irascible and impatient, especially during the conglomerate era, to buy the concept of team play. "I could never find the team, because they were always behind my back stabbing me," Horner said.

Sam Kalish had been Horner's boss at Revlon International in the 1960s, when Horner was the director of planning analysis and research. After four years at Revlon, Horner's poor timing brought him to Helena Rubinstein in 1972, three months before Colgate-Palmolive acquired the company. At thirty-three, Horner had an important job, vice president of marketing of the international division, but he did not have the patience to teach the Colgate brass the cosmetics industry. When David Foster, the chief executive officer of Colgate, asked Horner for a detailed report on why the industry was focusing on the prestige department stores in upper Manhattan, Horner didn't take him seriously. An hour before his presentation he borrowed a fat printout on drugstore sales from Herb Morris, the company's vice president of sales, whom he had run into on an elevator. He carried it in to Foster, presenting it as an analysis by a prestigious research company, Skelly and Yankelovich, and bluffed his way through the meeting.

Horner sensed it would be profit suicide for companies such as Rubinstein, Arden, and Factor, whose strength was in drugstores, to change their character by going after a bigger slice of the upscale department-store business. These companies were blindly following Revlon, who invested heavily in the department stores partially because of Charles Revson's desire to outdo Estée Lauder. Revson's strategy was to try to establish an upscale image in a high-fashion store with a fragrance such as Norell to have greater power and clout when he introduced less costly products such as Charlie in the mass outlets. The trickle-down theory worked for Revlon as long as Revson was alive and creating the superb mass-appeal fragrances and cosmetics that paid for his costly confrontation with Lauder in the prestige stores.

The rush to the prestige stores led to the American designer fragrance explosion from 1975 to 1982. Well over fifty designer fragrances were launched, but only five—Halston, Karl Lagerfeld's Chloe, YSL's Opium, Ralph Lauren's Lauren, and Oscar de la Renta—achieved significant volumes. Chloe was manufactured by Arden, Opium was Squibb's great triumph, and Halston was NSI's lone fragrance success. Oscar and Lauren were more the work of entrepreneurs and were precursors to Giorgio's success in the 1980s. This explosion of higher-priced, made-in-America fragrances shifted the industry's emphasis away from France and also made the department stores the critical arena for new products. Spurred by the introductions, the fragrance industry enjoyed a 9.5 percent growth between 1977 and 1981, reaching the $2 billion mark.

Doing business profitably in better department stores was almost as difficult for a fragrance manufacturer as finding a marketable fragrance. Department stores have limited main-floor space and the cosmetics companies who wanted a piece of that real estate had to pay a premium. To acquire and maintain favorable space, manufacturers were required to spend between 15 and 20 percent of their net sales for a variety of promotional and point-of-purchase costs. The manufacturers kicked in for the salaries of the line (sales) girls and, in the most prestigious stores such as Bloomingdale's, paid 100 percent of the girl's salary even though she was a Bloomingdale's employee. These in-store expenditures are not nearly as steep in drugstores or mass merchandisers because they are for the most part self-service, without many gimmicky gifts-with-purchase.

Even more costly for the cosmetics and fragrance companies, the merchandise is sold to the stores on consignment. If a fragrance fails to sell, the store ships it back. The department stores agree, in turn, to the industry's 40 percent markup, considerably less than the 50 percent and higher markups in apparel. The stores also agree never to take markdowns on a prestige fragrance because reducing the price of a fragrance compromises its snob appeal. These are the ground rules, and each manufacturer does battle with each store trying to get the most space, best location and terms.

Invariably, Estée Lauder has the best real estate, primarily because the company's sales are greatest. Competitors wanting to get instant notice go into a powerful store such as Bloomingdale's willing to be exploited and lose money. They figure if they manage to look good at a marquee store, they can impress all the visiting out-of-town buyers and then balance their losses in Bloomingdale's and Saks with profits in, for instance, Dayton's in Minneapolis or Burdine's in Miami.

Allan Mottus, an industry consultant who has worked with a number of manufacturers, including Norton Simon and Bijan, observes,

> Bloomingdale's is the noisiest and loudest of the stores and Saks is the most prestigious. You can make a profit at Saks, but I'm not sure about Bloomingdale's. Bloomie's adds on so much to the expenses that you must pay p.m.'s [promotional monies] up the yin yang. When Fendi came out, it had to buy its own rugs and paid about thirty thousand dollars. The other expenses at Bloomingdale's include advertising in newspapers and catalogues, and they hit you with everything in the world. Everybody goes in there willing to be raped, and it's not that Bloomingdale's is doing something strange and different. Everybody has their eyes wide open, and that is just the cost of doing business with Bloomingdale's.

Lauder and Revlon, plowing millions into their department-store divisions, drove up the cost of doing business in the department stores, which started to maximize their demands and become lecherous. New ventures found it especially tough going in the 1970s when these costs spiraled. Actress Polly Bergen had carved out a $6 million volume selling her line of turtle oil cosmetics to the better stores, investing $4 million of her own money; but by 1973 she was forced to sell out to Fabergé and her line soon disappeared.

Bergen remains bitter:

> The department stores were all whores. If you are hot on Monday, somebody else is hot on Tuesday and all they want is the hottest and latest. They want to work with your money. I only had the

best triple A store accounts and I was sitting with one-point-two million dollars in receivables and I was only doing three million in volume. They pay ultimately when they decide to and take their discount. Cash flow in this business is murder; but they just didn't pick on me, they are sweet enough to treat everyone that way.

For companies like Rubinstein, which had the financial support to market both at the prestige and mass outlets, the double-edged distribution game didn't work. Their hamstrung marketing departments seldom came up with great fragrances and when Rubinstein saw its Anne Klein Blazer lay a badly scented egg in the department stores, it drained capital and attention from the more profitable drug business. "The industry got hung up on space in the department stores and we sold ourselves a bill of goods," Horner says. "Only Charles was able to do the multibrands and validate his drugstore business. Only Lauder was working with sensible ground rules in the 1970s. They decided they have no place else to make it and we better make it in the department stores, so they played smarter, better, and more clever."

In a company where an executive in a blue shirt was considered rebellious, a wise-cracking, authority-challenging up-and-comer like Horner didn't stand a chance. His suggestions to his boss, Helena Rubinstein CEO Peter Engel, went unheeded. "Ralph Lauren came to us in 1974 broke and needed some money and we tried to convince upper management that a Polo fragrance would be a very good thing for us. Engel wanted to prove that he was the consummate negotiator and felt we shouldn't give him eighty thousand dollars up front, but only fifty thousand, and we blew the deal." Lauren later signed in 1976 with Warner Communications and Polo became a leader in the men's category.

Horner was not enamored of the new executive talent Colgate was sending Rubinstein. "Rubinstein was a dumping ground for Colgate's garbage. These were people they didn't want to fire, guys who had given twenty-two years of loyal service who hadn't screwed up enough to get kicked out, so we got these finance guys. I saw the same thing at Arden and at Charles of the Ritz. You had two kinds of people there, the bright young guy who came in and spied for the big company or the old loyal guys."

When Kalish took the Factor job, he hired Horner and made him his assistant and international troubleshooter. For eighteen months Horner shuttled back and forth to Japan, helping maintain that division's high profitability. Horner was promised he would be made president of Orlane, the fine French treatment house NSI acquired in 1976, but he was never given the post. He watched Mahoney pump up Kalish's ego with praise when the company had three good quarters consecutively and then watched him dismantle Kalish when Maxi bombed. After Kalish was fired, Horner and the rest of Factor were in limbo awaiting a new boss. George Evanoff was dispatched to be the interim president and Horner scoffed at his suggestion that he become his assistant and analyst. Horner, lobbying for international president, rejected Evanoff's offer "to ride sidesaddle over Factor. He was horrified that I had the temerity to eschew this opportunity so he sent me off to renegotiate my contract."

Horner took his severance package, leaving the corporate cosmetics world in June 1978. He finally had become a president, but not exactly of a Fortune 500 company. American Jojoba Industries was a collection of twenty-three affluent farmers from Texas and Bakersfield who were growing jojoba beans in their hot, desertlike fields. When processed, jojoba oil was worth fifty-five dollars a gallon, had cosmetics applications, and was marketed as an environmentally sane substitute for whale oil, long used by the cosmetics industry. The group, called California Farm Management, had approached Max Factor about a coventure while Horner was still there. Although he hated driving to Bakersfield for meetings and was hardly comfortable with a group of farmers who "must have been allergic to natural fibers," Horner joined the group in September, going to work for $3,000 a month and 25 percent of the startup company's stock. Horner quickly created a skin-care line called Nature's Secret from the jojoba oil. The line was sold by mail order and Horner was starting to build a business using an advertising approach unusual for the cosmetics industry.

Blue Boy magazine, a gay "skin" magazine, wanted Nature's Secret advertising and made Horner an offer he never should have considered. Although it had not been created for the men's market, the product could go both ways; and Horner decided to take the free advertising and give the magazine 15 percent of the sales generated from the ads. Operating in Los Angeles, Horner figured the Bakersfield group would not find out about his strategy.

"I went to Tom Kelly, a fine photographer in town, and we got the most nongay-looking model and shot the guy coming out of a shower with a towel wrapped around him. He wasn't looking swish and was saying jojoba was 'the oil of my skin,' and he 'couldn't live without it,' and the orders came rolling in."

However, at California Farm Management's 1979 board meeting, Horner's marketing strategy kicked up some dust. A stockholder from Texas brought *Blue Boy* to the meeting and started showing the group the kind of pinups they didn't post in their offices. Using a heavy Texas accent, Horner describes the wrath of a joboba farmer, "I've never seen shit like this in my entire life. I don't give a shit, I'm worth forty-two million and I don't want to make money this way."

Switching back to his own nasal New York accent, Horner continues, "About this time the four other guys move to his side of the table and start screaming at me and we have this war of wills. I get pissed off and say, 'If you don't like it, buy my goddamn stock.' They asked me to leave the room and they bought my stock which I paid nothing for."

While Horner was bowing out of the jojoba business, Roth was asked to leave his senior vice president's job at Max Factor in May 1979. Having survived the Kalish era, Roth was let go during Linda Wachner's reign. Although at the time it was a blow and he had trouble facing it, the move led to Giorgio.

As bombastic as Horner is, Roth, slightly stooped from a chronic back ailment, has a melodious voice and rarely shows emotion. He had joined Revlon in 1962 as advertising director of the international division and met Horner as he was leaving in 1969 to join Factor.

During the Maxi launch at Factor, Roth proudly told *WWD* that the Maxi television commercials cost in excess of $100,000 to produce, whereas the industry average was somewhere between $30,000 and $75,000. The $3 million Maxi 1977 Christmas television blitz caused Roth to boast, "You will never see one of our network spots before four thirty P.M. or after eleven P.M.; we're strictly prime time." The Maxi experience would soon humble Roth.

In 1971, Roth was having problems finding exciting clothes for the models in the Max Factor ads. He discovered Giorgio, with its kicky, innovative designs from Halston, Stephen Burrows, and Zandra Rhodes, and he began to wardrobe the Max Factor ads with outfits from the store. Roth is a detail-oriented nitpicker, like Fred Hayman and unlike Horner, who would prefer to get things done quickly to meet deadlines and financial objectives.

When Roth began to question why Factor's ad agency (Wells, Rich, Greene, Inc.) fees doubled in 1979, he soon was out of a $78,000-a-year job. Two months after he was dumped by Wachner, Roth had formed his own consulting company, International Marketing Group (IMG) along with Jerry Rosen and Joe Forkish, and was looking for clients—preferably entrepreneurs—who wanted to get into the fragrance and cosmetics business. He accidentally met Fred Hayman while crossing Dayton Way to pick up his shoes at the Artistic Shoe Repair shop across the alley from Giorgio. Fred asked him what he was doing and told Jim that Gale was working on a fragrance. Roth wanted a crack at marketing Giorgio and immediately set up a meeting with Fred to discuss the possibility of a licensing arrangement.

The Giorgio team was being assembled, a team that would exceed anyone's expectations. Roth, now a millionaire, summarizes, "If you listen to Fred, he did it all; if you listen to Gale, she did it all; if you listen to David, he did it all. If you listen to me, it was a four-part deal. I have done things on a bigger scale at Factor but nothing ever this successful. We were all Cinderellas who pooled our talents. And we were lucky."

Giorgio was not the first Cinderella to make it to the ball. If the fledgling Giorgio team had had the time to do a marketing study of the industry in 1980 they would have found a useful prototype in Parfums Stern. Milton Stern was another unlikely player who was able to go up against the giants, spending substantially less than $1 million to launch his successful Oscar de la Renta fragrance. Ironically, the Stern family sold their company to Avon in 1987 for $160 million. The Haymans would be the fragrance entrepreneurs of the 1980s and would sell to Avon for $165 million.

From 1960 to 1976, Stern was the U.S. distributor of the French perfume Cabochard. The business never exceeded $3 million. Stern had a reputation of being penurious and difficult, but fully understood the ins and outs of doing business with the better stores. While fragrance marketers were taking beauty editors to lunch at La Grenouille and La Côte Basque, Stern's idea was to order up a sandwich from the deli in his building and conduct the interview in his office. His wife, Bernice, worked with him; and, by fragrance-industry standards, Stern was running a shoestring operation.

Stern, at sixty-five, saw two niches in the fragrance market in 1976 that kept him from retiring. First, the distribution patterns of the fine French fragrance houses had broadened and, second, the drug companies who had invested in the industry did not understand the importance of limited distribution. The industry was on a volume kick and most new fragrances were launched in a thousand doors. Stern sensed the better stores were hungry for an exclusive fragrance and he plotted a launch in fewer than three hundred doors and only the most prestigious specialty stores such as Saks, I. Magnin, and Neiman-Marcus.

There was also a positioning opportunity after the glut of life-style fragrances spawned by Charlie, and Stern accurately perceived the need for a romantic throwback. He saw a chance to go against the trend and build a nice little business by hooking up with Oscar de la Renta, the designer who personified romance.

Oscar was launched in August 1977, in 290 doors. Stern's concept of limited distribution worked. Rather than negotiate with the fragrance buyers and their bosses, the divisional merchandise managers (DMMs), Stern insisted on dealing with the store's senior management. After all, he was offering them an exclusive in their market and he wanted to have the store as a full partner. Buyer and DMM positions experience rapid turnover, but there is more stability in the higher echelons. Stern focused his attention on these people because he wanted their long-term commitment. Oscar had no national advertising budget, choosing to focus its promotional budget on heavy in-store sampling programs and scented inserts in store catalogues and billing statements. Stern also got de la Renta involved, and his in-store appearances not only charmed the consumer but, more important, made the girl behind the counter feel indispensable.

The fragrance did $2 million the first year; Stern decided to get management help and go to the bank in an effort to make Oscar a big brand. His son Michael was working on Wall Street as an investment banker and, after studying his father's strategy, decided to make a career switch. Said Stern:

> He asked me to help arrange the financing because he was having problems with the bankers convincing them for this new venture. Their attitude toward a new fragrance was that it was highly speculative. I knew nothing about the fragrance business, but I sat down and reviewed it and saw his growth was coming with the blue-chip accounts and there was great stability; these were not mom-and-pop stores. He was getting repeat business and there was door-to-door growth which was tremendous. I put together a plan and we presented it to the bank and they went along and we got our seven-hundred-fifty-thousand-dollar line. I realized something exciting was happening.

The Oscar business doubled each year and Stern moved to Paris in 1979 to start an international Oscar de la Renta business. He semi-retired in Monte Carlo, leaving Michael to run the U.S. operation. Oscar was the first prestige scent ever to do over $1 million in Neiman-Marcus. By the time the Sterns sold out, they had built a $100 million fragrance mini-empire, with Oscar de la Renta's fragrance accounting for $35 million in sales in the U.S. The company created a second de la Renta fragrance, Ruffles, which bombed; and it had marginal success with Perry Ellis's fragrances. It has had no success with a Valentino fragrance.

Michael Stern ran the company (now under Avon) until he resigned in April 1989. He still thinks there is room in the industry for future Milton Sterns:

The consolidation in the industry makes it easier for new entrepreneurs. When there is a concentration of companies, the special touch and individual attention that the brands had before is more difficult to sustain. The parameters for success and the risks and rewards become much larger. Milton Stern was happy with a two-million-dollar launch; he could pick his spots and his niche. A company like Avon or any of the large companies is looking at bigger numbers. They are shooting for ten-million-dollar launches to make that brand successful. Dad risked everything; he put everything he had on the line, and he grew slowly. Fred Hayman started off with scent strips and Milton started with a limited number of accounts and in-store promotions because he couldn't afford national advertising. They were both smart enough to recognize what worked well and then to take advantage of it quickly. That's the sign of a great entrepreneur, to have the common sense to recognize the opportunity and then bring in people to support them.

CHAPTER EIGHT

Screaming and Sniffing: Birth of a Fragrance

The Haymans' business fared better than their marriage. Their thriving retail operation fixed Fred's salary in fiscal 1979 at $254,000 and Gale's at $159,000. Their equity in Giorgio was estimated at $2,327,350 and included the land and building, which they had purchased in 1979 for $1.2 million. The Charleville apartment was appraised at $501,150 and they owed $156,000 on the mortgage. The antiques and furniture in the house were appraised at $248,850 and their total assets as of July 31, 1979, were $3,197,190, according to court records.

In 1979, after almost two years of trying to find her fragrance, Gale Hayman was on the verge of giving up. Karl Lagerfeld, the designer and creator of Chloe, then a $15 million brand, had lunch with Gale and told her it took him two years to find Chloe. "After two years, forget about it, cut it off," he advised Gale, whose frustrations had grown the more she worked with perfumers.

Said Gale:

I didn't articulate as a perfumer, but as a layman. A fragrance is such an intangible. It's not like a fabric; you don't see it. Fragrance is all in the mind; it's very cerebral and emotional. It's a matter of interpretation. I may say I want a sexy and warm fragrance, but to you it may smell entirely different. I say this smells sugary but, to you, not at all. It's very subjective and can drive you crazy.

The fragrance project and Gale were not high on Fred Hayman's list of priorities. The Giorgio store was reaching the apex of its popularity and Fred's efforts with the Rodeo Drive Committee were increasingly visible as he became the street's spokesman. While Gale was tinkering with a fragrance, Fred was facing the biggest threat of the day—banks on Rodeo Drive.

Chester Firestein, the former Max Factor chief executive officer, had chartered a bank, among whose shareholders was Fred Hayman, who put up $2,000. Fred was horrified to learn that Firestein was planning to open the bank's first branch on Rodeo Drive. The location was to be the prime northeast corner of Rodeo Drive and Brighton Way. The lease had already been signed when the Rodeo Drive Committee took their concerns to the Beverly Hills City Council, trying to pass a zoning ordinance prohibiting banks from taking large ground-floor retail space on Rodeo. The committee feared it could damage the street's high-fashion image.

Firestein tried to assuage Hayman by taking him to lunch at Hillcrest Country Club. He brought a $2,000 check to give back to Fred, who wanted to resign from the bank's board over the Rodeo location. Firestein tried one last ploy to keep Fred and the committee at bay.

I said, "Fred, I hope there is no fallout against you. There are a lot of our shareholders who also shop in your store and when it becomes known you have dropped out of the bank and have become hostile to us, I just hope they will continue to shop in your place." This was the ultimate chutzpah ploy on my part, and there was a long silence from his end of the table; but he dropped out and they lost the fight over our lease.

Firestein's bank at 400 North Rodeo Drive folded five years later, replaced by Capital Bank. However, no other Rodeo stores have been converted to financial institutions as feared. Rodeo remains safe from places where people could save their money.

Fred's business interest in launching the Giorgio fragrance was aroused by the chance street meeting with Jim Roth in May 1979. The outsider's enthusiasm for a Giorgio fragrance gave a degree of credibility to Gale's concept. Roth's inquiry into the possibility of signing the Haymans to a fragrance licensing deal was a chance to shift the financial burden of launching the scent. Roth proposed a licensing arrangement to Fred contingent on the ability of Roth's group to raise the necessary capital—$2.5 million—through a public offering.

The prospects for a Giorgio blockbuster fragrance were hardly bright given the circumstances. There was Gale's frustrating inability to find a fragrance and Fred's lack of enthusiasm for the project. Understandably, he did not believe other retailers would carry a fragrance spawned by a retailer. There were Roth's fragrance-industry credentials—somewhere short of impeccable after the Maxi disaster and his firing. Roth was joined by David Horner, rapidly going broke putting his four children through private school after he was forced out of the short-lived jojoba venture. It was not exactly the nucleus for a winning team.

The team's best asset was the growing mystique of the boutique. Judith Krantz's *Scruples*, the novel about a boutique on Rodeo Drive, was published in 1979. The first-time author used Giorgio in the novel as the ultimate competition for her heroine's boutique. Krantz interviewed Hayman to find out how much volume her fictitious retailer would have to hit to become the queen of Rodeo. She misrepresented herself as a journalist from *Cosmopolitan* magazine doing a story on retailing. Krantz studied Giorgio's small dressing rooms and decided to make the Scruples boutique much more opulent than Giorgio. Spider Elliott, the Scruples manager who lusts for heroine Billy Ikehorn, says,

> And Giorgio's is the number-one retail specialty store in the country, including New York City. . . . They have four thousand feet of selling space, which means four million dollars a year just on clothes and accessories. . . . In comparison, our local Saks, which has one hundred fifty thousand square feet, only did twenty million dollars in 1975, so you can see how well Giorgio's is using its space. There are dozens of women who spend at least fifty thousand dollars every year with Giorgio's, customers from every wealthy city in the world.

Krantz started shopping at Giorgio after moving to Los Angeles because the Haymans carried Halston exclusively. Later Krantz's tastes drifted toward Chanel sweaters and Yves St. Laurent evening clothes, but *Scruples* was her first book and she was awed by her first publication party, which, at Fred Hayman's insistence, was held at the Giorgio boutique.

> Fred had the photographers and every star was there. Even though it was my pub party, my mouth was hanging open. It was

hard to believe I was connected with this and I walked around in a total daze. I was embarrassed when Charlton Heston came in and immediately the photographers grabbed me and threw Mrs. Heston into a corner and put me on his arm. I had never done this before and I thought I had to talk to him. He was staring at the cameras while I was busy trying to have a conversation with him. I said the most stupid thing, "How does it feel to be a movie star?" and he said out of the corner of his mouth, "It's a living." When I go to a party now, I just smile and look straight ahead. I learned that smile and you don't want to be caught by the photographers talking.

Scruples was on the best-seller list for fifteen weeks and then eventually sold over thirty million copies in twenty-two languages. The book became an eight-hour CBS mini-series in 1980 and tourists arriving on Rodeo Drive went to Giorgio looking for Scruples and posed for photos outside the store.

Inside the shop the discreet love lives of the owners were keeping the salesgirls guessing. Gale's new lover was Igor Stalew, a big, blond, mustachioed video and commercial producer whom she had met while grocery shopping at the Santa Glen Market near their respective apartments in West Los Angeles. When they first met, Gale told Stalew she was a shopgirl at Boulmiche, a boutique at the corner of Rodeo and Little Santa Monica. Stalew was UCLA-educated and, although he grew up in Beverly Hills, had never been inside Giorgio. Active in liberal campus politics as a student, he considered Rodeo Drive "bourgeois stuff."

Stalew had been married at twenty-four, to an older Spanish woman who had four young children, and the marriage lasted six years. His relationship with Gale took about six months to develop.

When I first met Gale she was wired. As she got to be more relaxed, some lovely things began to happen that really attracted me to her. When she started to laugh it was contagious and you couldn't stop her from laughing. She would tell me her husband would never allow her to laugh and she would look at me before laughing and I would laugh with her and say how wonderful that somebody could laugh this way. She was told [by Fred] that it's not polite or elegant to laugh in public. I said, "Are you crazy? What kind of aesthetics do you have? Laughter is the most elegant thing in the world."

Closer in age to Gale (he is four years younger), Stalew started taking her to dance clubs, foreign films, and art galleries. After about six months, they began to see each other exclusively. Said Stalew,

> She had been with Fred for twelve years and I got the impression that this woman had never known what love was. She didn't know what it was to be touched. Someone had not opened up to her or become vulnerable to her. They were together for twelve years and something must have worked, but I didn't consider it a romantic relationship. I wasn't in their bedroom with them; but I don't care, this was a woman I found who needed love. She was starved for love and wanted to open up to new ideas.

Stalew was eager to make Gale more outdoorsy and athletic. During the 1980 Christmas holidays they went skiing together in Banff and Lake Louise in Alberta, Canada. Barreling out of a ski class, Gale lost control and returned to Los Angeles with a broken leg.

Fred had found a more athletic girlfriend, Betty Endo. They lived near each other in Beverly Hills and a mutual acquaintance suggested they go jogging together. Endo grew up in Brigham City, Utah, near where her Japanese-American parents were interned during World War II. Working as a secretary for Steve McQueen and then Clint Eastwood, she had spent fifteen years on movie locations and hated the ephemeral nature of location romances. High-fashion and black-tie social events were not part of Betty's world until Fred started shaping her as he had done with his other long-term lovers. Betty moved into his Charleville apartment and Fred became her full-time occupation.

The Haymans' most important new business relationship was with Jim Roth, David Horner, and Joe Forkish. Although a Giorgio fragrance was nowhere near final selection, the IMG team was putting together a marketing and fund-raising plan that would put Fred and Gale Hayman in the fragrance business with just a $150,000 investment. On February 26, 1980, the Haymans agreed to license the Giorgio and Giorgio Beverly Hills logos to Parfums Giorgio Ltd., a proposed California limited partnership managed by Roth, Forkish, and Horner. The licensing agreement gave the Haymans a 5 percent royalty on gross sales of the fragrances and written approval of all advertising, promotion, and sales decisions. In addition, the general partners had to spend at least 15 percent of their gross sales on national and cooperative advertising. The Haymans agreed to purchase two units at $75,000 each to show their financial commitment and were to receive a 4 percent interest in the limited partnership. The licensing deal was contingent on the successful subscription of twenty-four units at $75,000 per unit by December 31, 1980.

Although Allen & Company, a prestigious New York underwriter, produced the impressive seventy-three-page subscription memorandum, the document had fiasco written all over it. The five-year plan gave a realistic estimate of a $941,000 loss (pretax) in the first year, reaching $14 million in sales by 1985, with a 20 percent pretax profit of $2,826,000. However, to savvy investors worried about a recession and interest rates approaching 20 percent, a fragrance with the name of a Beverly Hills boutique must have seemed either a joke or a risk not worth taking.

On December 7, 1980, a cocktail party for about 150 prospective investors was held at Roberta and David Haft's sprawling Beverly Hills home. Henry Rogers, a respected public-relations man, was interested in the project and arranged the guest list, which included affluent entertainment people such as Quincy Jones, Jeff Wald, Pierre Cossette, and Alan Livingston. Roth had tried to get Giorgio's impressive customer list from Fred Hayman, who did not cooperate.

According to Roth,

> The day of the party we got a call from Allen & Company that they were pulling out of the deal because Herbie Allen was in some kind of litigation [the David Begelman affair] and they didn't want the exposure on the West Coast. The party was being canceled. Just before the party David and I decided we wouldn't say that Allen & Company had pulled out and we did a dog and pony show totally unrehearsed and I was a nervous wreck. When the party was over we solicited maybe five units, and the next day we were on a plane to New York with our attorney demanding to see the Allens.

The private placement had cost Forkish, Horner, and Roth $25,000 each, which it appeared they had lost. Horner was "climbing the walls" because he was already broke, Roth was able to live off a condominium he had recently sold, and Forkish had a steady income from his Max Factor job. Forkish was in London on Factor business but stayed up until 4 A.M. to get the bad news on the placement party. Fortunately, IMG's attorney was able to salvage the $75,000. The group reprinted the prospectus and spent the first half of 1981 trying to solicit investors on their own.

Not only was IMG ineffective in raising capital, the group was frustrated trying to work with Gale to select a fragrance. Forkish was supposed to have the best nose and was working directly with Gale. In February 1979, Gale started working with IFF, telling the perfumery staff that her fragrance preferences were, ". . . Oriental, Chloe, sexy, musky, violet . . . glamorous with some sandalwood and sweetness." Submissions began and by June 1979, a jonquil floral fragrance emerged that Forkish loved and was ready to accept; but Gale had some reservations. She told the perfumers it should be longer lasting with a warmer dry-down and mentioned the way Chloe and Halston permeated the air. Then Gale told the perfumers she wanted some notes of Coty's Complice fragrance to be introduced into the dry-down. (There are three stages of a fragrance, the top note, the middle note and the dry-down. The top note is the most effusive and is the scent when first applied to the skin. Most purchases are made based on the top note. The middle note is the scent when the mist settles on the skin. The dry-down is the scent after the fragrance has been on the skin for about five minutes and has dried on the skin. The dry-down is the way the fragrance will smell on the user for the rest of the day and should be consistent with the top note and the middle note.)

Forkish remains frustrated about the experience of trying to please Gale:

> We were working on this specific note, jonquil. It's very effusive, because we wanted a blatant scent. This was our idea; it came out of our document [marketing plan]; it wasn't her idea. She wanted to do a fragrance that was much softer. She wanted to do something that was rosy and old-fashioned, a knockoff of a fragrance called Complice. She gave me a sample bottle of Complice and said, "This is what I want." It was a nothing fragrance by Coty. It got to the point where we were in Paris working with the IFF perfumers who started to knock off Complice, and she started to see her memory for that fragrance was not terrific and she saw that we were right and she was wrong. She was speaking out of ignorance. It didn't mean she couldn't learn or that she didn't recognize a winner, but she really didn't know what she wanted. She kept running around saying, "We are never going to have a fragrance, it's never going to be right," but we were real close on that jonquil fragrance, and if I were going to do a fragrance today I would resurrect that jonquil scent.

Gale recalls wearing Complice and that she did tell IFF's great perfumer Bernard Chant that she liked the fragrance, but she was disappointed in IFF's offerings. "They didn't come up with anything modern, powerful, strong, nothing that says, 'Wow!' I have got to get turned on by it. It just can't be another smell, the world is filled with nice fragrances; we need something socko. I wanted something commercial but exciting. Women were becoming assertive and I wanted that personality in the fragrance."

The game Forkish played with Gale was not nearly as dangerous as the corporate tightrope act he was trying to perform. As a senior executive at Max Factor, Forkish was engaging in a conflict of interest; and if news of his involvement in the Giorgio project reached Factor's top brass, Forkish would be in trouble. The prospectus ended up on the desk of Robert Kamerschen, Factor's chief executive officer, in January 1981; and Forkish was promptly terminated. He had the choice of staying with Roth and Horner or seeking more steady employment. With one young child and another on the way, Forkish dropped out of IMG and took a job at Mattel, the toy manufacturer. Forkish's career would later come full circle. After stints at Mattel and Jovan, a fragrance company based in Chicago, he ended up back in California and lost money in 1987 with a failed Chris Evert shampoo line. In 1988, Fred Hayman needed help in developing his new fragrances and hired Forkish as a part-time consultant. Later in 1988, Forkish was named vice president of fragrance development of Fred Hayman Beverly Hills, Inc. He gives Roth, Horner, and Fred Hayman all the credit for Giorgio's success while giving Gale "zero" credit.

Giorgio was not the only project Roth and Horner were working on. They were forced to take some odd marketing jobs to pay the $900 rent on their small office at 113 North San Vicente Boulevard. A quadriplegic, who was hoping the drug DMSO would help his spine, hired IMG to start Health Science Laboratories, a company that would try to market DMSO as a topical healing aid. The venture never took off because the client died. There was another client, Sam Bennett, in the California Apparel Mart. IMG did his quarterly promotions, which barely paid the bills. Horner recalls, "We would boil eggs in our coffee pot and split a can of tuna fish for lunch. We didn't spring for anything. We did our own typing."

The best prospect Roth and Horner had was Giorgio, but they couldn't raise the money on their own and Fred Hayman continued to balk at the suggestion that he put up the money himself to launch the business. Roth and Horner began devising an inexpensive way of entering the fragrance business while continuing to work with fragrance suppliers on submissions for Gale.

There are only about a dozen fragrance suppliers in the industry. Having turned down two of the most successful, Roure Bertrand Dupont and IFF, it was time for Giorgio to seek submissions from other houses. These companies do not charge for their submissions; they make money only when their scent is selected. Word travels fast, and most suppliers were not eager to submit their best fragrance to Giorgio. The hard-to-please little Beverly Hills boutique had no track record in the industry and could waste a lot of time.

Fortunately, Roth and Horner had not burned all their creative supply sources. Turning desperately to Frank Buchwalter, their former Max Factor colleague, Roth and Horner were able to gain entry into Florasynth's well-established library of fragrances. A former Revlonite, Buchwalter had headed Factor's research-and-development department for four years until Linda Wachner took control and started shuffling the lineup, replacing Buchwalter with Monroe Lanzet. Disappointed with corporate life, Buchwalter became a consultant. He was a friend of the Friedman family that owned Florasynth. During his twenty-three years at Revlon, Buchwalter got to know and work with Jack Friedman, the president of Florasynth. Friedman and Florasynth's top perfumer, Harry Cuttler, together with Charles Revson, worked weekends in the Flora-synth perfume laboratories creating Charlie. The team came up with the scent that turned out to be the most successful second guess in the industry's history after Revson threw out three hundred kilos of the original scent he had decided on. Friedman and his son Freddy enjoyed working with Revsonian entrepreneurs but disliked working with con-glomerates that wanted to panel test their fragrances before making commitments. Florasynth did all the Revlon fragrances, including Jontue, Ivoire, and Bill Blass, and it was always Revson or, later, Paul Woolard, who made the decision. Florasynth created Jungle Gardenia, the white floral fragrance that helped established Germaine Monteil as a serious fine fragrance house in the 1960s. The company also sired some big flops, one of which was Stampede, a men's cologne for Sears. It was discontinued soon after it was launched.

Coincidentally, Jack Friedman was a friend of Charlie Allen of Allen & Co., and over lunch Allen had shown him the private placement for Parfum Giorgio Ltd. Friedman, who had no faith in boutique fragrances, advised Allen not to get deeply involved in the Giorgio project.

Buchwalter agreed to help Roth and Horner and immediately contacted Jack Friedman, who didn't want to personally handle the Giorgio account, but did agree to work with Buchwalter in shaping a fragrance for the boutique. Friedman assigned his son, young Freddy, the account. Freddy had tried teaching while still a student at Boston University, but he had enjoyed working in the Florasynth laboratories as a teenager and joined the family business. He spent a few years in the lab before he got involved in the sales side of the business in 1980. Friedman, garrulous, energetic, and slightly paunchy at twenty-five, was given the Giorgio account and started sending samples to Buchwalter, who sent them to Jim Roth.

Every year, Jack Friedman would work on one special fragrance and in 1976 he, along with Cuttler, had developed a complex white floral fragrance that they called Cinq Fleurs (five flowers). "We tried to develop a multifloral fragrance that would be diffusive and strong like an Oriental, like a Shalimar or a Youth Dew. No one had done a multifloral with that kind of strength," Friedman recalls. Friedman's wife, Lorraine, adopted the fragrance as her favorite; but Jack's efforts to peddle the powerful jasmine and rose-dominated scent to the industry were futile. Soon after it was created, Friedman tried to sell the scent to Germaine Monteil and Helena Rubinstein, but it didn't test well and was turned down. Variations of Cinq Fleurs were submitted to Revlon for Scoundrel but were rejected. Yves St. Laurent Parfums considered the scent for Paris but passed on it. Max Factor could have had it for Missoni but instead picked a far less heady scent. After each rejection Cinq Fleurs was altered slightly, but the Friedmans never gave up on the fragrance, realizing the highly diffusive and powerful scent was waiting for an entrepreneur to take a chance on it. When Frank Buchwalter came asking for a good fragrance in November 1980, Cinq Fleurs was pulled off the shelf forever.

When Buchwalter sent Roth and Horner samples of Cinq Fleurs in January the samples were numbered J-9186, and it was about 90 percent of the fragrance that would eventually become Giorgio. The last 10 percent in the development of a fragrance, the fine tuning, is the hardest part—and Gale agonized over the refinements for seven months before giving it her final approval in July. How the fragrance went from the Florasynth shelf to the Giorgio boutique has become a sensitive and debatable topic within the Giorgio inner circle. The cajoling and jockeying to produce the fragrance were early signs that the Giorgio team was a far from harmonious marketing machine. When the fragrance became successful several years later, assigning credit for its creation became part of the tug of war that eventually undermined the team. As with any blockbuster fragrance, establishing the creator is almost impossible because anyone associated with the project wants a share of the limelight.

In Giorgio's case, here was a group hungry for recognition. Gale had worked under Fred's long and deep shadow for fifteen years and wanted full credit for the fragrance. Roth and Horner had failed at Factor and wanted to shed their image as cosmetics-industry retreads. They believed their imput at Giorgio should not be upstaged or besmirched by the Haymans. Until 1986, when they bowed out of Giorgio, they let the Haymans joust with each other for the credit and quietly remained in the background. In the early 1980s, Fred often gave Gale credit in print for working on the scent and pushing the company in that direction.

Was Gale the sole mastermind for Giorgio's creation, as she forcefully claims? Did Roth and Horner deserve any credit? What was Fred Hayman's role? Millions of dollars and several pints of bad blood later, the answers vary with the storytellers. Evidence suggests the credit should be spread out. After all, luck is something created by no one.

Gale's account of the creation of Giorgio starts with her taking a break and shelving the project temporarily. She realized after two years of working with Roure and IFF that she was too intense and this intensity may have been backfiring. She needed a break. She was recuperating from her broken leg but always knew she would go back to the fragrance venture. Roth and Horner were encouraging Gale to try more samples because if she didn't find a fragrance, they didn't have a client; and they needed the work. Gale agreed, at Roth and Horner's urging, to start testing fragrances again and found herself inundated with samples.

> Now submissions were coming through from companies that I never heard of before. I would see the boxes on my desk and I would open them and return them to Jim and David and say no. One day I got three boxes on my desk. One company was Givaudan, the other was Florasynth, and the third I can't remember; it could have been anybody. I opened the first and I wrote no. The Florasynth sample, I loved it immediately and I kept it aside and sent the other two boxes back. I took home the Florasynth sample. It was a fabulous fragrance, absolutely sensational, it smelled like what I had been looking for. I was shocked and almost afraid to say anything—could this be true?

The next morning Gale says she found the packing slip with Fred Friedman's name on it, called him in New York, and told him this was the first fragrance she really loved. Next she called Roth and Horner. "I told Jim and David I loved it. I told everybody, 'We won't look at anything else. Stop the submissions. This is the fragrance I want to work with. I was really happy and I went into Fred's office and he is on the phone and I was saying, 'We got the fragrance! We got the fragrance!' and he said, 'Okay, okay.'"

The Giorgio offices at 9595 Wilshire would shortly be reeking of

Gale's discovery. Gale, still on crutches, was driven to the office by Joseph, who tended bar at Giorgio and occasionally chauffeured the Haymans. Joseph helped her out of the car, and as she struggled to navigate the curb with her crutches, she dropped a shopping bag. It contained three vials with differing versions of J-9186. Joseph got a strong whiff of the scent and reacted favorably. In the office, the smell of the smashed sample bottles immediately permeated the air. Heads turned in Gale's direction and staffers began to ask what fragrance she was wearing. Giorgio had passed its first unofficial test and met Gale's criteria.

Gale wanted a drop-dead, entrance-making fragrance. When a woman walked into a room, everyone should instantly recognize her scent as Giorgio. The original Florasynth samples were powerful, but Gale says she wanted to make the topnote richer and started working with Buchwalter and the Florasynth perfumer, Harry Cuttler, to make the scent more diffusive. "I was making it richer from the beginning. I couldn't get it rich enough. I love this fragrance. I want it bigger and better and I wanted to exaggerate it a thousand times before it was launched."

Gale tested the fragrance on her friends and their positive feedback further convinced her this submission should be bottled as Giorgio. She also listened to negative criticism, and her frequent demands for change based on people's reactions practically drove Buchwalter and the Friedmans nuts. Perhaps the most important feedback came from Roz Katz, whom Gale had met in the early 1970s. They had become good friends, although outsiders couldn't figure out what they had in common. Katz was wearing the Florasynth sample to a luncheon at the Waldorf and following lunch was walking past St. Bartholomew's church on Park Avenue on her way up to the Plaza Hotel. "I met one of the most interesting men in my life in front of St. Bart's. He gave me the standard pickup line most men use, 'Don't I know you?' but then he said, 'Wow, what fragrance are you wearing?' He walked me up to the Plaza Hotel and it took a week before we started dating. I have been wearing the fragrance ever since, but nothing that wonderful ever happened again." Gale had sent Katz many fragrances but this sample was long-lasting and did not have to be reapplied, and Katz liked the unusual, flowery scent.

Gale's test panel included Loretta Swit, Maureen Dean, Grace Robbins, and noncelebrities such as her friend Steffi Dilworth (née Bekassy) and Berkeley author Susanna Hoffman. Robbins enjoyed the sample so much she would decant it into empty Contac decongestant bottles to prevent spilling and breaking when she traveled to Acapulco.

Although Gale gives Roth and Horner no credit for helping find the fragrance, she is more generous in other areas:

They were in the industry and they knew their aspect of it. Jim and David brought the cosmetics expertise. David was terrific with numbers and Jimmy was terrific with advertising and he coined the two slogans we would later use. But the actual selection of the fragrance, they had nothing at all to do with it. David was neutral about the Florasynth sample, Jimmy thought it was too sweet, and David's wife Katrine didn't like it. David was neutral and said, "Whatever Gale wants." By this time Fred was still not really behind the fragrance.

Roth's and Horner's version of the story varies more than slightly. After failing to raise funds a second time early in 1981, they came to Fred with a revised start-up marketing plan. If he put up $200,000, IMG could get Giorgio into about forty department store doors and also do a small mail-order business.

Horner recalls, "Fred liked our idea but he said he couldn't go ahead without a fragrance and he said, 'I'll give you ninety days to help Gale find a fragrance. If you find a fragrance I'll put you on retainer.' There was no way he wasn't going to get a fragrance. We called up Buchwalter, told him, 'Here is what we were doing,' that we were desperate."

The samples of J-9186 were given to Gale and she "hated" it at first, according to Horner. However, Gale agreed to work with the scent at Fred Friedman's urging, as well as test others. Roth's description of how the scent was selected makes the Giorgio group sound like the gang that couldn't smell straight:

Roz Katz, one of Gale's closest friends, wore it and got compliments and she called Gale and said she loved it. This helped sway Gale to make the final decision. We did all the testing [at shopping malls and with panels], but Gale made the final decision. We tested over three hundred fragrances. Gale is a fickle lady and over an eight-month period she worked on every one. While we were working on the packaging with Fred in one room, she was in another room working with fragrances. Fred didn't fight her, but he couldn't go for her bullshit and they would have fights over the refinements and finite things. She didn't know how to articulate what she liked and that frustrated him. She would pull shit if we came up with something we liked. Fred and Gale would fight in about half the meetings with some kind of little tiff. It was never vitrolic; they each had great respect for one another.

By June we didn't have the fragrance, but the party was scheduled for November and he said to her, "If we don't have [the
fragrance] soon, I'm calling the whole thing off." We had been
working with the Florasynth sample for many months and kept
bringing it back up to her and she kept making modifications. The
fragrance was a little bit off from the original submission. We
pushed it, tested and retested, and we finally convinced her.

Roth and Horner admit to a little trickery because Gale was rejecting
the fragrances they sent her. They had Florasynth send the exact same
samples directly to her only with a different label. In the area of testing,
Horner admits to dummying more than a few questionnaires to impress
Fred during the ninety-day period he had established for discovering a
scent.

After testing the J-9186 sample around their office on San Vicente,
in shopping centers, and at the Marina City Club through Horner's wife,
Katrine, who was selling memberships to the Marina Del Rey club and
high-rise condominium, Roth and Horner presented their research to
Gale who, they maintain, continued to dislike the Florasynth sample:

It wasn't even a discussion. She still hated it. We went to Fred
and told him, "We would like to do a test and she is just not
receptive. We would like your agreement that if we get decent
results you would intercede in our behalf," and he said yes. So we
wrote up about three hundred questionnaires in our office with
blue pencils and red pencils and we falsified them. I had my kids
signing them and about eleven different people with all kinds of
handwriting. If Fred ever knew this he would die. Jimmy didn't
want to do this but we were desperate. The fact that I learned
about Fred and Gale—unless you take them by the hand, neither
will make a decision. If you give Fred the ammunition and hand
him three hundred questionnaires, that gives you a push.

Horner maintains Fred took the questionnaires at face value, showed
them to Gale, and forced her to pay attention to the Florasynth submission. Roth says,

Gale did play a role once she was comfortable with the consumer's
acceptance [of the Florasynth samples] and then she got on the
bandwagon. If she didn't select that fragrance, there were no

others for her. She was cornered, she was issued an ultimatum [by Fred]. We have the bottles and the package picked and ordered and the fragrance not selected and we were way behind, considering it was summer and Fred had scheduled the Giorgio's anniversary party that November.

Gale labels the Roth-Horner chronology a "disaster." "It's a lie. Oh, God, unbelievable . . . they manipulated the whole truth." The idea that Fred could pressure her into finally choosing a fragrance was totally out of character with their working relationship which, she maintains, was still excellent in those days:

There was no pressure on selecting the women's scent. The party had nothing to do with the fragrance. It was the twentieth anniversary of Giorgio. Jim and David were anxious, but they were not in a position to pressure me. They weren't in the company; they had no clout. They weren't part of our company. They were only part of the team if I found a fragrance. They had no authority. They pushed and nudged and kept getting more submissions. That's not pressure. Nobody said I ever had to have it at such and such a date. The only one with any power was Fred, and he wasn't interested in [the fragrance].

Gale says of the falsified questionnaires, "Those falsified questionnaires are a moot point. I had already selected the fragrance. Fred and I sat there and we said, 'Fine, that validates my selection,' and we went for it."

Florasynth officials are careful about what they say. Since their success with Giorgio, the Friedmans have tried to remain friendly with all the Giorgio combatants. They continue to do business with Fred, Gale, and IMG.

Harry Cuttler, the venerable perfumer, is less political. He likes to say perfumers are treated like mushrooms: "They keep us in the dark and feed us bul!shit." In the case of Giorgio, Cuttler credits Gale with being the obstinate force behind the selection of J-9186.

They [Roth and Horner] had to please her and I would give her a lot of the credit. Most of the conversations I had were with Gale. Frank, Jim, and David would make comments, but the person I had to please was Gale. I took what they said in stride, but I paid extra-special attention to what she was telling me. She was looking for a strong and lasting aesthetic experience and she had the outlook of someone new to the industry and she was looking for something nobody else would be looking for; she had fresh eyes. Once she was hooked on this one [J-9186] it took months to fine tune and it was very discouraging working on it so hard, and she wasn't happy. I think anybody would have settled for a hell of a lot less and we gave her beautiful versions that she turned down. She made us do things that we didn't think it was possible to do. We pushed the topnote and got it to a point we never thought we could reach.

The Friedmans acknowledge that IMG saw the J-9186 samples first and that Gale originally, while still in her cast, did not like the fragrance. At their suggestion she took the fragrance home and tested it on her friends before being won over. They encouraged the testing because they feared if left to her own nasal devices she might play forever without choosing a fragrance. Florasynth would hold on to a fresh, newly blended sample and let it age five or six days before presenting it to Gale, especially near the end, when they were trying to enrich J-9186. Gale would call demanding the sample, and the Friedmans would tell her they had sent away for a new secret ingredient. By allowing the sample to age six days, they made the sample richer. "One of the good things about Giorgio, the older it gets the better it smells. That's what happens when you use lots of naturals," Fred Friedman said.

Gale surprised the Florasynth perfumers on several occasions. When a batch of samples of the J-9186 wasn't smelling right, Gale insisted it was off and, upon closer inspection, the scent makers discovered that an ingredient had crystallized and they had to alter their sophisticated mixing and brewing.

Perhaps Gale's most important contribution was her unwillingness to change the high concentrations of expensive natural ingredients in the fragrance. After she had approved the rich version of J-9186 and Florasynth started shipping drums of the cologne and perfume for filling, Buchwalter, at Roth and Horner's urging, continued working with Florasynth's perfumers to develop an identical-smelling but less costly synthetic version of Giorgio. Gale ranted and raved about the cologne's power and argued with Fred, Roth, and Horner to not change the concentrations no matter what it cost—and she won out. Horner figures the synthetic version would have cost the company a dollar a bottle for the cologne version versus the $3.50 cologne Gale had selected, giving Giorgio the dubious distinction of having the highest cost of goods in the industry.

If the synthetic version had been used, the company could have saved millions on its costs. However, it is doubtful the fragrance would have been as successful.

The average cologne contains between 12 and 15 percent essential oil (the actual perfume essence). The rest is water and alcohol, which actually deliver the essential oil to the skin. The average perfume is stronger, containing 25 percent essential oil, but is far outsold by the cheaper colognes. Giorgio contained much stronger concentrations of essential oils. The Giorgio cologne actually had perfume strength, with 25 percent essential oil. Its key ingredients were absolute rose at $5,000 a kilo and absolute jasmine at $3,000 a kilo. In addition to rose and jasmine, Giorgio contained orange flower, chamomile, sandalwood, and patchouli, in combination with many other subtle notes. Not since the days of Lauder's Youth Dew had anyone tried to make such a heavily concentrated scent. The Giorgio customer was going to get a lot of fragrance for her money. The fragrance was long-lasting and, unlike many other scents, remained true to its original character for almost as long as a woman wore it.

By June 1982, Roth and Horner were on a retainer with Fred; their contract stipulated they would receive 3 percent of the pretax profits based on increments of $50,000. When the profits hit a certain point, their profit-sharing would remain steady, without graduating. As the deal was based on profit increases of only $50,000, it was obvious there was little faith in the business becoming large. IMG showed Fred a plan in which the business would hit $6 million in volume within three years and throw off $2 million in profits. In addition Fred agreed to pay Roth and Horner a monthly retainer of $7,000. Recalls Roth, "With Fred giving us seven thousand dollars a month, it kept us going and we signed exclusively with Fred. We put on our gloves and it was good to be back working in the industry. We were both willing to start over, to work morning, noon, and night, seven days a week."

CHAPTER NINE

Under the
Big Tent

The Haymans were finally in the fragrance business and for less than $300,000. The modest plan Roth and Horner presented to Fred called for a mail-order campaign and initial retail distribution solely in the Giorgio boutique. Fred liked starting small, testing the fragrance's viability in his own store. He understood better than anybody the power of exclusivity. If the fragrance was any good and available only at Giorgio, consumer demand would build.

Gale had selected a rich, costly scent and it was priced appropriately high. The entry price point was thirty-five dollars for the three-ounce "extraordinary" spray cologne, fifty dollars for the one-quarter-ounce perfume, and one hundred fifty dollars for the one-ounce perfume. Giorgio, with its thirty-five-dollar entry price point, was above the standard bearers of the day—Opium, Oscar de la Renta, and Ralph Lauren—whose entry price points were still in the twenty-to-thirty-dollar range for smaller-size eau de toilette versions, which Giorgio did not market.

In an effort to save on packaging costs, Roth and Horner had discovered Charles Huschle, the owner of Imaginative Packaging Ltd. Huschle had been supplying fragrance companies with bottles for thirty years and represented glassmakers in Europe and the Orient. He considered himself a midwife to entrepreneurial start-ups such as Giorgio. A graying maverick, who when not working on bottle projects was on his sailboat in the Caribbean, Huschle wanted to break the French monopoly in producing the industry's beautiful glass bottles. He believed viable alternatives to the French bottles were available in Spain, Italy, Germany, Taiwan, and Japan; and he aggressively pitched fragrance companies, trying to convince them that a Spanish glassmaker could equal a Frenchman's quality at a third of the cost and with a much faster turnaround time. Prior to scoring with Giorgio, Huschle had been "midwife" to the marketers of Polo, Lauren, Oscar de la Renta, and Geoffrey Beene's Grey Flannel.

Most prestige fragrance companies hire a bottle designer, quite often Pierre Dinand in Paris, and have a $200,000 private mold tooled. The Giorgio team designed their own bottle, primarily because of financial and time limitations. Roth and Forkish (while he was still with IMG) saw a Baccarat bud vase they liked in Tiffany and immediately checked out books from the Beverly Hills public library about Mandarin vases and Phoenician pottery. The Giorgio bottle evolved from these graceful silhouettes of the female shape. The major bottling companies such as Pochet of America look for big runs. They did not embrace the Giorgio project; it was a start-up venture with an initial order for just five thousand one-ounce perfume bottles. Huschle, however, was hungry for the business. Roth and Horner contracted him through Fred Friedman to have their bottle blueprint translated into glass.

Huschle flew to California in May 1981, and the Giorgio bottle design was modified in an airport lounge.

We went over the blueprints at the Ambassador Club at the L.A. Airport at midnight. My plane had been delayed and my original plans to spend a day in L.A. had to be canceled. Once they decided to launch the fragrance at the party in November, it was essential to get the molds to Spain so we could make the deadlines. They gave me the blueprints for the three-ounce cologne, the quarter-ounce perfume, and the one-ounce perfume and I made modifications. I thought the bud-vase design was exquisite, but the angles were too sharp and needed to be rectified. I see all the P.R. about the Haymans. Gale had nothing to do with the bottle. We finalized the bottle that night at the airport and sent it off to Spain. I give Roth and Horner all the credit; the Haymans couldn't have done it without them."

The original Giorgio bottles were made by a Barcelona glass manufacturer called C.R.E.P.A.L., S.A. The first shipment of bottles made it to Los Angeles on deadline in October 1981, with some fancy flying.

Huschle flew to Barcelona on a Thursday, packed the bottles, and put them on a TWA flight to London. A Concord flight got the bottles to New York on Friday afternoon and by Saturday the bottles were in Los Angeles ready to be filled.

Kolmar is a company specializing in cosmetics-industry production and filling. Roth and Horner had the perfume bottles delivered to Kolmar's Riverside, California, plant. Before the bottles were to be filled, Roth and Horner wanted to test the glass and were more than surprised at the test results. Roth said,

> We were tapping the bottles first on a laminated table and finding the corners were breaking. Then we started tapping lightly with a pencil and we still broke the corners. Invariably, one of the four corners would get a pin hole or break. This was about two A.M. now and it was still too early to call New York and rip Huschle apart. We stopped tapping because if we kept up there wouldn't be any bottles left to fill. We started filling the bottles with a few girls in white gloves who filled the bottles gently by hand and we held our breath.

Luckily the initial fragile bottles did not result in any insurance claims, although about a dozen bottles were broken and returned to Giorgio. Modifications were made to round out the shoulders of the perfume bottle and the breakage problem was solved. The initial bottle orders were for five thousand one-ounce perfume bottles, fifteen thousand one-quarter-ounce perfume bottles, and twenty-five thousand three-ounce cologne bottles.

The design of the outer package (carton) was competitive. About fifteen package designers submitted variations on Giorgio's yellow-and-white striped logo. Fred disliked them all and decided to use as is the thick, bold, yellow-and-white stripes that decorated the store's awnings, the Giorgio shopping bag and stationery. Fred felt strongly about his gaudy stripes, not realizing that the perfume industry usually packaged its product in muted, sophisticated hues of blue, red, gray, lavender, and peach. No fine fragrance had the audacity to march in with yellow-and-white stripes. Those stripes would jump out of the fragrance cases and would set Giorgio apart in the next five years. The House of Harley, a small packaging company in New York run by Natalie Harley, made the first boxes, charging a premium for the small run. There were problems with the printing and stamping on the boxes, but deadlines were met and it was time, finally, to put the fragrance in the store. The process had been started in 1977 and now, in the fall of 1981, Giorgio was ready to enter the fragrance arena.

The first two bottles of Giorgio ever sold were filled in David Horner's kitchen in Marina Del Rey. Inexperienced at cellophane wrapping, Roth burned his fingers over a hotplate in their makeshift bottling and packaging setup. Carol Doumani, a customer of Giorgio, told Fred her husband had business connections with the royal family in Saudi Arabia. He was going there and Carol thought it would make a nice gesture to present the fragrance as a gift. Roth and Horner trotted to Doumani's home in Beverly Hills with the perfume bottles and an American Express credit card slip and the sale was consummated.

The fragrance went into the boutique in mid-October and in the first ten days did $15,000 in sales, well beyond the projections. Gale instructed the Giorgio salesgirls to take a soft-sell approach.

> I told the salesgirls, "If we can get this fragrance in the consumers' hands, we can sell it. All you have to ask our customers is if we can spray it on their wrists." Because it smelled great, I thought ninety-five percent would buy it. I told the salesgirls, "Don't tell them it smells wonderful or it's terrific, forget that. Just ask them if they would like to smell our new fragrance." And sure enough women would smell their wrists and say, "This is really great."

Fred was putting his years of hotel management and catering skills to work organizing a grand Giorgio twentieth anniversary party. The fragrance was to be officially launched at the party, but the scent was secondary to the boutique's twentieth birthday. The store was now generating almost $6 million in annual sales and Fred wanted to thank his large and loyal clientele. Agonizing over the guest list, Fred didn't want to exclude anyone; but there was room for "only" a thousand under the yellow-and-white striped tent that was to be pitched in the parking lot of the American Savings & Loan Bank across the street from the boutique.

Patrick Terrail was hired to coordinate the party and carry out Fred's whims. Terrail is a strong-willed Frenchman, whose family owns the three-star Tour d'Argent restaurant in Paris. Terrail started Ma Maison, the 1970s Hollywood lunch spot on Melrose Avenue, famous for the Rolls-Royces parked at the entrance. Orson Welles had a secluded side table and literary superagent Swifty Lazar often held court in a more obvious table in the middle of the room. Wolfgang Puck, who went on to make pizza chic at Spago, got his start as a chef with Terrail. Terrail and Hayman had met in 1971 and were impressed with each other's ability to attract and service affluent, high-profile customers. Terrail was included at dinner parties at the Charleville apartment and had catered smaller Christmas parties at Giorgio, but he had never put together anything on this grandiose a scale.

The tent had to be yellow-and-white striped and Terrail conducted a nationwide search for a big enough circus tent with those colors before finding a sixteen-thousand-square-foot tent in Oregon. Next, Terrail had to keep egos in line. Fred's concept was to have the party catered by five top restaurants in Los Angeles, a group that included Jimmy's, The Bistro, La Scala, the Beverly Wilshire Hotel, and Ma Maison. The chefs from these restaurants would all be at the party preparing their specialties and sharing the culinary limelight normally reserved for themselves. Fred insisted on two important Giorgio touches inside the tent—the 1952 Rolls-Royce Silver Wraith with Giorgio logo license plates and twinkly holiday lights. "If Fred wants it one way, then you must give it to him," Terrail says.

> Fred wanted his Rolls inside the tent and I thought it was a good idea to stack the fragrance in the trunk of the car. What's wrong with the idea? To do it, you must get the gas tank out because it's a fire hazard. We got the gas tank disconnected and towed the car in. That car is identified with Giorgio and is part of the image so he is right to do it, but it just makes my life miserable.

The party was held Sunday night, November 22, and Terrail had a crew of four hundred, including thirty-five valet parking attendants. This small army worked around the clock the night before erecting the tent and the three thousand or so bee lights Fred wanted strung from the tent's ceiling. Motorized cherry-pickers were rented so the workmen could get to the top of the tent and string the lights. Two chandeliers made up entirely of the bee lights were fashioned to illuminate the dance floor. Terrail was relieved to find that the lighting worked after testing it. The only detail Terrail forgot was bathrooms for the workmen, who sought relief at the Beverly Wilshire across the street.

The "very black tie" party turned out to be the social event of the year and the local press gave it lavish coverage and praise. It was not a night of understated elegance. The Beverly Hills High School Marching Band strutted and stomped, eighty pounds of caviar were chomped, the flow of Taittinger champagne was torrential, and smilax vines festooned throughout added to the extravagance.

By Hollywood standards the star list came up short of an A. The competing event that night hosted by Elizabeth Taylor to benefit the Simon

Wiesenthal Center was partially to blame. Among the names turning out for Giorgio included Charles Bronson and his wife Jill Ireland, Henry Mancini, Mark Harmon with Cristina Raines, Loretta Swit, Pamela Mason, John Dean, Hal Linden, Stella Stevens, Hugh O'Brian, Rosemarie Stack, Persis Khambatta, Lorne Greene, and former California governor Edmund G. Brown. There was a birthday-party festiveness about the event not usually associated with a commercial venture, although some of the Hollywood people knew exactly why they were there. Pamela Mason recalls,

> That was a nightmare of a night. There were four hundred fifty thousand people all in a tent and it's what we [Hollywood crowd] call a rat fuck. You are either invited to a rat fuck or a party, one or the other. When Fred invites you, it's usually a party; but on this occasion it was actually a rat fuck. By that I mean it's just a crowd of as many people and press. The party was done for publicity and with the damn trail of television cameras you can't walk without falling on your nose. If you say yes to *E.T. [Entertainment Tonight]* then you have to say yes to CNN and it's open season. But as a result he was exploiting that fragrance fantastically.

Merv Griffin was the master of ceremonies and made a little speech describing Fred and Gale as the "Ma and Pa Kettle" of Rodeo Drive. Fred wore tails and the evening was, in effect, his coronation. He had begun hosting parties at the Beverly Hilton in 1954, and after twenty years of playing maître d' at Giorgio, had emerged as Beverly Hills' most tastefully flamboyant host. The *Los Angeles Herald Examiner* dubbed him the prince of style and status. The tent was filled with his old Beverly Hills friends and, with Griffin and bandleader Freddy Martin entertaining, memories of the difficult Ambassador Hotel years were rekindled. Henry Berger was quoted in the *Herald Examiner*, "Fred is the most brilliant businessman, public relations man, and goodwill ambassador there is. Put these three things together and you come up with miracles like tonight."

Fred's rambling, rah-rah ("There is nothing like Rodeo and nothing like Beverly Hills") thank-you speech named just about everybody in the tent and included the florist, country sheriff, and the people he was paying handsomely to be there. He saved his thank you to Gale for last. "And, foremost, I thank Gale. You are the most unique and marvelous partner; without you Giorgio could not be."

Gale said simply, "The only thing I would like to say is, without all of you there wouldn't be a Giorgio, and I thank you from the bottom of my heart."

Griffin sang a song especially written for the occasion. Written by

Norman Gimbel, "You Know Who Wears It," was composed by Jack Elliott
and was sung with a bossa nova background.

> The scent seduces, it fills the night
> The scent reduces the will to fight and
> You will follow wherever she may wander to and
> you will do for her whatever she may ask of you . . .

It may not have been George Gershwin, but the message was clear:
the Haymans were launching a fun, seductive fragrance with as much
hype as possible. Prestige fragrances had always been serious, but Giorgio,
with its heavy-handed scent, had a lighthearted appeal. Every woman at
the party was given a generous one-ounce gift of the perfume, adding to
the spiraling costs of the party. When asked by reporters how much the
party cost, the prince of style and status sniffed, "Discussion of money
is vulgar." Horner would be vulgar and reveal the party cost: $260,000.
He and Roth thought spending that kind of money on a party was wasteful
and a big ego trip for Fred. They had hoped Fred would be equally lavish
and willing to spend $260,000 on advertising and marketing. They failed
to recognize the publicity value of the party. The generous social column
coverage and mentions of the new fragrance stimulated local consumer
interest in the scent. A spread in *WWD* favorably compared the Giorgio
bash to YSL's Opium party, which until that time had been the most
opulent fragrance launch party in the industry. Retailers nationwide who
rely on *WWD* for new-product information found their curiosity piqued
by the new Beverly Hills fragrance.

Fred's approach to the fragrance industry was still cautious and
conservative. In a *WWD* article published November 20, 1981, Fred said
he had hoped the fragrance could do $3,000 a day during the Christmas
season in the boutique and between $250,000 and $500,000 the first year
in mail orders. He said he had invested about $300,000 (a figure Horner
says is too high) to develop and promote the fragrance to this point,
exclusive of the party. "The more I knew about the perfume industry,
the more monstrous it seemed to me," Fred said. The idea of taking
returns (fragrance that does not sell in the stores and is shipped back to
the manufacturer), paying for co-op advertising with the stores, and
adopting the costly point-of-purchase programs used by other manufacturers did not appeal to him. "I didn't want to set up a sales organization.
I am not Estée Lauder. I'm just a little merchant," he said.

Fred didn't realize it but he had assembled the nucleus for a po-
tentially dynamic fragrance company. In Gale, he had a tireless product

developer who was consumer-driven and not bound by the stale dictates of the industry. Jim Roth understood the mechanics of the fragrance business, had a thorough knowledge of advertising, and was detail oriented, a crucial asset. He was also a diplomat, unlike Horner, the financial firebrand whose emotional outbursts gave the company a sense of urgency and the necessary toughness to deal with major department stores. Fred knew the Giorgio concept, the importance of exclusivity and prestige marketing. He would become the silvery, dapper Giorgio spokesman and image maker.

Hunger was another factor that contributed to the young company's dynamism, and Roth and Horner were working as if they had never eaten at The Bistro or a fine Beverly Hills restaurant before. Constrained by limited working capital, they came up with a new way to reach consumers. A prestige fragrance had never been sold successfully via a mail-order magazine campaign before—primarily because there was no way to effectively sample the fragrance. Roth had dabbled with mail order earlier in his career and was pushing Giorgio in that direction. In the mid-1970s he had experimented with scent strips to sample Halston and Geminesse fragrances in regional magazines and in *McCall's*. However these ads had not been accompanied by mail-order envelopes. No fragrance manufacturer had ever made an effort to massively sample a fragrance in magazines and then have customers respond by mail. Scent strips in national magazines were to be the innovative high-impact marketing hook that would put Giorgio under the noses of millions of women in 1983.

Scent strips were being promoted by Arcade, a Chattanooga, Tennessee, paper company that took existing microencapsulation processes developed by 3M and applied them to fragrance. The scent strip was merely two pieces of paper bound by glue and containing scented capsules. The microencapsulation involves coating microscopic molecules of fragrance oil with plastic resin. When the bond is broken, the capsules break and scent is released, behaving exactly as if it had been spritzed into the air. Arcade, who would later trademark the term ScentStrip, by 1988 had sold over three and a half billion to the industry.

The first Giorgio ads in early 1982 ran in small regional magazines such as *Texas Ultra, Palm Springs Life*, and a group of magazines called *The Good Life* that were mailed into the most affluent zip codes in six cities, including Dallas, Philadelphia, Houston, Boston, and Los Angeles. *Texas Ultra* was to become one of the most successful magazines for Giorgio and was discovered by Fred through social connections. *Ultra* was the toy of Houston millionaire Harold Farb and his publicity-starved wife, Caroline, who got plenty of press attention during her marriage and subsequent divorce from Farb. Fred was introduced to the Farbs through Houston socialite Joan Schnitzer, who attended the Giorgio party with Cartier president Ralph Destino. A Giorgio ad in *Ultra* cost $11,000 and would bring in $35,000 worth of orders in January 1983.

The first Giorgio fragrance ad featured two attractive women with three men in black tie. It was staged as if the men were putting the make on the women at a Hollywood party and a photographer was shooting the action. Most of the models were Roth's friends; the ad cost just $700 in modeling fees. Jack Demorest, the West Coast advertising manager for *Vogue*, was one of the three men in the ad, but the hair of a beautiful blond was blown across his face. Demorest would later do significant business with Giorgio for the magazine. Madison Mason, an actor, did the ad and was paid with a Giorgio gift certificate. The one professional model wore a black dress slit between her cleavage and her hair was windblown. The tag line, "You Know Who Wears It," was intended to have one meaning but it took on a second interpretation. Peggy Lancaster wrote the line. Her small advertising agency, Scott Lancaster Jackman Mills Atha, had the Giorgio account because she knew Roth. The line was meant to imply the beautiful, monied, fun people were wearing Giorgio perfume; but many, including Fred and Gale, took the literal meaning—the fragrance smelled so strong that you literally knew who was wearing it.

At first, scented blotters were mailed to Giorgio's customer list— about twelve thousand names—in January 1982. Postage alone was $15,000, but orders began to trickle in. These blotters were then blown into the pages of the regional magazines (*Good Life, Ultra*). The blotters were manufactured by Orlandi Perfume Specialties of New York and were used by the industry mostly as a sampling vehicle in statement enclosures to department-store charge customers. They were cumbersome because they fell out of the magazines and also uneconomical because postal authorities, claiming the blotters were actual product, would tax national magazines with second-class mailing permits. Thus Giorgio was restricted to regional publications with third class permits such as *The Good Life*, which had a controlled circulation and was delivered free. The scent strip, however, could not be taxed by postal authorities and would allow Giorgio to go into national magazines with the May 1983 edition of *Vogue*.

Without a sizable advertising budget, Roth and Horner were looking for deals. The Good Life Group agreed to give Giorgio its first ad free, but if the returns on that first ad were to result in a break-even situation, the magazine would get a contract from Giorgio. The results were over-whelming, with sacks of thirty-five-dollar cologne orders rolling in. *Ultra*, a slick ninety-thousand-circulation life-style magazine about high living, oil-boom Texans, was pulling between 0.6 and 0.8 percent in orders, a good return considering a quarter of a percent is figured to be the break-even rate. *Texas Ultra* was given a contract. *The Good Life* magazine ads were also pulling and suddenly stores in those markets started calling Giorgio headquarters and asking if the fragrance would be available to them. Consumers reluctant to order through the mail were starting to ask for it at retail.

Inside the Giorgio boutique, a little fragrance counter was set up along the Dayton Way wall across from the bar, and suddenly both the locals and the tourists were lining up to buy the fragrance. Busloads of tourists were invading Rodeo and during the days preceding and following the Rose Bowl game on New Year's Day in 1982 visitors came into the store and sampled the fragrance. The boutique became a national testing ground and told Roth and Horner the fragrance had immense potential in both urban and rural America. There were few things in Giorgio priced as low as thirty-five dollars, yet now a small-town midwestern woman could amble down Rodeo with the little yellow-and-white shopping bag showing she had bought something at Rodeo's most famous store, the one *Scruples* was written about. In purchasing the fragrance, she was taking home a slice of the fast and opulent life-style she had momentarily glimpsed through the lens of her Instamatic.

The fragrance's surprisingly fast start was due purely to the quality of the scent, Gale believed. Fred was impressed with the success of the fragrance in the store but also saw it as a distraction from the primary Giorgio business, selling women's and men's apparel. He was concerned about the increasing telephone calls to the store from consumers ordering the fragrance. In a memo to all Giorgio personnel on August 3, 1982, Fred wrote, "As mail orders increase, I do not wish the Giorgio Sales Staff at the store to spend their time taking perfume orders, they should be selling clothes, which is our main living." Meanwhile, Horner was pressuring Fred to pay the salesgirls a 5 percent sales commission on every Giorgio fragrance product they sold. At first he argued with Horner but then relented. Horner said,

We almost came to blows when I told him we should pay a five percent commission. Our numbers in the store were blowing my mind. At one point we were doing eight hundred thousand dollars in the store [annually] and the profit was about five hundred thousand. We had a fifteen percent cost of goods and there were no other expenses. With our sales taking off I wanted to pay the girls selling the fragrance ten percent commission. He finally relented and gave five percent on the cologne but nothing on the moisturizer. When the moisturizer didn't do well he asked why. These were the kinds of conversations we would have repeatedly.

Horner was convinced Giorgio was doing well because of Beverly Hills' sex appeal. He had learned the "every woman wants to be a high-class hooker" marketing theory at male-dominated Revlon. This denigrating notion earmarks women as pouty vixens who use fragrance as one of their tools to nab men. Horner subscribed to Revson's theories and saw Giorgio playing to America's sexual fantasies. Beverly Hills was a potent aphrodisiac:

> Beverly Hills says sex better than anything else. Beverly Hills is the resting and living place for all those people you fantasize about. Our advertising said nothing of us being a small, quality emporium on Rodeo Drive. Who knows that Beverly Hills is a city of thirty thousand where the average age is sixty-two? People thought sex is always up-to-date in Beverly Hills, and fantasy is, too. They had read Judith Krantz and Harold Robbins and knew where the fucking and sucking was taking place. People in Nebraska must have been saying, "If I put this fragrance on, my teamster husband will come home, take off his white T-shirt, I'll put on my gold lamé caftan, and he'll impale me with a golden dildo, while swinging from a chandelier." The people in Ypsilanti, Michigan, must have believed that would happen if they bought the best-selling fragrance in Beverly Hills.

Both Roth and Horner were eager to test the fragrance in a major department store. Although they had yet to advertise in a national magazine such as *Vogue* or *Cosmopolitan*, their regional magazine ads and Giorgio boutique business had encouraged them. In the first six months the business was running at the rate of $1 million annually and was showing slightly better than a 10 percent pretax profit. Few fragrances show a profit in their launch year and most are lucky to see the black before their third year.

Fred had doubts other retailers would want his fragrance because of the competitive nature of retailers. Saks Fifth Avenue to Fred was America's premier carriage-trade store and his first choice for Giorgio's national retail debut. There were encouraging signs that Saks might want to carry Giorgio. Before Giorgio was launched in Beverly Hills, Fred had wined and dined Margaret Hayes at The Bistro in 1980 when Forkish arranged a meeting. Hayes was running Saks' cosmetics operation and expressed an interest in the product. Gale and Fred met Arnold Aronson, the chief executive officer of Saks Fifth Avenue, at the European collections in the fall of 1981 and Aronson's wife asked Gale what fragrance she was wearing and seemed impressed.

Surreptitiously, Fred started calling Aronson in late spring 1982 to remind him of their meeting in Europe and to ask if Saks were interested in carrying Giorgio. It was the last solicitation Fred or anyone at Giorgio would ever make. Aronson never returned the phone calls and Fred's ego was bruised. The snub would be much more devastating for Saks, eventually costing the store millions of dollars and lost market share to arch foe Bloomingdale's. Aronson maintains that he was being elevated from Saks' CEO to president of the parent company, BATUS (British American Tobacco United States), and wanted to leave any merchandising matters to Mel Jacobs, who succeeded him in October 1982. Giorgio's lack of New York industry presence, along with the Haymans' anonymity in New York social circles, prevented them from gaining entrée to the Saks management. Fred was unwilling to contact the Saks middle management first and work his way up to the senior executives; after years of running a successful store, he was accustomed to dealing with people in power. In addition, Giorgio's loud fragrance and wild yellow-and-white stripes did not suit the traditional image of a store such as Saks. The Saks snub was a lucky stroke for Giorgio, because it led the fragrance to Bloomingdale's.

Margot Rogoff, the aggressive and high-pitched press-relations director for Bloomingdale's, was vacationing in Los Angeles. Her friend, Elaine Klein, an advertising saleswoman for *Playbill* magazine, was having breakfast with Roth and Horner. Klein had sold space to Max Factor and had known Roth over the years. When he heard a Bloomingdale's executive was in town, he invited Rogoff to the Giorgio boutique and presented her with the fragrance. Rogoff had met Fred Hayman on a previous visit through restaurateur Sylvia Wu (Madame Wu's), and was immediately enthusiastic about the fragrance. Rogoff recalls,

I'm talking to Fred and said, "I'll make you a deal right on the spot. We are doing an American promotion in September and if I get Giorgio into Bloomingdale's, would you do a swap and put the Bloomingdale's fragrance in your windows?" He said, "Sure, anything," and from the boutique I called Mike Blumenfeld, the store's vice president of cosmetics. "Michael, how are you? I have great news for you. I'm at Giorgio on Rodeo Drive," and he interrupted me and said, "What is that?" Fred is standing over me, so I continued. "Giorgio is coming out with a fragrance and what could be better than to have Giorgio of Beverly Hills be part of our American promotion?" Michael kept saying, "What is wrong with you, what are you talking about?" I said, "I will find out all about it," and hung up. I told Fred I can't promise him anything, that I'm just

Bloomingdale's P.R. and this has to go through Mr. Blumenfeld and his boss Mr. Gribetz.

Loaded up with Giorgio sweatshirts, towels, and the fragrance, Rogoff returned to New York to present her discovery to Blumenfeld. A curt New Yorker who intimidated the buyers below him, Blumenfeld had risen through the ranks at Bloomingdale's and had seen a number of fragrances come and go. He wasn't buying Giorgio. A great-smelling fragrance was not reason enough for Bloomingdale's to get behind something new. Blumenfeld wanted to know where the newcomer's money was coming from and how much there was to support the heavy allowances Bloomingdale's demanded. He knew retailers' fragrances as a rule did not do well. Bloomingdale's own Bloomies fragrance took three years to develop and was doing so little volume that the time and money spent to create it were hardly justifiable.

Not deterred by Blumenfeld's sagacious negativity, Rogoff called Paulette Weisenfeld, Bloomingdale's twenty-seven-year-old women's fragrance buyer, to her office to test the fragrance. Weisenfeld's mother, Eliette Beddouk, had worked in the fragrance industry as a training specialist for Coty, Chanel, Hermès, and Halston; and Weisenfeld had inherited her discerning nose. When she sampled a fragrance she had a quick love/hate reaction. Her standing with Blumenfeld was not at an all-time high. Natchez, a fragrance utilizing scented earrings and marketed by a woman from Mississippi who thought she was the southern coming of Charles Revson, had been brought into the store by Weisenfeld in the spring of 1982 and was a fiasco. Another Natchez could be Weisenfeld's Waterloo. She was looking for a winner to rebuild her credibility, and when Rogoff presented her with Giorgio she became intoxicated by the fragrance and started wearing it.

Weisenfeld had never been to California and had planned a week's vacation to Los Angeles and Palm Springs. She was traveling with Meryl Friedman, the store's buyer of men's fragrances. Rogoff got on the phone to Hayman, told him Weisenfeld would be visiting and to get out the Rolls-Royce and any other tricks that would impress her. The only impression Giorgio had made on Weisenfeld to this point were the Merv Griffin and television game-show credits—"clothing supplied by Giorgio, Beverly Hills."

After driving in from Palm Springs, Weisenfeld and Friedman had lunch at the Brown Derby at the corner of Rodeo and Wilshire. Friedman, in a holiday mood, convinced Weisenfeld to try a piña colada and before lunch was over she had three. Friedman says she got Weisenfeld "bombed." She walked into the Giorgio offices at 9595 Wilshire Boulevard in sneakers and a sweatsuit and was treated like visiting royalty by Fred and his staff. She found Fred charming. They spoke French a bit and began to develop an unusual rapport. Lauding the fragrance, Weisenfeld told Hayman when she returned to New York she would speak to her boss, Robin Burns, the group manager of fragrances, and lobby to introduce the Giorgio fragrance in the fall. As the fragrance buyer, Weisenfeld rarely received the doting attention that Burns and the decision makers above her got from big companies in the industry. Fred's well-honed skill at making people feel important was about to pay off. Said Weisenfeld,

> They loaded me up with all the typical Giorgio things, which started my mind working. They gave me a satin jacket, a hat, a towel, a tote bag. They were not trying to buy me, but in a sense were saying all of this is available to you as promotional material, and this started me thinking. We could do yellow-and-white awnings, topiary trees, models dressed in yellow satin jackets, and turn this into a typical Bloomingdale's extravaganza. Well, when I got back to New York I was the only one who saw it like that.

Burns thought the fragrance was unusual, highly distinctive, and powerful. Unlike many new fragrances that had the familiar smell of successful ones before them, Giorgio clearly was not a me-too scent. Bloomingdale's had a history of pursuing new products throughout the store, but the store did not need another new scent in the heated and competitive fragrance arena, and it certainly was not hungry for an exclusive new fragrance from a company with a limited budget. The store was locked in a tug of war with Saks and Macy's Herald Square for a bigger slice of manufacturers' investment dollars. Fragrances in the late 1970s and early 1980s had been launched at Bloomingdale's and Saks simultaneously, but only one store would get the coveted *New York Sunday Times* full-page break ad and a personal appearance by the designer or whoever was doing the fragrance, e.g., Estée Lauder. Manufacturers picked one store into which to pour their promotional dollars for the two-week launch period. The other store would have no hoopla unless it was willing to spend its own money, an unlikely scenario.

Burns was the golden child in Bloomingdale's cosmetics hierarchy. She joined the store in 1974, coming into the cosmetics department as the men's fragrance buyer in 1979. In a relatively short time she built Polo into the number-one men's line, supplanting Aramis, which had been the top-selling men's prestige scent in virtually every U.S. department store since the late 1960s. Burns could do no wrong in Blumenfeld's eyes, and it was clear to Weisenfeld the only way to get Giorgio into the store was to win over Burns, who could finesse it past the Blumenfeld barricade.

Horner and Roth were calling Weisenfeld wondering why they were not getting any progress reports. Fred was insisting on setting up a dinner on his next New York buying trip with Marvin Traub, the high-profile chief executive of Bloomingdale's, and Lester Gribetz, one of his senior merchants and Blumenfeld's boss. Weisenfeld recalls, "Fred wanted to meet with Marvin but there was no way. Fred was not a captain of industry and he felt he deserved to be meeting with the big guys, but there was no way I could get him access to Marvin Traub. The only people who could gain him access were Robin or Mike, and through Robin I worked to win Mike over."

Fred, Gale, Roth, and Horner convinced Burns during dinner at La Côte Basque. Now at least Weisenfeld had a partner, a prerequisite for bringing new fragrances into the store. "The classic line in the cosmetics department at Bloomingdale's is, 'You need someone higher up to be your partner, because if it goes bad, you don't want to be out there in the storm alone.' Robin was my partner but Mike wasn't. We decided we were going to do it without Mike because we really believed in it. Mike would have never let me do it myself, but he signed the order because he liked Robin."

Fred wanted nothing short of an extravaganza to launch Giorgio at Bloomingdale's. However, his idea of flying in Hollywood celebrities and hosting a big party in Bloomingdale's elegant sixth-floor restaurant, Le Train Bleu, was never given serious consideration. Burns and Weisenfeld never asked Blumenfeld to stage a party because they doubted Traub or any of the store's senior executives would show up even if it were approved. Weisenfeld did not want to blow the whole deal over Fred's damaged ego and was able to tap dance around his demands by suggesting that perhaps an event could be staged in the less hectic spring season. Her hope was that Giorgio would do so well that Traub and senior management would be excited enough about the fragrance to get involved with Fred.

The initial Bloomingdale's order was for about $40,000. Weisenfeld thought it was too much and too risky. Horner chastised her for being conservative. He was not happy with the tiny space allotted the fragrance. Still, this was Giorgio's big chance and Horner and Roth were prepared to spend as much time and energy on the Bloomingdale's sales floor as necessary to make their yellow-and-white-striped mark on the industry. For Fred, who had spent his early years working in New York, and Gale, who had been born and raised there, this was a homecoming. Giorgio was entering the big time.

CHAPTER TEN

Yellow-and-White Stripes at 59th & Lex

The June 21, 1982, issue of *People* magazine summed up the Haymans and Giorgio in six meaty paragraphs and three splashy photos. In one of them, Gale, in a cleaved and flowing posthippie suede dress, posed sexily atop the pool table next to Fred. Wineglasses filled, both stared lovingly—into the camera, not each other's eyes. Here they were in the store that had inspired *Scruples* and provided probably one-tenth of the gowns hanging from celebrity shoulders at the Academy Awards show, the article by Suzy Kalter said.

The Haymans had become grist for *People*'s mill by catering to Hollywood with flair. The store's sybaritic perks, including the oak bar, pool table, and 1952 Rolls-Royce "delivery truck," had become Beverly Hills bellwethers. Publications also wrote about the Haymans' unusual partnership. Fred was quoted by Kalter, "If your marriage fails, it doesn't mean your friendship fails. We like each other, see each other socially, and even entertain together."

The fragrance, although less than a year old, was starting to make its impact both in the store and on the Haymans. Sales of Giorgio's apparel and accessories had flattened before the scent was introduced; its acceptance brought in additional volume and new customers. The entire store got a much needed lift from fragrance sales that averaged

$50,000 to $70,000 a month. Giorgio had a hot item, an item carried nowhere else on Rodeo Drive or in America.

Gale's confidence and ego were being fed by the women who were buying the fragrance in the boutique and telling her how much they enjoyed it. "It was important for me after the big party when women came into the store and bought it for themselves and also for their friends. Harriet Deutsch [wife of Armand, a Ronald Reagan chum] would buy gifts and that really pleased me."

Gale started working on ancillary products as soon as the women's fragrance was finalized. "The body cream took three months, the moisturizing cream took three weeks, and the candle was an entire year. The bath gel was hard. It was a nightmare. Every time it hit the water, the smell would evaporate; it didn't diffuse. To get it right we had to change the formula." Gale was not satisfied with just spinning out new products. Each had to have a point of departure. She insisted collagen and elastin be added to the body moisturizer so it would have treatment benefits. She balked at Roth's suggestion of doing bath powder, saying it was old-fashioned; but went ahead and, instead of making it white, came up with the idea of giving it a flesh tint.

Gale also was working on a men's fragrance, a project that took three years and caused much tension in the Giorgio camp. She had ideas for other new products: scented hangers, drawer liners, potpourri, and, eventually, shampoo and styling mousse. However, after the struggle they had just been through to come up with the women's fragrance, Roth and Horner were not eager for Fred to give her the green light on many line extensions. They also realized that successfully launching the women's scent at Bloomingdale's was the company's major objective in 1982 and the ticket to future business throughout the U.S.A.

On Monday, August 16, 1982, the dark-suited businessmen having their quiet power breakfasts in the Plaza Hotel's staid Oak Room had their turf invaded by a large, noisy group. In the midst of this decorous room were David Horner and Jim Roth, having breakfast with six young, beautiful women. Horner and Roth were presenting their mostly blond companions with tight pastel terrycloth jogging suits and tester units of the Giorgio fragrance and moisturizer. The pumps on these counter tester units were stuck and as Horner fumbled with them he exhorted the women to be aggressive in sampling customers. These were Giorgio's in-store models and this was their training session. At a nearby table, a group of Estée Lauder executives were giggling watching Horner fidget with the defiant pumps. Giorgio's in-store models were chosen by Bloomingdale's but paid ten dollars an hour by Giorgio to spray and sample customers as they moved through the cosmetics department. If Giorgio were to be discovered in New York, the vehicle would not be a splashy ad in

The New York Times, a television commercial, or a bus poster. It was up to these women to get the fragrance under the noses of harried New Yorkers who pass through Bloomingdale's labyrinth of special shops, endless aisles, and escalators.

Roth recalls, "David and I went into our dog and pony show and convinced these girls they would be selling the best-selling fragrance in Beverly Hills. They believed in it and they went into that store and started grabbing wrists and spraying. These models were made to feel as if they were the movie stars."

The models hardly looked like movie stars in their ill-fitting jogging suits that bulged in the wrong places. Susan Fried, the assistant fragrance buyer, was assigned to watch over the Giorgio launch and immediately saw customers react to the fragrance rather than the Giorgio name. "The models were saying, 'Giorgio is a very exclusive boutique in Beverly Hills' and then would repeat the advertising tag line, 'You know who wears it.' The people would then ask them, 'Who?' They would say it's the largest-selling fragrance in Beverly Hills, but the appeal was the juice, absolutely."

There was no advertisement in *The New York Times* to announce the arrival of Giorgio at Bloomingdale's. Whereas other manufacturers gladly paid 100 percent for the *Times'* "co-op" launch ad, the Giorgio policy was different. There were no co-op advertising dollars for Bloomingdale's, but Giorgio, Inc., would pick up all the costs for the models and would pay a 5 percent commission to the person behind the Giorgio counter. Roth and Horner felt an ad in the *Times* was merely a way of placating the store and would not be as effective as an in-store model actually spraying the heady fragrance among the Bloomingdale's hordes. The Giorgio promotional budget was directed at intensive in-store sampling and scented national magazine inserts. No other fragrance manufacturer had ever sampled as aggressively as Giorgio would over the next three years, investing $4 million on in-store models alone in 1985.

The 1982 fall period could not have been a better time to launch Giorgio. The industry was in a slump, with the prestige market showing no real growth, due partially to the recession and a glut of fragrances already on the market. The consumer was confused by the overabundance of designer names, many of which meant nothing to the average fragrance user. Wall Street analysts were critical of the industry, noting that in a business so highly dependent on promotion and new-product development, companies were trimming budgets because of the economic downturn.

"Giorgio hit a wonderful window in the industry in 1982," analyzes Allan Mottus:

Other people were not advertising and prestige brand distribution was proliferating all over the board. The stuff was coming in from Miami and these diverted designer fragrances could be bought everywhere, and the consumer was tired of the designer brands. Giorgio didn't have to apologize for good taste. It was extremely loud and glitzy and a taste level that Americans like. They were looking for an alternative.

Fragrance manufacturers had reached their creative nadir by 1982, providing retailers with nothing bold and different. The three major new fragrances launched that fall were Raffinée from Houbigant, Niki de Saint Phalle from Jacqueline Cochran, and Gianni Versace, named for an Italian designer who was hardly well known in Los Angeles at the time, much less in Peoria. None of these scents would excite the consumer, although Saint Phalle's vibrantly painted, entwined-snake bottle was a curiosity. The spring 1982 launches were slightly more viable, with Ombre Rose and Vanderbilt cracking the top ten in some important stores. These were not breakthrough fragrances, though; and one was a blatant knock-off.

Vanderbilt was the signature fragrance of socialite Gloria Vanderbilt. Bob Ruttenberg teamed with George Friedman at Warner/Lauren Cosmetics to introduce it as a follow-up to Lauren and Polo, fragrances the company had launched in the late 1970s. Ruttenberg had worked at Revlon and had watched Revson perfect the knockoff strategy with Charlie, which was a copy of Revlon's own Norell.

Charles could recognize something and knock it off before anybody recognized the fragrance was going to be a winner. With Vanderbilt, we knocked off Oscar de la Renta; we did that by design. We saw Oscar was a good fragrance—a winner in very limited distribution—and we wanted to knock it off and take it mass and that's what we did. Stores that couldn't get Oscar put up signs that said, "We don't carry Oscar, but we have Vanderbilt." It was a fantastic strategy and everyone in the industry knew it.

Compared to these scents, Giorgio was special. Weisenfeld knew if Giorgio were to be discovered among the 120 fragrances Bloomingdale's already carried, the newcomer would have to have an exuberant saleswoman behind it. Diana Romanello smelled Giorgio and was more excited about it than were the other saleswomen in the fragrance department.

Romanello had been selling seven other lines and her base salary of $75 a week plus commissions afforded her and her husband a small apartment in a housing project in Greenpoint, Brooklyn, where roving desperados stole the garbage at night. Romanello would do such a good job with Giorgio that in three years she would earn $100,000 annually and would buy a house on Long Island.

Romanello did not have much to work with at first. The fragrance department at Bloomingdale's was small and recessed and other manufacturers already had laid claim to its limited real estate. With 120 fragrances packed into fewer than twenty existing cases, manufacturers literally were battling for inches, and there was not an inch left over for Giorgio.

Weisenfeld and Burns found a spot for Giorgio on the fringe of the cosmetics department adjacent to the jewelry area. There they erected a four-foot-square cube, painted it yellow and white, put a couple of small topiary trees around it, and starting selling Giorgio. The models were restricted from walking throughout the department because of the territorial imperative that rules the cosmetics domain. Complaints about one company's model invading another's space are common, and Weisenfeld often had to mediate between line girls squabbling over real or imagined space invasions.

Despite Giorgio's small, out-of-the-way location, the fragrance rang up over $1,800 the first two days. The Friedmans took Roth and Horner to lunch at Le Cirque on the launch day to celebrate. Weisenfeld was also ready to celebrate. Toward the end of the first day she saw Blumenfeld and Gribetz walking down B-Way, the main aisle in the cosmetics department, and she asked them to guess how much business Giorgio had done. When she quoted them the figure, "their eyes almost dropped out of their heads," according to Weisenfeld, who gave them a smart-alecky, "I told you so," response.

By the end of the first week, Giorgio had produced $5,000 in sales and Burns couldn't believe it. "I thought it was a mistake. For a fragrance nobody ever heard of, and in that small piece of real estate, that was astounding. It outsold any other fragrance we ever had in that position. I thought it was a fluke, maybe one customer bought a lot of bottles."

It was no fluke. Over the fall season and into the critical Christmas season, when over 50 percent of all fragrance business is conducted, Giorgio continued to sell at a rate far above the meager space and location alloted to it. Not wanting to infuriate the manufacturers of Opium, Lauren, or Oscar de la Renta, the store's top-volume scents, Burns conjured a way of getting Giorgio more space without displacing the others. She asked the display department to create a yellow-and-white striped wooden cart that could be wheeled through the store as a sort of mobile fragrance outpost. When the two models pushing the cart passed through an area, they would blast Giorgio.

The cart, that small PT boat with its big cannon, clicked; and when Bloomingdale's Christmas season went on the books, Giorgio had a $400,000 volume and was among the top five fragrances at the vaunted 59th Street flagship. No fragrance had ever done over $1 million there. Even Opium, the store's leader, achieved almost $2 million in all twelve Bloomingdale's stores. Based on Giorgio's half-year volume, Horner was predicting Giorgio would become the flagship's first million-dollar scent. He started asking for (soon he would be demanding) case space and better locations. Bloomingdale's management recognized what they had but wanted to keep Giorgio their secret for as long as possible. Giving the company space and location was not the way to do it. When reporters from *WWD* called Weisenfeld, asking for current rankings for their annual Christmas round-up story, they did not get a totally honest answer. She said,

> I was told to keep the lid on Giorgio for the first Christmas because no one believed it. They [senior management] thought it was a fluke. Why announce Giorgio's success and get everyone else upset? At the time, having exclusives with a well-known name was one thing; but with a little-known company like Giorgio, it was another. It was an anomaly. It was frustrating for David; he knew how much Giorgio was doing and he wanted it announced.

Horner was the field general, making sure Bloomingdale's was supplied and moving forward. If he weren't in the store, he would call Weisenfeld daily, often twice a day, to get an up-to-the-minute report about the day's business. When merchandise was running low, Horner would fly to New York on the weekends with stock to make sure Bloomingdale's was supplied. The company had no warehouse facility in New York, but Florasynth kept an ample supply at its Manhattan office and Fred Friedman became Giorgio's unofficial sales representative, running boxes of the fragrance through Manhattan to feed Bloomingdale's growing demand.

Back in Los Angeles, Fred was not happy with the service level of the mail-order-fulfillment house contracted by Roth and Horner. Fred felt the orders were not being delivered in a timely manner. He wanted the three-to-four weeks cut down to five-days-to-a-week, and he wanted personalized notes from him included with every order. In addition, he was unhappy with the way the fragrance was being wrapped, often in the wrong color paper and never in the Giorgio signature stripes. Bottles were breaking and Hayman was pressuring IMG to take the mail-order operation in-house. After all, the boutique had its own small-scale in-house mail-order operation that could be handled by one person. However, the idea was a little too entrepreneurial for Horner, who thought it would stretch the company's limited personnel.

Fred was insistent, so while Horner was in New York keeping tabs on Bloomingdale's Christmas business, Jim Roth set up a mail-order operation in a new office at 9250 Wilshire Boulevard. It would become a family affair.

Roth recalls,

We turned that office into a perfume factory on weekends. We used to fill the bottles on Saturday with David and his kids, and on Sunday I would come in and cello-wrap the boxes. Katrine [David's wife] would use a turkey baster to fill those bottles. We practically worked around the clock and during December 1982, we worked every single day until two A.M. until we got too tired or got a headache from being around that scent. I used tape guns to seal the boxes but had to pound the tape and both my hands got bloody.

Charles Hayman, Fred's oldest son, was running the shipping department and Betty Endo, Fred's girlfriend, was typing labels. In addition, ten people from a temporary employment agency were handwriting and typing labels, as in its early days the operation was not computerized. Fred was not on the production line, and after one of his infrequent visits to the office he vehemently objected to having both the Giorgio and IMG logos on the door. Roth and Horner were irked. "We are not on your payroll; we have to have our name on the door," Roth argued. "But he threatened us with all kinds of shit and we took it off the door but kept it on the building's directory." Roth and Horner also had a major run-in with Fred over the cost of the cologne. It was high-priced at thirty-five dollars, but Roth and Horner felt it needed to be priced at forty dollars to cover the high cost of goods and to bolster its snob appeal. Fred, who has always been sensitive about pricing, thought forty dollars was a stretch. Roth and Horner were right. As soon as the cologne went to forty dollars, sales grew even more dramatically, and the first year ended with a $125,000 pretax profit. Fred recognized the Roth and Horner contribution with a $25,000 bonus not stipulated in their contract.

Giorgio's retail launch in 1982 did not set any fragrance industry records: the scent's $1.5 million volume caused little concern among the competition; the tiny space in Bloomingdale's was easy to miss and the mail-order campaign had yet to hit the mass-circulation magazines. The first Giorgio scent-strip ad in the May 1983 issue of *Vogue* would let the industry and retailers all over America know that Giorgio was an ambitious new entry with a unique marketing hook.

The mail-order advertising campaign of January 1983 produced $250,000 in revenues using only regional magazines. The first scent-strip ad in the May *Vogue* cost the company $106,000, which covered the space, production of the ad, and payment to Arcade for 950,000 scent strips. Later, Giorgio's scent-strip orders would grow so large that Arcade would not be able to maintain consistency of the scent, and at Fred's urging the company would switch to 3M, who pioneered the technology but charged considerably more for the strips—sometimes as much as fifteen cents each.

One day while driving down the San Diego freeway, Roth came up with a better advertising slogan than the current, "You know who wears it." He pulled off the freeway and wrote, "Giorgio, the best-selling fragrance in Beverly Hills," which became the line used over the next two years. To check the claim, Horner did some quick calculations of what Opium, Lauren, and Oscar de la Renta's volume were in the Beverly Hills stores such as I. Magnin, Saks, and Robinson's. The exercise convinced him Giorgio was the best seller. The new ads, although simple, were extremely effective. They showed only a product shot of the bottle and box, with copy touting the fragrance's exclusivity, "available only at Giorgio and Bloomingdale's." Here was a precious slice of Beverly Hills glamour now available not just to the rich but also to Middle America. The powerful scent released by the scent strip was the clincher.

Vogue, Bazaar, and *Town & Country* charged Giorgio for two full-color pages of advertising, but the scent-strip exposure was worth it. The *Vogue* ad brought in $197,000 in orders, against the $68,000 cost of goods, for a net profit of $21,000. That same month, the scent-strip ad in *Ultra* magazine brought in $44,000 in orders and the company made an $18,000 profit. "We sat there and said, 'If we can get twenty thousand net profit out of every magazine, let's run with it,' so we started expanding," Roth said.

Regional and national insertions allowed the Giorgio scent to be smelled and tested all over America during the summer and fall of 1983. *Town & Country*'s July issue garnered $138,000 in orders and a healthy $50,000 in profits. *McCall's* and *Vanity Fair* were not as fruitful, failing to pull with the consistency of *Ultra, Bazaar, Town & Country*, and *Vogue*. The mass-circulation magazines, *Glamour* and *Cosmopolitan*, brought them little more than break-even money; but they were important for visibility. Many women who sampled the fragrance in the magazines were not mail-order customers and were beginning to ask for the fragrance at their local department stores. Pent-up demand was building, and Fred started getting calls from both small and large stores requesting distribution.

Bob Renberg, of Renberg's in Tulsa, Oklahoma, was among the first and most insistent retailers to come after Giorgio. The Renberg family has been in the retail business in Tulsa for seventy-five years, building Renberg's into a $30 million, four-unit operation with an emphasis on quality, service, and fashion. Renberg's wife, Nancy, had grown up in Beverly Hills and was visiting her hometown in December 1982. One day, while sitting around record industry executive Howard Stark's pool, Renberg got a whiff of Mrs. Stark's Giorgio perfume and the vacation was over. "Fred had just launched the fragrance to his own clientele and when I called him he said he wasn't interested in selling to retailers. When I got back to Tulsa I told my fragrance buyer that this fragrance is going to be incredible and we have got to get it before we get squeezed out because we are in Middle America."

Renberg kept calling Hayman and when he found out he was in New York negotiating with Bloomingdale's he grabbed his fragrance buyer and got on the first plane to New York. Fred agreed to see him at his suite at the Tuscany Hotel, where Renberg laid out the portfolio of exclusive fragrances his store had carried over the years, including Bal à Versailles, Oscar de la Renta, and Lauren. "Fred was upset because he couldn't get Saks to give him an audience and I couldn't believe it. Anybody who had an understanding of fragrances should have opened their doors and rolled out the red carpet and lined it with gold. I convinced him I had to have it and he said, 'You can have it because you're not going to hurt any of my other future accounts.'"

When Bloomingdale's wrote a substantial order for Giorgio, Fred told Renberg he couldn't get him the fragrance then because of production limitations. Renberg was not to be denied and made a formal presentation in Fred's Beverly Hills office with schematics of the fragrance department and how Giorgio would be given the star treatment. Fred was impressed and, during the last week in October 1983, Renberg's became the unlikely second store in America to carry the fragrance.

Said Renberg,

> The Giorgio cologne spray quickly became the number-one stock-keeping unit in our store. Never in the history of our store was

anything in such demand. Even during the war, when silk stockings were the most desired product because of rationing, it was nothing to match Giorgio. Nobody needs another bottle of cologne to put on your shelf; but this fragrance brought some fame to people in Tulsa who would never come into contact with what you might call "the beautiful people."

Renberg's wracked up sales of $138,330 that Christmas season, and by the end of 1985 may have done the most Giorgio business in America on a per capita basis. The store was doing $707,391 with the Giorgio women's scent and $114,791 with the men's brand—incredible figures, considering Tulsa only has four hundred thousand residents. The seventy fragrance cases in Renberg's four stores carried over seventy-five fragrances, but Giorgio, at its peak in 1985, represented 30 percent of the total fragrance business at Renberg's. "Everybody was buying it. The wealthy ladies bought it and, pretty soon, the people who cook and run errands for them came into the store to buy it. When the black people started coming in and buying it we knew we had a universal fragrance and we couldn't keep up with the demand."

The typical distribution pattern for a prestige fragrance starts with the premier carriage-trade stores in America—Saks, Neiman-Marcus, Marshall Field's, and I. Magnin—and then spreads to the larger-volume department stores such as The Broadway in Los Angeles, the May Company, and Dillard's in the Southwest. Giorgio's early distribution pattern was atypical, but in keeping with this maverick venture. Fred was afraid of size from the start and was more comfortable in dealing with smaller stores and people he knew. Every fair-size city in America has its own special small store catering to the rich with expensive imports, and Fred commanded Roth and Horner to go into these stores before venturing into the major department stores.

Horner disagreed with Fred but had no choice. "I thought the guy was out of his tree. We went into Balliet's and the main store has a neon pig on its roof, but Fred knew the owner and that made it a quality store. We did volume in these small stores but not nearly as much as in the big stores. The whole thing was folderol."

While staying at the Plaza Athenée in Paris on his European buying trips, Fred had become friendly with Leo "Buddy" Rodgers, who owns Balliet's, a fine Oklahoma City speciality store. The "neon pig" is a piggybank sign that lights up at night on top of Sooner Federal Bank across from Balliet's. When Rodgers heard about Giorgio and saw it at Bloomingdale's, he leaned on Fred for the scent, hoping that a new fragrance would help the store during the oil depression. Rodgers's office window looks out on the Penn Square Bank, which went bankrupt on July 5, 1982, and was a daily reminder of how depressed the oil-dependent Oklahoma economy was.

Giorgio not only helped get Rodgers out of the doldrums, it shook the store's stately chandeliers. Rodgers said,

> People started buying Giorgio like mad. It was like a woman in the Depression in the late twenties, the women couldn't afford a new hat so they had seamstresses sewing new bows to update their look so they could feel good. Giorgio was a shot in the arm that everybody needed right now. I've never seen acceptance like that. We had farmers and cowboys who couldn't even pronounce it, along with the wealthiest women and men coming in for it. I knew it would be good, but not that good.

The most business Balliet's had ever done with a fragrance was $350,000 with Oscar de la Renta. Giorgio rocketed to $600,000 in its first year in the store and became not just Balliet's number-one fragrance, but the highest-volume producer of any line in the store, which did only $10 million in total. The exclusive was a big part of the bonanza, but Balliet's had to pick up the launch costs and pay 100 percent of the advertising, almost unheard of in a business where retailers seldom spend advertising dollars unless the fragrance manufacturer kicks in half or more.

The third small store to carry Giorgio during the 1983 Christmas season was Korshak's, in Chicago, a store that stocked the same Italian and French designers as Giorgio. Unlike Balliet's and Renberg's, which had developed fragrance departments, Korshak's was experimenting with fragrance and had just put in a four-hundred-square-foot counter. Giorgio did $64,000 at Korshak's in December 1983, representing about 70 percent of the store's total fragrance sales, according to Hope Rudnick, Korshak's general manager.

I. Magnin's flagship on San Francisco's Union Square was the only other store in the U.S. to have the fragrance during the 1983 Christmas season. Steve Somers, Magnin's young CEO, was always looking for a way to shed Magnin's stodgy carriage-trade image and make the store more competitive with Macy's California. Since the 1950s, Magnin's cosmetics and fragrance department had ranked among the best in the U.S., partially because Van Venneri, the store's cosmetics divisional merchandise manager, had a talent for discovering special upscale lines. In her thirty-five years at the department's helm, and with Estée Lauder among her early discoveries, Venneri had built the Magnin cosmetics business to around 15 percent of the store's total, an unusually high percentage. Normally the cosmetics area of a fine speciality store contributes around 10 percent of total sales, while a department store's cosmetics area contributes between 5 and 8 percent. By the early 1980s, though, Venneri was semiretired and serving as a consultant to Magnin's, and Macy's was making serious inroads into Magnin's cosmetics business.

Magnin's sister store in the Federated Department Store chain was Bloomingdale's, and at a principals' meeting at Federated's Cincinnati headquarters on October 25, 1983, Bloomingdale's chairman Marvin Traub told the group his fragrance business was strong and being led by a powerful new scent. Somers pulled Traub aside after the meeting and quizzed him about his star scent.

Somers was baffled that Bloomingdale's quiet winner was Giorgio. He had met Hayman in Paris and given him a ride in Magnin's Rolls-Royce, reserved for shuttling the store's merchants to fashion shows. Somers considered Hayman an "L.A. phenomenon," but had been impressed with his markdown selling strategy of giving the salesgirls an extra five dollars as an incentive to sell markdown items. Venneri had told Somers about Giorgio, but he hated the idea of selling another retailer's fragrance: "I told Van, 'It will be a cold day in hell before I buy another retailer's fragrance. Don't even mention it to me again.' Why should I perpetuate another retailer's name?" After hearing Traub's report and visiting the Bloomingdale's counter in New York, Somers quickly ate his words. "They had these girls spritzing and people were loving the scent and going over to their little counter and they had more people buying it than you could shake a stick at. I called Fred the next day and had Elaine MacNeil [Venneri's successor] call the two henchmen [Roth and Horner], but Fred said they wanted to roll it out in the spring. I said, 'No way, I want that stuff soon for the Christmas season.' "

Hayman and the henchmen went to San Francisco and were wined and dined at Trader Vic's by Somers and his team. Sonja Caproni, Magnin's well-respected and strikingly attractive fashion director, understood more than hemlines and haute couture. She paid attention to Fred, and by the time the Giorgio gang went back to Los Angeles they had agreed to open Magnin's Union Square flagship in time for the Christmas season and received a hefty $100,000 order. The merchandise was trucked from Beverly Hills the Friday before Thanksgiving and Somers and his merchants were at the dock at 7 A.M. Saturday to meet the truck, unload the merchandise, and set up the display with its yellow-and-white awning.

As Somers recalled:

In that first day we had no advertising, just the girls spritzing and we did twenty-five thousand dollars. No one knew we would have the fragrance and it was the scent that sold it. We were spraying the fragrance everywhere and the store smelled like shit. We even sprayed the elevators and people were gagging on the elevators, it was so strong. That Saturday night we had to wash the elevator walls with Clorox to get it out because the people were complaining, but no other fragrance company had ever done twenty-five thousand on their launch day—not Givenchy, not Dior, not Armani—and they hyped it considerably more.

Magnin rang up over $300,000 in Giorgio business in December alone. However, Somers paid for an ad in the *San Francisco Chronicle* that did not help his business. The three-quarter page was a blatant piece of competitive one-upsmanship and read, "What can't you buy at Macy's, Saks, and Neiman-Marcus and is only available at I. Magnin? Giorgio."

The ad's content was a violation of the Robinson-Pattman Act, a federal trade law that mandates manufacturers treat all retailers evenhandedly. The act was designed to protect small retailers who do not have the buying power of the larger chains. The act restricts manufacturers from setting unreasonable criteria for the purpose of restrictive distribution. The act is seldom enforced in the cosmetics industry, which by its very nature of exclusive launches and select distribution violates the act. This ad, however, made Macy's look bad and the Macy's brass in New York had lawyers look at the situation and Giorgio was threatened with a lawsuit, according to Horner. Hayman and Somers thought the ad was cute at first but after the threat, Hayman called Somers. "Fred was always nice with me but this time he went crazy about the ad. Horner got on the phone and went berserk also saying we can't do that." To salve Macy's wounds, Giorgio agreed to open a few Macy's branch stores early in 1984.

The Giorgio business in New York during the 1983 Christmas season finally was starting to draw the attention of the industry itself. Initially, executives from the major cosmetics companies had seen the yellow-and-white stripes at Bloomingdale's, smelled the fragrance, watched the models spritzing, and derisively thought the whole thing was cheap, loud, and unsophisticated. A reflection of that thinking was evident at the Fragrance Foundation Awards dinner on June 15, 1983, at New York's Sheraton Centre. The event is the industry's version of the Oscars; awards are given for the best new fragrances in several categories. Giorgio was a nominee. Fred and Gale attended the black-tie event and sat with Robin

Burns. Houbigant's Rafinée was the winner for the best women's prestige launch, while Vanderbilt was the winner in the mass market. Armani won the packaging award. The evening wasn't a total loss for Giorgio, though. *WWD* photographed the Haymans and quoted Fred, in what must have seemed an arrogrant statement, considering Giorgio's lack of recognition at the dinner. Fred said, "Staying humble is the toughest part of the fragrance industry. As a retailer, I find it hard to say no to people who would like to have us in the store."

Retailers identified Giorgio's potential much quicker than the fragrance industry did. The industry's high level of snob appeal accounted for much of that blind spot. Barbara Gyde, acting co–general manager of Sanofi Beauty Products, observes, "No one could believe Giorgio's success. Everyone in the industry is so snobby and thought the fragrance was too strong. I would always hear, 'I don't know anyone who wears the fragrance,' but little by little the industry woke up. Once Bloomies started giving Giorgio large space and the other manufacturers were getting pushed aside, we knew it was a huge hit."

Weisenfeld, in a June 17, 1983, *WWD* survey of the New York fragrance business, for the first time listed Giorgio along with Lauren, Oscar, and Perfumer's Workshop as the strongest 1983 performers. However, it was not until the height of the Christmas holiday season, when Diana Romanello was selling Giorgio like "six-packs of beer," that Giorgio vaulted to number one at Bloomingdale's and the industry got the message that Giorgio was for real.

The effect of achieving the number-one fragrance ranking at Bloomingdale's could be compared to winning the singles tennis title at Wimbledon for the first time. You've arrived, and even if you don't win another match, your name is recognizable. The battle for number one at Bloomingdale's was being waged by Opium, Oscar, and Lauren and was getting heated. Lauren, which had been number three, had overtaken Oscar and was within reach of number one until Giorgio came along. Bob Ruttenberg was masterminding Lauren's ascent for Warner/Lauren and was determined it would be number one at Bloomingdale's. It never got there:

> In my mind I knew being number one at Bloomingdale's was just an ego trip because, clearly, Bloomingdale's is not the most profitable store in the world, and it may be the least profitable, but it was ego driven for me. We were chasing Opium and all of a sudden I'm pushed down to number three because of Giorgio, so I start spending more promotional money because of Giorgio, which I thought was a real flash in the pan. A few months later I meet

with Robin Burns and she tells me we moved back to number two and I asked her who number one was and she said, "Giorgio." I said, "Giorgio what?" It's not possible, I thought. But she pulls out computer printouts and I can't believe it. We spend hundreds of thousands of dollars on advertising and promotions, on models and samples. I'm gearing all my efforts in Bloomingdale's and I'm still number two, but now the distance between number one and number two has grown greater than the distance between us and number three. This is only after Giorgio's first year and they are off in a corner in a location that I wouldn't have taken for free. I'm really pissed; I'm spending like a bandit; I've got Ralph Lauren's name and Giorgio is kicking my ass. I said, "This is a phenomenon."

Ruttenberg could not escape the Giorgio cloud over his head:

Everywhere I go, I'm smelling Giorgio, and it's really eating me up. I use to smell Lauren everywhere; now it's Giorgio and it's showing me I don't have a great handle on the industry, though I thought I really did. I'm visiting my son at his camp in Vermont and we are walking through the woods on Parents Day and I smell Giorgio. Here I am in the woods, I must be hallucinating. We go to lunch and this lady is sitting two tables away and is wearing Giorgio. I said, "How long ago were you walking in the woods?" and she says, "About a half hour ago," and I said to myself, It's coming out of the trees now. I was getting depressed, visiting the son I adore, but hating being at his camp.

Ruttenberg wasn't the only one struggling with Giorgio, trying to comprehend its popularity and control its growth. The Bloomingdale's cosmetics merchandising staff had never seen a fragrance do what Giorgio was doing. Giorgio's growth was pushing it into a realm beyond the number-one fragrance in the store. It was starting to approach the volume figures of premier cosmetics and treatment lines such as Estée Lauder and Clinique. Suddenly the entire fragrance category was being looked at differently. Giorgio was a mass-appeal fragrance with limited distribution and Bloomingdale's was the beneficiary of its success. Until now, fragrance had been considered an impulse purchase. Now people made special trips to Bloomingdale's because that was the only place they could purchase Giorgio.

Bloomingdale's was building a new store in the Valley View Shopping

Center in suburban Dallas, and the store was going to open with Giorgio in October 1983, the first store in Texas to carry the brand. Arline Friedman, who merchandised the branches and later succeeded Mike Blumenfeld, said,

> Customers were calling us before the store was open saying they must have Giorgio. "I'm driving in from Oklahoma and I must have it for my wife, I beg you, I'm pleading with you." We had customers come to the construction site and we found a man in with the construction workers begging us to sell him some [Giorgio]. We told him, "We can't sell you anything yet. There is nothing here yet; we only have hardhats."

The Texas appetite for ostentation would propel the Valley View branch past Bloomingdale's in New York to become Giorgio's top-selling door in 1984 and 1985.

Back in New York, Weisenfeld became Bloomingdale's treatment buyer and Meryl Friedman was promoted to buyer of women's and men's fragrances. Weisenfeld had successfully launched the Giorgio fragrance and wrote the first $100,000 order of her career when Giorgio did its first scent strip with Bloomingdale's in the store's April 1983 lingerie catalogue. She wrote the order with hands shaking, despite David Horner's cool predictions that the catalogue would produce $400,000 in volume. It did, and Meryl Friedman was able to approach her new job without temerity, ready to place huge orders. She would, however, have to be as much psychologist as fragrance buyer in order to maximize the Giorgio business.

Friedman, along with senior management, developed a specific marketing plan for each Bloomingdale's branch store and knew how each dollar would be spent on Giorgio. Each branch had its own separate advertising, direct mail, and in-store activity plan. Bloomingdale's had never tooled a marketing program this carefully for an individual fragrance, but this was the only way to "monitor the monster." It was clear that to get the maximum out of Giorgio, additional space would have to be found; and management started creating Giorgio outposts outside the cosmetics department. Although Bloomingdale's had pioneered the outpost concept with lines such as Estée Lauder, it was on a small scale compared to Giorgio, which at its height in 1984 would have eight outposts in the 59th Street flagship.

Space and location are the issues creating an adversarial relationship between retailer and cosmetics manufacturer. Giorgio's astronomical growth at Bloomingdale's, from nonentity in August 1982, to $3 million a little more than a year later, had its effect on the Giorgio team. Their egos were growing in proportion to their success and the Californians were becoming contentious and demanding, with good reason. They were doing more volume than many lines with significantly more space. Fred and Horner saw the figures at 59th Street and began to exert some leverage, making Meryl Friedman's job that much tougher. Friedman said,

> Fred became demanding because he knew the commodity he had and became impossible to deal with. Every time we wanted to do something that was easy in August 1982, now it became difficult. "How clean will my cases be kept? Will my cases be dusted? What kind of people will sell my product?" He was particularly questioning our standards and they were very high, but were being tested all the time. It became frustrating—how can we please these people?

Accompanied by Horner, Fred would make unannounced visits to Bloomingdale's branches, which failed to provide the excitement of the Lexington Avenue flagship.

> After seeing Fresh Meadows with Fred, David called me and said, "We are closing it down; it's over." I said, "David, good morning. How are you today?" He then said, "We look terrible at that branch. We are in half a case." "Calm down, David. Let me speak to the department manager." Fresh Meadows is our smallest branch and has a total of five cases for women's fragrance. Giorgio had half a case and it was a major presentation, but not in their eyes. A case is a case, relativity meant nothing. They never pulled out; they threatened they would. David was a real hyper guy and if Fred was pinching him he was jumping that much higher. I would always get this picture in my mind of a marionette. Every time Fred would kick him he would react and kick us. It was a knee-jerk reaction to what Fred was doing and saying. We went through this anxiety and trauma repeatedly but always ended up kissing and making up.

Presentation and image were Fred's main concerns, and if Giorgio didn't look good Fred was not bashful about complaining to Traub and Gribetz. He saw Bloomingdale's as an extension of his Rodeo Drive boutique. Horner's major concern was keeping Giorgio liquid with ample cash flow to keep up production and meet the growing demand. The company was operating from funds generated by the business and without any bank loans. Giorgio's terms were designed by Horner to ensure steady cash flow, and they were radically different from those of other fragrance companies. Retailers had always bought fragrance and cosmetics on consignment, but Giorgio did not accept returns. This policy greatly simplified bookkeeping and forced the stores to buy wisely. Whereas most companies gave retailers sixty to ninety days to pay for their receivable merchandise, Giorgio had a thirty-six day rule. Bloomingdale's and other Federated stores seldom paid their bills on time. When Bloomingdale's payments were running late during the first Christmas, Horner called Blumenfeld and threatened to set up a little wagon outside Bloomingdale's and give the fragrance away for free. He reasoned it was acceptable because he wasn't getting paid by Bloomingdale's. After repeated threats of cutting off Bloomingdale's supply, the payments became more regular. Arline Friedman says it was almost impossible to keep up with the Giorgio paperwork because of the constant shipments, and that the store never intentionally tried to delay payments, a contention Horner doesn't buy. Other Federated stores, Foley's and Burdine's, would later delay payments and Horner did cut off their shipments to enforce the thirty-six day rule.

While Fred Hayman, David Horner, and Jim Roth were building a $15 million fragrance business in 1983, Gale was working on new products and getting a divorce from Fred. She filed for divorce on April 12, 1983, after she and Fred reached a settlement agreement on January 28, 1983. The divorce was granted on September 9, 1983, and would contribute to the breakup of the couple's business partnership and eventually lead to the sale of Giorgio.

The Haymans' relationship was perplexing. Their separation was old news by 1980, though many had been surprised by it and even more amazed at the stability of Fred's and Gale's working relationship. On the surface, there still seemed to be plenty of respect and affection between them. On October 13, 1982, Fred was honored by the Maple Center of Beverly Hills as Man of the Year. Gale took a full-page ad in the event's program. Her ad read, "ADVENTUROUS CHIVALROUS GENEROUS FABULOUS No tribute can ever equal everything you are or everything you have been to me. Love, Gale." "Our business relationship was still good at the point of the divorce. Good? Are you kidding? It was great. We would be meeting constantly and Fred didn't make a decision without me. He would review with me after meetings with Jim and David and we were in sync. My feeling was to manage the growth, I had no interest in growing the company quickly at all."

Gale said Fred had hoped to end the separation and become reunited but she balked. She was in love with Igor Stalew, traveling with him to Mexico and Big Sur, going to underground nightclubs and to Lina Wertmuller movies. Stalew was encouraging Gale to stand up to Fred. He didn't like the public's perception of who was the driving force behind Giorgio:

> Gale was an equal partner with Fred but she was getting five percent of the credit and doing fifty percent of the work or more. I began to say, "Gale, you are getting a raw deal." I am the significant male relationship in her life and she would come home to me depressed and I would say, "Why are you so depressed? You have created a great fragrance." She was having a hassle with Fred, always being put in her place and getting put down.

Gale maintains,

> He didn't want the divorce in the beginning and he had hoped we would go back together after the five years. And he asked, "Are we going to go back?" and I said, "I think it's best this way." Then he said, "I want a divorce," just like that. I said, "Fine, let's draw up the papers." I went to a girlfriend who was an attorney for advice on a divorce lawyer. I told her I wanted a nice fellow who isn't going to make any waves because I don't want to upset the company. The fragrance is just becoming successful and I didn't want to do anything to upset this fragrance. I didn't want to have a really powerful lawyer. It wasn't smart. I was very stupid, too trusting, naïve.

Gale hired Stephen Miller of Miller and Nolan, a small local law firm. Fred was represented by his close friend, Leo Ziffren, who was the Giorgio corporate attorney and had represented both Gale and Fred. Gale did not challenge Ziffren's status, although his objectivity would become an issue in Gale's future lawsuits against Fred.

The property-settlement part of the divorce agreement was standard, with Gale getting half of their assets. The six checking accounts were split and Gale got a half interest in her large new apartment with swimming pool in West Los Angeles, in addition to half of the Charleville home where Fred lived. However, the most important possession the Haymans shared was Giorgio, Inc., and it was here that Fred fought for control and Gale gave in.

Fred asked for 60 percent of the Giorgio stock, which Gale rejected outright. Not realizing how vulnerable she would become, Gale buckled to Fred's insistence on control of the company. She testified in a later deposition that she didn't feel threatened by allowing Fred to have control; she thought it would merely satisfy his ego. Gale stated,

> I was used to him—his ego needs. I thought this was one more need to placate his ego, and it didn't look particularly unusual coming from Fred, because Fred was—is—a very demanding man and he needs to always feel in control and powerful, and he has a very large ego. To me this was like if it makes his ego feel good, fine—and if he keeps peace in the business, fine. I had no idea that placating his ego and keeping peace in the business would allow him and give him the right, the legal right, to force me out of the company.

The trust agreement Gale signed on January 28, 1983, gave 49 percent of the stock ownership to both Gale and Fred. However, it named Fred the trustee of the remaining 2 percent of the outstanding stock, thereby giving him voting control of the company during his lifetime. In the event of his death, the 2 percent would go to Gale, who would become the successor trustee. The trust agreement had no codicil protecting Gale's job in the company, and Miller made that ominous point to her:

> When we got the divorce my lawyer said, "If he has control, he can fire you," and I went to Fred. He said, "Gale, I would never do that, don't you trust me? Oh, come on, Gale, we were married, we built this business. How can you say that? I would never do anything to harm you." I then said, "I'm just telling you what my lawyer said," and he got very angry and intimidating and he said I had a shyster lawyer who wants to create a battle. I told him this business is very important to me and I agreed to it.
>
> I agreed to give him control, and it was total stupidity. I gave him the two percent out of love, the marriage, and respect that he was older, all these things. My lawyers said, "Don't do it," but I trusted Leo Ziffren. He was the corporate attorney and he handled the divorce for Fred and I trusted him because he was the corporate attorney.

In Fred's November, 1986, court deposition he stated,

In 1983 when Gale and I finalized our divorce proceedings, I reluctantly agreed to each of us getting forty-nine percent of the stock of Giorgio, with my having an extra two percent during my lifetime. I believed that I was entitled to a much greater percentage of the business since I had owned Giorgio for years before we were married. I hoped at the time that even though our personal relationship had resulted in divorce, that we could continue to work together in business.

Fred's hopes were not realized. Although the Giorgio fragrance would soar to $50 million in 1984, the Haymans' deteriorating business relationship would dampen the euphoria.

CHAPTER ELEVEN

The Scent of the Century

In 1984 America was hungry for Giorgio, and the company started to satisfy that appetite. By expanding distribution in cities such as Los Angeles, Atlanta, Houston, Cincinnati, Minneapolis, Chicago, Miami, and Philadelphia, Giorgio was on its way to becoming a national phenomenon. The company now had the cash flow to support a national roll-out and spent almost $6 million on advertising—$4 million on scented inserts alone and a little over $1 million on the magazine space.

The national press finally recognized that Giorgio had become the biggest news in the fragrance industry since the introduction of Charlie in 1973. The April 16 issue of *Newsweek* headlined its almost full-page life/style piece on Giorgio, SCENT OF THE CENTURY? capitalizing on a quote from Fred, "I'm convinced we have the scent of the century."

Giorgio was a volatile commodity in the few department stores that were lucky enough or smart enough to land it. This success at retail was stirring a volcano back in Beverly Hills. For five years following their separation, the Haymans had been able to temper their personal differences and stay focused on the business. However, by 1984, as they battled not only for control of the business, their struggle was visible both inside and outside the company. The ambition that had been instrumental in transforming a hole-in-the-wall boutique into a nationally recognized logo was now a threat. Gale was no longer content to work in Fred's shadow, and he was not ready to share the spotlight. Fred believed the company should have one spokesman and that was he. Roth and Horner found Gale disruptive and gravitated toward Fred, who had hired them and who had fiduciary control of the company.

Ego and greed, according to Gale's later court depositions, led to the confrontation between Gale and Fred.

The divorce became final on September 9, 1983. It was at this time that the perfume which I had created and developed became the number-one selling fragrance in the United States. Since I was the individual who developed the fragrance, I was getting more and more publicity and attention as the sales of the fragrance increased dramatically. Mr. Hayman and I had been able to work together in the company throughout the divorce proceedings. However, as I received more and more publicity and credit for the development of the fragrance, Mr. Hayman became more and more jealous of my success. Mr. Hayman became unreasonable to deal with and refused to follow any of my recommendations for the business of Giorgio. Strange behavior started to occur. Among those strange actions, Fred Hayman would routinely order me to leave fragrance meetings, directly in the presence of the executive staff, before the meetings had started. Of course I refused, and Mr. Hayman would later accuse me of insubordination. Mr. Hayman's actions, without provocation, were humiliating and denigrating to me in the presence of Giorgio executive employees. Mr. Hayman, with the active counseling and participation of Mr. Ziffren [Giorgio's corporate attorney], commenced to contrive and instigate concocted confrontations and disputes.

According to Fred's 1986 court depositions, the fighting began in late 1983, when Gale tried to usurp control.

I had become ill on a flight back from Europe with Gale. Even though I told her that I felt very sick, for two hours she yelled and screamed at me, stating that she questioned my ability to head Giorgio and that she felt I surrounded myself with "inept" people. I was hospitalized upon our return to Los Angeles, and out of work for several weeks. While I was absent, Gale was in charge. When I returned, Gale demanded that she be included in every decision made. For example, when I informed her in December 1983 that

I had worked out a contract with a chemist with whom we worked on fragrances, Gale screamed at me. She demanded copies of all correspondence addressed to or from me.

In February 1984, Gale and I were in Atlanta for the opening of our fragrance at a leading department store [Rich's]. While we were inspecting the various stores, along with the head cosmetics buyer for the store, Gale stated in the buyer's presence that I could not go to Europe or New York to buy clothes for our Beverly Hills store. She told me that I should "take a two week vacation," while she and another employee went to Europe. I felt embarrassed and humiliated.

Fred wasn't the only one embarrassed. This cat fight was not part of the image Rich's executive team had expected. Tracy Scoggins, the fragrance buyer, wanted the scent badly and convinced Allen Questrom, the store's chief executive officer, to visit Giorgio while in Los Angeles for the men's wear show. Rich's was able to get a $400,000 order and distribution in eight branches, but had to agree that Questrom, as the store's top executive, would host a gala party to launch the scent. The Questroms hosted the party for Fred and Gale in the beautiful Buckhead mansion that Allen's wife, Kelli, had redone in ultramodern black and white. The next night there was a get-together at Tony's, a posh Atlanta eatery. Later in the week, a black-tie event called the Beaux Arts Ball featured Fred Hayman as a guest of honor. By the end of launch week, the Haymans were ready to wrangle. Scoggins recalls, "She and Fred were sitting around and were fighting over something stupid. I tried not to listen but they were snapping at each other and I was embarrassed."

The spat had no impact on Rich's Giorgio business. Although the fragrance was launched in January, probably the deadest month in retailing anywhere, Giorgio did unbelievably well. Planned to do $1.5 million its first year at Rich's, the scent reached $3 million in just eight of Rich's eighteen branches and was on its way to becoming well over 20 percent of Rich's total fragrance business. Manny Roth, Scoggins's boss and the divisional merchandise manager of cosmetics, said Fred was just learning the cosmetics business in early 1984 and hadn't become a maven yet. "The most difficult part was convincing Fred to place Giorgio in more than one of our branches. He was trying to parallel his success in Los Angeles with his one store which could pull customers from all over the city. We spent a lot of time convincing him Rodeo Drive was unique and didn't represent the rest of America. That was a big hurdle and was like pulling teeth." The fragrance had soared to $5 million by 1985 and marked the first time Rich's had a storewide fragrance promotion, i.e., displays, mannequins, and banners throughout the store, including the restaurants. Scoggins describes Giorgio's customer acceptance as a "feeding frenzy."

Giorgio's timing for the roll-out could not have been better. There was no other fragrance on the market with a West Coast image. While other industries had recognized California's marketability, the fragrance industry was oblivious to the Pacific Basin and the California life-style that revolved around conspicuous chic. The auto industry in the early 1960s had even produced car models called Malibu, Belair, and Newport. The relaxed, glitzy California mentality was easily understood by an American consumer who, in 1984, had job security, increased stock holdings, and was in a bullish spending mode.

Annette Green, the executive director of New York's Fragrance Foundation, put Giorgio's timing in perspective:

> When Giorgio came along, everyone was watching the nighttime soap operas. Beverly Hills' glamour was reaching the population and they wanted an instant status symbol that reflected the glamour of Hollywood. The fragrance made such a strong odor statement and it was concurrent with a time when people wanted immediate gratification. They didn't want a fragrance to develop slowly. What people smelled is what they got, and they wanted to be able to say who they were and what they wore.

Gale's point of view, that assertive women wanted a high-powered, entrance-making fragrance, was on target and would soon encourage other manufacturers, such as Calvin Klein Cosmetics, with Obsession, to use high concentrations of essential oils in their cologne versions. Purists in the industry blame Giorgio for starting this cloying trend and liken Giorgio to loud, heavy-metal rock music.

Maurice Raviol, a perfume-industry veteran who has worked on the supplier side with PFW and, more recently, Robertet, believed Giorgio was not for the true fragrance lover but for an anosmic woman whose sense of smell was suddenly jolted to life by Giorgio. "I like to get my fragrance experience as a subtle, elusive whiff of something beautiful. For it to be lucid I want to be sitting with a woman over dinner and smell her and then I can smell my food. In three or four minutes her scent is suddenly there again. With these metronomic fragrances [Giorgio, Passion, Obsession], they don't change and you are overwhelmed and you don't smell your food." Raviol maintains women who live in big cities have lost or at least have diminished olfactory senses because of odor pollution (bus fumes, car exhausts, etc.). Fragrances such as Giorgio break through the pollution barrier to impress them and their men.

The day-to-day running of the company was now important to Gale, and she was expanding her territory. Like a blast of Giorgio, she began to penetrate parts of the business from which she previously had been excluded or in which she had been uninterested. She hired a UCLA accounting instructor to come to her home twice a week to teach her how to read profit-and-loss statements and to understand costs of goods. Business books were now part of her nightly reading. Buying and merchandising the boutique no longer interested her and she was grooming Marguerite Schaefer to succeed her so she could devote full time to the fragrance company. Creating new cosmetics and fragrance products for the company had become Gale's passion. The divorce settlement clearly separated her interests from Fred's and to protect those interests she no longer was content to allow Fred to manage the business side of Giorgio alone. After all, the fragrance was making Giorgio, Inc., a big, soon-to-be-international business. It was her creation and she wanted to shape the company's destiny along with Fred.

Gale's friends, including Susanna Hoffman, were pushing her to stand up to Fred. Hoffman had met both Hayman and Horner and did not like either man. She considered Fred arrogant and thought he ran Giorgio, Inc., like a "feudal lord." Horner she felt was vicious, had contempt for women, and thought of Gale as a little cocktail waitress from New York. Horner reminded Hoffman of Iago, the professional soldier in Shakespeare's tragedy, *Othello*, who had clawed his way from the lowest rank and was now within reach of the top. Hoffman warned Gale that Horner could try to knife her and she was right. Hoffman said,

> Part of their vested interest was keeping Gale submissive. I'm not a strident feminist, but I was perplexed. "Gale, why are you putting up with this?" I encouraged her to stand up for her rights even while she was creating the fragrance. After Fred would make a public speech, Gale wanted to say something and I encouraged her to get up and say something gracious as Fred did. She was intimidated by it all and she needed the encouragement. Gale didn't have the education and background of women who had moved themselves forward in the world and taken their equality. She had no role model.

According to Gale, Fred saw things differently after the divorce. It was emotionally painful for Fred to see her around the company every day and he started to build a case of insubordination against her that would lead to her ouster, Gale maintains. He was trying to keep her in her place and also exact some revenge for the failed marriage. Gale says,

The divorce triggered the end of our business relationship; it was the total reason. As soon as I agreed to the divorce settlement, it was a different atmosphere; it was day and night. He was not satisfied with anything I did. I was ahead thirty-three percent in the women's store, but he said he didn't like the clothes. He would say, "I don't care if we're ahead, I don't like the clothes." It became very difficult; I couldn't do or say anything right. I didn't give him a hard time; I couldn't understand it, and he was becoming abusive. In 1984 Fred staged a reason to force me out of the company and he built a case. It took one year with his lawyers.

In 1984, Jim and David started observing the difficulties I was having with Fred and they started to go to his side because he had the power. They didn't become hostile to me at all, but I think they clearly helped Fred build a case against me. If you read the court papers, you will see the charges against me. The affidavits are ridiculous. Obviously they were fabricated and they wanted me out. There was no case against me. Fred said, "I want her out. How do I get her out?" And they said, "She has to do something. There has to be cause." On the contrary, I was working my ass off and my track record was pretty good. I created the product that made all the money in the company. Prior to that we were a small company, but now they had got it [the fragrance] and decided they didn't need me anymore. Fred was emotional. He didn't want the divorce. He sought revenge and this was his revenge. He also wanted this to be one company with one voice.

With Fred and Gale's relationship reaching the boiling point, Roth and Horner were caught in the middle of a lean and increasingly mean company. Early in 1984 they started to build an organization to handle the spiraling growth. Will Ferguson, an eleven-year Max Factor veteran, was hired to run operations and did a yeoman's job overseeing shipping, mail order, and production. Ron Chavers, only twenty-five, was hired as vice president of sales, despite his lack of experience. He almost turned down the job because he didn't want to be fired in six months for not knowing what he was doing. Horner wanted to hire Chavers; he wasn't "Lauderized" and wouldn't have to be untrained.

All major fragrance companies have a sales force that carefully monitors inventory, because the goods are in the stores on consignment. These salespeople constantly try to cajole the stores out of returning old merchandise and try to wheedle more space out of store executives. They also, based on inventory levels, write reorders for the buyers to approve.

Horner thought the system was ridiculous and expensive. Giorgio was not going to blindly follow the industry with a full-fledged team in the field, especially as the company would not accept returns other than damaged merchandise. "When I went into the stores I told the cosmetics buyer, I'm a third of your business and you should pick up the phone and call me because I have only fourteen stockkeeping units and you are the buyer. I'm not spending one hundred thousand dollars a year for a traveling salesman to visit your eleven stores to find out what some pipsqueak fragrance-department manager making seventeen thousand a year needs to run her business. If you want the goods, call me," Horner would tell and sometimes yell at store executives.

Horner and later Chavers accompanied Fred on tours of the stores. Ever conscious of Giorgio's image, Fred did not want to open in any department stores that were not in keeping with his standards of shop-keeping, exclusivity, and snob appeal. If a major department store was in a mall with a J. C. Penney or Sears, Fred sneered and balked about selling that branch. If a shopping center had a tire center, as many do in suburban and rural areas, it was not considered Giorgio's milieu. Fred, who rarely had shopped other stores in Beverly Hills, much less the malls of Middle America, was now getting an education. Horner got to know which shopping centers had tire centers, and he would instruct limo drivers to approach these centers from entrances where Fred would be spared the sight of a Goodyear or Goodrich logo. Horner was thinking volume and Fred would later dub him the "king of schlock."

"We were buddies. We drove around the country. We ate together, got drunk together, and took walks, and I was his confidant," Horner recalls:

> I was the only person who didn't go for his Swiss tyrant shit. He was hell-bent on impressing me and I would tell him to go fuck himself. He knew that I had some knowledge about wines and one night in Miami he bought a bottle of a Côtes du Rhône wine for two hundred dollars. Wherever we went I got the best treatment and I got close to him, but close with him is doing it his way. We would spend ten hours a day together and he would be lecturing me on his good taste and what we needed to do. At five A.M. he would be up and would want to talk about the business. He was worried about his image and would walk into a store and make "pronounciamentos" about the store's walls and carpets. I would remind him of the threadbare carpets in Giorgio. . . . If he yelled at you, you could yell at him and he would stop. I would ask him, "If you're such a fucking maven, why do you need me?"

According to Horner, Fred, wearing Nikes and a blazer, would tour stores in Southern California as if he were Napoleon picking the sites for his next conquest. He smirked at J. W. Robinson's branch stores in Palm Springs, Panorama City, and Glendale and let store managers there know how he felt. Horner had a T-shirt printed up that said I WENT MALLING WITH FRED HAYMAN.

As dated and ugly as some of Robinson's branches were, giving Robinson's the Southern California exclusive in February 1984 was the second most important distribution decision Giorgio, Inc., made after going with Bloomingdale's in 1982. Robinson's would become the largest Giorgio account in the U.S., peaking in 1985 at $11 million; but the relationship with Robinson's would backfire for Roth and Horner.

Robinson's, with its young, assertive chief executive officer, Michael Gould, was the exciting store in Los Angeles in 1984, taking market share away from archrival Bullock's. Gould was not afraid to invest in the trendiest European merchandise (such as Giorgio Armani) and he gave his sales-promotion department, headed by John Funck, a budget big enough to advertise aggressively. Linda Grizzle, the fragrance buyer, and Vic Gassman, the divisional merchandise manager, were going after new fragrances and using the launch excitement to build traffic throughout their department. They believed the fragrance industry revolved around newness, and when Grizzle saw the Giorgio scent strips and the action at Bloomingdale's, she knew that Giorgio was the most exciting news in the business. Skeptical at first, Gould went with his fragrance merchandising team—Grizzle, Gassman, and Hank Schubert, the group manager—to a meeting at Giorgio. Gould was a bit uncomfortable when Fred walked into the meeting with Fawn, the healthy and growing German shepherd that had become Fred's constant companion after he was robbed outside his Charleville garage. Gould was not a dog lover, but he and Fred soon would become pals.

Horner and Roth were convinced that Robinson's was a better choice than Bullock's, given Bullock's underdeveloped fragrance business. Without telling Fred, they primed the Robinson's team on how to impress Fred and win the line. Fred was invited to Gould's executive suite for a formal presentation. Gould's suite had been transformed into a Giorgio wonderland with daffodils, products, props, and displays. Lunch was served on yellow-and-white striped tablecloths. Fred was impressed and on December 7, 1983, Grizzle got a phone call from Roth welcoming Robinson's into the Giorgio family.

There was some concern that if the fragrance were carried by a major Southern California store, the fragrance business within the Giorgio boutique would be diluted. The Robinson's flagship store was just a mile from

Rodeo Drive. The fears were unfounded. In the first three weeks of February 1984, Robinson's rang up $270,000 in Giorgio sales in fourteen doors while the Giorgio boutique had sales over $100,000 during the same period—almost double the figure for the same month in 1983. Gould was amazed and was quoted in *WWD*, "Giorgio has been our number one, two and three fragrances this month. It's been the single most important launch in my six years with Robinson's in any product category."

Schubert and Grizzle had predicted Giorgio could hit $1.5 million the first year, making it Robinson's number-one scent, ahead of Oscar de la Renta, which had been the fragrance kingpin at $1 million. After the first month, Schubert revised his Giorgio forecast to $3 million, but that was still too low. The scent ended the year reaching a startling $4.8 million. "Our entire women's fragrance department was only four and a half million to five million and Giorgio was running fifty percent of our total in its first year. I couldn't believe it," Schubert said. By 1985, Giorgio became the biggest vendor in the cosmetics department, surpassing Lauder, Clinique, and Lancôme—the first time a single fragrance line ever did that in any major department store in America. Women's fragrance had represented 20 percent of Robinson's total cosmetics business before Giorgio; but with Giorgio, fragrance was now 39 percent. In addition to the sheer numbers, having Giorgio exclusively was a morale-builder for the store's employees, and Gould made sure the residual side effects were maximized in his frequent pep talks. He also used Giorgio as a hook to get other manufacturers to do exclusives with the store.

Schubert and Grizzle studied the Giorgio figures daily trying to comprehend the phenomenon. They discovered something Fred Hayman didn't want to hear. Giorgio's primary customer at Robinson's was not a bejeweled Beverly Hills woman being driven in a Rolls-Royce to the Wilshire Boulevard Robinson's flagship. Rather, she was a housewife who drove to the Puente Hills Mall in a Toyota, schlepping her kids through the mall in a stroller. Among the best Giorgio doors at JWR were Cerritos, Westminster, and Puente Hills, all stores in the heart of middle-class suburbia. Robinson's most fashionable and upscale stores in Beverly Hills and Newport Beach failed to rank in the top five. It was obvious that Middle America was buying a scented slice of a life-style they had only dreamed about or seen on television.

The Giorgio figures in New York were equally startling. They were reaching their peak at Bloomingdale's in 1984. Robin Burns, the divisional merchandise manager who left the store in the spring of 1983 to become Calvin Klein Cosmetics president, noted that Giorgio created a new tier in the Bloomingdale's hierarchy. The top rung had been filled with scents such as Opium, Lauren, and Oscar, all doing around $1 million. The next tier contained lines such as Chanel and Halston, which had volumes between $500,000 and $1 million. The third tier was a wide base of all the fragrances that come and go. Giorgio would be in a tier all by itself. Giorgio did almost $2 million in 1984 at the 59th Street flagship, and in Dallas it did a whopping $2.5 million.

Lester Moran, the Valley View Dallas store manager, had worked at Bloomingdale's in New York and had seen his share of fads:

> Giorgio was the wildest trend since I was in the business twenty-two years ago. We were the only store in Texas to have Giorgio at the time and we had one guy call up a few days before Christmas and he told us to hold one bottle of Giorgio for him because he was driving three hundred miles to get it. After living in Texas for a few years I got to know the Texas mentality. They like ostentation and to be first with trends so they came from all over to get Giorgio.

Due to Giorgio's huge volume, the cosmetics department at Valley View accounted for 16 percent of the entire store's volume, whereas in a typical Bloomingdale's branch the department would account for between 7 and 10 percent. Giorgio was between 60 and 70 percent of the total fragrance business at Valley View, whereas in New York's flagship Giorgio was a "mere" 30 percent of the total fragrance business.

Burns studied the Giorgio success. She would later incorporate several of the marketing techniques (scent strips, exclusivity) into Calvin Klein's successful Obsession fragrance for men and women. Burns analyzed:

> Giorgio was drawing a customer to Bloomingdale's that might normally be shopping in a mass outlet [drugstore]. It was a fragrance with a mass appeal, but with limited distribution, and the department store was benefiting. People were actually getting in their cars and going to buy it, unlike most fragrances, which are impulse purchases. It ranked as our third top cosmetic line. It was rivaling Clinique—forget about the competition with the other fragrance lines. Giorgio was a humbling experience for the retail community and an enlightening experience for the manufacturers. It shook the industry hard and it needed it. The industry was lethargic and got into a rut. A sameness was being applied to distribution, to product, to the type of advertising. Giorgio rocked the boat.

The envious and jealous fragrance industry could not ignore Giorgio any longer. Several members of the Fragrance Foundation's board of directors felt Giorgio deserved a special award at the June 1984 awards dinner. Due to Giorgio's small distribution (fewer than two hundred doors), a faction argued that Giorgio did not qualify for the unusual award. Dr. Fernando Aleu, the president of Puig of Barcelona, the marketer of Paco Rabanne, was serving as the foundation's president. Aleu, a Spaniard and a former doctor, is probably the most disarming and charming executive in the industry, and he recognized Giorgio's sensational success. He thought Hayman was an "international romantic who went after the buck, but did it with flair," and he backed the faction that wanted Giorgio to get the award. The foundation voted to give Giorgio a special plaque acknowledging the foundation's "admiration" and "secret envy." Aleu was amazed at Fred's gratitude. "Two days after we voted on it, Fred somehow found out about it, and two days later I heard our French secretary say, 'It wouldn't fit through the door.' Fred had sent me a huge bouquet of flowers that literally couldn't get through the door. There must have been sixty thousand gardenias and [it] took up half my office. It was very embarrassing but I loved it."

Fred was ecstatic over winning the special award, and both he and Gale marched up to the stage to receive it. Gale, wearing a low-cut leopard-print dress, was photographed with Michael Gould and Bob Miller; and her photo, not Fred's, appeared in *WWD*. The award clearly meant more to Fred than to Gale. "The award was nice, but to me the sales of that fragrance were pivotal. I don't put much importance into awards; it's what sells that counts. It was nice but it didn't mean anything, it didn't gratify me," Gale commented. Neither did schmoozing and socializing with the other leading manufacturers in the business. Gale felt it was a waste of her time. Fred hung the plaque prominently in the boutique.

As 1984 progressed, the Haymans' relationship continued to deteriorate. Horner maintains that the Haymans almost had a swing-out at the Louisville Airport in April after a visit to that city and Cincinnati to launch Giorgio at Shillito/Rikes. Horner testified in a November 1986 deposition:

> Gale Hayman initiated an argument with Fred Hayman in my presence and in the presence of a senior representative of a major Giorgio retail account [Ms. Janet Block, the vice president of public relations for Shillito/Rikes]. The argument had nothing whatsoever to do with Giorgio's business with Shillito/Rikes. Rather, the argument had to do with profit sharing for the employees at the Giorgio Rodeo Drive store, in the course of which Gale Hayman severely criticized Mr. Hayman's entire management philosophy and acumen. Mr. Hayman asked Gale to please hold the matter for discussion at a later date. She refused and continued to yell

and argue with him. I escorted Ms. Block out of earshot as best as I could.

Block, now retired, remembers spending two days with the Haymans escorting them between Cincinnati and Louisville. Although she remembers the restaurants where they ate, she has no memory of Gale's alleged antics. "I don't remember David taking me aside, I probably tuned it out. I don't force myself if I don't belong. If he took me aside, he did it successfully."

Block's friend, *Cincinnati Post* society columnist Mary Linn White, portrayed the Haymans as a happily-divorced-but-still-working-together couple in her April 17, 1984, column. She wrote, "Everyone at the Treasure Aisle preview party at Corbett Tower would have sworn that Fred and Gale Hayman are married. The names are the same, they seem on excellent terms, very supportive of one another, and involved in one of the hottest shops on storied Rodeo Drive in Beverly Hills."

White used an unattributable quote, which turned out to be inaccurate. "The Haymans, who 'get along much better' since their divorce a year ago after 12 years of marriage, live apart but travel together, host parties together, are partners in the store."

The Haymans' travels in Europe that spring were far from harmonious, according to Fred, who started looking for a way to rid himself and Giorgio, Inc., of Gale. "When we both went to Paris, after I refused to 'take a two week vacation,' she said that there would be no tickets for me to attend the fashion shows. At one point, I told her that I was fifty-nine years old and for the sake of my health I wanted to split our business relationship," Fred testified.

On our 1984 buying trip, she continually told me that she did not want me to go to Europe buying. I informed her that it was not her choice. She continued to do things which embarrassed me. For example, we went to a fashion show in Paris at which she had not arranged for us to have assigned seats. She nonetheless sat down at a reserved seat and refused to move when an usher told her it was someone else's seat.

In Milan on the same buying trip, she insisted we change the incentive compensation method we were using with salespeople. I told her that it was a matter we were working on with our lawyers, who specialized in incentive and pension plans. Her response was, "Fuck the lawyers. It is up to us." She would not stop discussing the subject. A week later in Rome, she told me during a cab ride that we could work everything out. I told her that I did not think we could. At that point, she said, "You are out of touch, passé, and old fashioned; and if you won't resolve things with me, you'll find me the aggressor and you can go fuck yourself."

When we got back from Europe, she demanded that the controller of the company show her every charitable donation to be made, for her prior approval. She continually criticized donations that I had approved, even including some donations that I made personally.

Gale made the first overture to separate their business partnership by attempting to buy Fred's interest in Giorgio. In March, Gale hired Washington, D.C., attorney William Casselman, who wrote Leo Ziffren, telling him of Gale's desire to either buy Fred's stock or have a third party acquire it. Fred countered by hiring attorney Marshall Grossman, a flamboyant Los Angeles litigator whose first big case had been a suit he filed against Playboy Enterprises in which Grossman himself was the plaintiff. Grossman's consumer class-action suit had turned out to be the first of its kind, ending in a $3 million settlement. When Dennis Stanfill resigned from Twentieth Century Fox, he hired Grossman to sue Marvin Davis, the studio's owner. The no-holds-barred, three-volume complaint led to a $4 million settlement for Stanfill. Fred was arming himself with perhaps the shrewdest attorney his money could buy.

On June 7, the Haymans and their attorneys met in New York and Grossman told the group Fred was open to any and all ways of effecting a separation of his and Gale's interests, including the sale of the company, or just the perfume division. Fred preferred to stay with the company if it were sold, but he would be willing to step aside and let Gale continue on if the new owner wanted her to stay with Giorgio. The meeting took an unbusinesslike turn as Fred described in his 1986 desposition: "When Gale suggested that instead [of negotiating a buy out], we get therapy together, I rejected that as unworkable. I indicated to Gale that it was my interest to separate our issues without either of us resorting to litigation."

Although Gale was giving him increasing grief, Fred had a lot to be thankful for during the summer of 1984. His dream of having a store in Manhattan was realized when a Giorgio fragrance boutique opened at 47 East 57th Street on August 22. The 1,750-square-foot store was costly to open and operate, with $600,000 invested in decorations and $10,000 in monthly rent. To make the shop a miniature version of the Rodeo store, a chandelier, celebrity photo wall, espresso bar, and yellow-and-white striped awnings were installed.

Hayman's son Robert had emerged as Giorgio's heir apparent; Fred persuaded Robert to leave the real-estate business in Boston and come to New York to manage the New York boutique. Robert had attended the University of California at Santa Barbara before transferring to Boston University, from which he graduated. Charles, a year older, had attended UCLA and was considered to be the brightest of Fred's children, but not the most pragmatic or business-minded. Fred was a strict father, instilling formality and etiquette in his children that made Charles and Robert seem more European than American, and certainly too stiff to be Southern California natives. Charles was book-smart, spoke fluent French, and his peers found him abstract and "spacey." Fred considered him "flaky" and never envisioned him as a businessman, but Charles would start his own business in Manhattan in 1988, transporting valuable works of art between galleries and collectors. Nicole, the youngest, wanted to pursue a singing career; and, although Fred initially discouraged her, he later would host a party to help kick off her career. Nicole worked in the Rodeo Drive boutique after attending UCLA. She looked older than her twenty-four years, and she often wore clothing that accentuated her small but buxom proportions. She found a voice coach, Arthur Joseph, and started singing in various clubs in Los Angeles while working at the boutique and later at Merv Griffin Productions.

Robert's swarthy good looks, his interest in business, and his strong desire to please his father were his primary qualifications to manage Giorgio's new boutique. As manager, Robert's responsibility was to get the New York store off to a good start, meeting Fred's volume goal of $2 million the first year. Fred was obsessed with the New York store, and if it did well, he planned to open similar shops in three or four other cities. His enthusiasm for opening Giorgio shops was not shared by Gale or Roth and Horner. Putting Robert in charge of the shop irked Gale. Of the three children, Gale was closest to Robert and had visited him in Boston. She wanted him to stand on his own and not be reliant on Fred. Robert was becoming a pawn in the power struggle between Fred and Gale.

Roth and Horner thought the New York shop was a bad business decision. They were afraid of jeopardizing sales at Bloomingdale's, just a few blocks away. Although the exclusive with Bloomingdale's had been broken in April, when Macy's Herald Square on 34th Street started carrying the brand, they feared the scent would become too available in too small a radius.

Fred was convinced the little shop, which was to carry special items not for sale in department stores, would bolster Giorgio's image in New York. Gale had developed a night treatment cream for the face, the first nonfragranced Giorgio product, which was to be launched first in the New York and Beverly Hills boutiques before going into the majors. Fred believed in testing products first in his own stores to get the stamp of approval from his special clientele before going to the general public in the department stores. The New York store was to be stocked mostly with Giorgio fragrances and gift sets, with the thrust of the inventory in gift baskets ranging in price from $17.50 to $400. "We want people to stop going to florists and candy stores and buy fragrances for gifts instead," Fred was quoted in *WWD* on August 24. Fred believed the boutique would give New Yorkers a taste of his Beverly Hills emporium. Casting as manager his son, who lacked experience running a boutique, was seen not only as nepotism but also as detrimental to business. Gale was furious with Robert's appointment and clashed with Fred over the shop's merchandising concept.

Susan Fried, the assistant fragrance buyer at Bloomingdale's, was named as co-manager of the New York boutique with Robert. She took the job hoping it would lead to a marketing post within Giorgio, but it didn't turn out that way. Fried describes the boutique: "It was a cartoon of a business, a ridiculous animation of life. The arguing, the politics. Robert and I got along fine but we were pitted against one another by Fred, and Robert wanted to please his father so much. I was amazed at what was going on."

Gale and Fried planned to have the fragrances share the space with glitzy costume jewelry and Giorgio's signature T-shirts and sweatshirts. Kenneth Jay Lane designed a panther brooch for Gale, to be sold along with a bottle of fragrance for $200. Fried recalls,

> Huge amounts of jewelry were delivered, but a week before the store opened Fred insisted all the jewelry be taken out of the store and returned. Fred overruled Gale and it was a bad merchandising decision. I think Gale really had the hook on how to bring the Giorgio image to New York and make it work. When the boutique was opened we did very little business. Many people came in expecting to see something fabulous and they saw a pretty little boutique with the Giorgio fragrance counter at Bloomingdale's in there. There was an ambience of Beverly Hills and we served espresso. I must have served three thousand espressos and I never want to drink or make another one in my life. The people who were coming in were advertising and P.R. people and friends of the Haymans, but not much else.

The New York boutique may have had the service and ambience of Rodeo Drive, but it lacked merchandise. How comfortable does a customer need to be to buy a bottle of cologne? Fried watched Fred lose his temper in the store and scream while Gale kept her cool:

> Fred would scream, "Get this off the counter," and, "This needs painting." Fred is very charming. I would never have gone to work there thinking Fred is a monster. He is very sophisticated, charming, and attractive, there is no doubt about that. But I think Fred is disappointed in any situation where he is not the center of attention.
>
> Sure, Fred helped Gale grow, but there is nothing going to stop Gale Hayman. Gale wouldn't have been a cocktail waitress all her life if Fred hadn't come along. She was a bright woman and assertive and has goals. You can't take a formless gray matter and make it into something. That's not to say they didn't have a close partnership and were not involved with each other. Maybe in Fred's heart he is not at the level that he is projecting to the world. Anger, egoism, fear, and insecurity—everybody has it. I didn't think that Fred could really believe all the things that he was projecting. If not he would be a much more consistently gracious human being and he is not.

While Fred was being psychoanalyzed inside the boutique, pickets showed up outside the New York store on August 22, 1984. They carried signs that read DAYTON'S THANKS GIORGIO. Most New Yorkers walking up 57th Street that day couldn't have comprehended the hoopla Giorgio was creating in the Minneapolis/St. Paul area, especially since the fragrance was not yet sold in the Twin Cities. The pickets were sent by Dayton Hudson Department Store, as part of a creative and aggressive campaign to convince Fred Hayman to sell Dayton's the fragrance.

John Pellegrene, Dayton's senior vice president of marketing, orchestrated the campaign. He understood the success of Giorgio in other markets and wanted Dayton's to have the Twin Cities exclusive. His strategy was to have the area's citizens and top politicians demand Giorgio via petitions and "Giorgio-Grams." It was the same kind of campaign cities wage to win professional sports franchises, but in this case it was the winning of a fragrance that would put Minneapolis in the fragrance and fashion major leagues.

Ironically, Beverly Hills and Los Angeles intimidated Pellegrene, who worked for Dayton's for nineteen years. "Hey, I have no hair and stretch marks. I could never work in L.A.—all those shirts opened to the navel—I would be too intimidated."

Dayton's started the campaign on August 9 with a full-page ad in Minneapolis's *Skyway News*. The ad was headlined, PLEASE GIORGIO, COME TO THE TWIN CITIES! The copy was tongue-in-cheek, but it was a serious effort by Dayton's. Part of the ad read:

> The pen is mightier than the nose. We know that there are plenty of people in the Twin Cities with extraordinary taste. What we need is proof. All you have to do is either:
>
> a. Fill out the Giorgio-Gram below, cut it out and get it to our Minneapolis store ASAP (that means by foot, bus, rollerskates, horseback, whatever).
>
> Or, b. Sign the petition. We want to send Giorgio a huge, very impressive petition, signed by thousands of anxious citizens.

Between August 1 and August 15, Fred received hundreds of telegrams from the Twin Cities. Prominent businessmen, local celebrities, and the mayors of Minneapolis and St. Paul were urging Giorgio to come to the Twin Cities.

On August 15, a fifty-foot yellow-and-white striped petition was stretched across the front entrance of Dayton's store. Boone and Erickson, the popular local D.J.s from WCCO Radio, set up at the corner of 7th and Nicollett to do live remote broadcasts from the petition site. A dixieland combo drew passers-by, and models dressed in the yellow-and-white striped outfits paraded with appropriately colored picket signs reading PLEASE, GIORGIO, COME TO THE TWIN CITIES. It was hard for Fred to resist four thousand signatures and six thousand completed Giorgio-Grams. The next day Boone and Erickson called Fred; he relented on the air and decided to sell to Dayton's. The following week, Pellegrene hired the models in New York to thank Fred and also sent him Matthew the Mallard, the store's mascot, in the form of a chocolate duck. A skywriter flew over Minneapolis, spewing THANK YOU, GIORGIO.

Dayton's had never gone after a vendor in any merchandise category the way it pursued Giorgio. The campaign paid dividends at the cash register, when Giorgio rang up $1.3 million in only seven doors during the fall and Christmas seasons in 1984, breaking all previous launch records and becoming the store's top-selling fragrance.

Although the Haymans were quibbling, their fragrance was rapidly becoming the best-selling prestige fragrance in America. In a September 1984 survey of twenty department-store chains representing 410 doors, Giorgio was named the top seller by nine chains representing 173 doors. Opium was ranked among the top five brands in more doors than any other fragrance. Lauder's White Linen, Oscar de la Renta, and Lauren rounded out the top five. At the time, Giorgio, in 225 doors, was still in very limited distribution compared to, say, Opium, which was in well over a thousand doors.

The scented-insert campaign had put Giorgio under thirty to forty million noses. Giorgio's mail-order campaign was the biggest in the industry by far, accounting for $12 million in sales.

Retailers both small and large wanted to carry Giorgio. Some would resort to buying the product at retail, reselling at their own store without making a profit. Others would attempt to get it through diverters, who specialize in buying up quantities of sought-after fragrances. Unlike more widely distributed fragrances, Giorgio was able to exercise tight control over shipping destinations. The company was working assiduously to control diversion, whereas Opium and Lauren had poor controls.

Quite often, diverters obtain the fragrances from the manufacturers who, under pressure to make their figures, will "dump" the goods through "alternative distribution." Selling to a diverter is tempting, a pure profit situation for the manufacturer; he doesn't have to spend money on commissions or other department-store charges. The downside is loss of control over final distribution. There is another theory that department stores divert to quickly get out of an overstocked situation.

Diversion is the gray area of the industry, and there is little proof that department stores divert. Bob Ruttenberg, whose Polo and Lauren fragrances at the time were getting hurt by diversion, said,

I have never been able to prove that department stores sell to diverters and I have been trying to prove it for twenty years. Some of my really good friends are in the department-store business and they say they don't divert. A & S had a reputation of doing it, but you can't prove it and I can't find one store that does it. There has been a lot of diversion caused by international distribution. It's simple, the way it occurs. You sell the fragrance to an overseas distributor and they lie, they phony up the records. It's what we call the U-boat theory. The boat is loaded with the product to go overseas and it goes to sea and comes back in about eight minutes and ends up in the hands of diverters.

The industry has pressured customs agents to watch for diverted goods and seizures have been made, but the problem still remains.

Fred was careful about security almost to the point of paranoia. He feared both diversion and copycats, companies that copy a fragrance and sell it for a greatly reduced price. He instructed Will Ferguson, the vice president of operations, to crush the drums of fragrance so not a drop was left after the bottles were filled. Security guards, some in plainclothes, patrolled the Giorgio warehouses and operations bases in Santa Monica and Cucamonga. Fred did not want Giorgio distributed outside his select few stores. The scent's prestige reputation could quickly be tarnished by sales at J. C. Penney or—even worse—drugstores and swap meets.

In an April 27, 1984, full-page *WWD* story by Jane Lane about Giorgio's phenomenal growth, Fred was quoted, "There are frustrations. A large purchase that was supposed to be for corporate gifts ended up transhipped to Texas. The fragrance was imitated. These problems are widespread enough to be bothersome and we sue diverters whenever possible. The diverted supply is about to dry up and we won the case against the imitator." The company would later hire Al Vetter, a detective whose job it was to track down diverters and help build a case that Fred would pursue with his lawyers. In 1988, Vetter cracked a counterfeit ring operating in Riverside and San Bernardino (California) counties, and he led police on the resulting raid.

Fred had much to protect. The Giorgio name was bankable and there was plenty of growth ahead through expanded distribution of the existing women's fragrance in both the U.S. and in Europe. A growing contingent of European tourists to Beverly Hills had discovered the Giorgio fragrance and gone home wearing it. New products were another way to grow; after about three years Gale had finally finished the men's fragrance and the night treatment cream. The men's scent was launched at Giorgio in Beverly Hills on November 13, 1984, and at Bloomingdale's a week later.

The development of the men's scent made the creation of the women's fragrance seem almost simple. In addition to Gale's input, there was Fred's involvement in the scent selection. Roth and Horner, whose stature had risen considerably in the company, also had much to say. Unlike the scent selection of the women's fragrance, for which Gale wants complete credit, she has no pride of authorship for the men's:

> I felt we were putting out the men's fragrance sooner than we should have, because the women's fragrance hadn't peaked. I would have waited until the women's peaked and had that men's cologne waiting in the wings, but instead we launched while the women's was still growing. They [Fred, Roth/Horner] forced it and they pushed me to meet a deadline. We didn't need anything new at that point; it was just a question of managing it and just a product here and there, with a few women's-line extensions. If I had longer and was not under the gun I would have held out for something a bit more special.

Florasynth was working exclusively with Giorgio, Inc., to develop a men's fragrance and Fred started giving his direction for the development of the scent in 1982 while he and Gale still had a sound partnership. Fred had been wearing Jicky, a light European lavender scent from Guerlain; and he mandated Florasynth to make a fragrance similar to Jicky, but longer lasting, with a more powerful topnote. Gale wanted Fred to have his own signature fragrance, but after a year the Florasynth perfumers were nowhere with the Jicky knockoff; every time they tried to strengthen it, they changed its character.

Florasynth was caught in the cross fire between Fred and Gale. The fragrance house had started sending submissions to both Haymans and, predictably, the two disagreed. Finally, Horner, who was eager to get into the men's market, asked other fragrance suppliers to make submissions. Horner said,

> She putzed around for two-and-a-half years with the men's fragrance and we started to work on it independently, screening submissions with Buchwalter. Fred wrote her a memo to either cooperate with us on the development or stop all together. Finally, we got close with a submission from PFW and she got into the middle of it with Jeff Miles [a sales executive at PFW]. She never liked the men's fragrance. Jimmy and I picked it, and it was the same thing with the women's. Fred enforced the deadline.

Packaged in the same yellow-and-white striped box, the scent, in its fluted flask bottle, was a complete departure from the women's cologne. It was not long lasting and had a mandarin orange topnote with spice and wood tones. Gale was quoted in *WWD* on October 12, 1984: "My concept was to marry the elegance of light, subtle European fragrances for men with the power and sensuality of American scents." The scent lacked that power, but made up for it with the name Giorgio, Beverly Hills. The cologne, priced at thirty-five dollars for four ounces, got off to a strong start in November in the Giorgio boutiques and at Bloomingdale's.

Gale's night cream also was launched in November and Fred predicted it would be "a hot item—perhaps as hot as the women's fragrance." The Extraordinary Night Treatment Cream cost forty dollars for a 1.7 ounce jar and was part of a four-product skin-care regimen. The basis for the products was a substance Gale called Bio-mol 20, a formulation that supposedly nourishes and tones the skin. Gale's skin-care plan would not come to fruition. Both the cream and Gale would be discontinued in 1985.

CHAPTER TWELVE

California Splits

Giorgio, Inc., finished fiscal 1984 with sales volume of $50 million and pretax profits of $20 million. The company planned to exceed $100 million in sales in 1985, an astonishing figure, far surpassing the growth rate of any start-up venture in the perfume industry. The success was making Gale and Fred Hayman rich. In 1983, Fred was compensated $712,000 while Gale took $474,000 out of the business. With the ascendance of the fragrance in 1984, Fred received $4,241,000 in salary and dividends totaling over $3,400,000. Gale's salary was $2,827,000 plus dividends of $3,416,000.

The Haymans may have been getting richer, but their relationship was deteriorating daily and Giorgio, Inc., was an increasingly histrionic place to work during the latter half of 1984 and early 1985. The company was becoming a movie set where a soap opera was unfolding not in front of the cameras but behind the scenes. Giorgio seemed, to the industry, press, and consumers, a smooth-running business as well as a sensational fragrance; but the company was being ripped apart by internal feuding and creatively it was starting to stagnate. Fred was this movie's protective executive producer and director, trying to control and nurture it into a classic. Horner and Roth were the ambitious coproducers, more interested in big box-office receipts than winning Oscars. Gale had become the troubled, petulant star who wanted to be the next great screen siren.

Her role in Giorgio would propel her to cosmetics-industry stardom and she wanted to shape the production. These divergent talents and goals meant trouble on the Giorgio set.

Meetings at the Beverly Hills and Santa Monica offices were getting out of control in late 1984 and early 1985. Gale wanted to be involved in much more than the creative end of the business and according to Roth and Horner was questioning Fred's judgment in front of employees. "If Gale had something to say she would take over a meeting and would be so disruptive, sometimes refuting the decisions of eight or nine people. She would come up with a different tangent and wouldn't let go and that caused Fred to throw her out of the meetings," Roth recalls. Gale would refuse to leave, challenging Fred's authority in front of the staff, according to Horner. Fred reacted like a puppy and took Gale's jabs, which further infuriated Horner. The needle Gale frequently stuck into Fred's psyche and back was that she had wanted to do the fragrance. Gale would use Fred's age and gender to question his grip on contemporary life-styles and marketing and say, "You are not a woman, you don't wear the products," according to Horner.

"David would go into Fred's office and say, 'How can you take that shit in front of everybody?' David would try to rile him up," Roth says. Horner adds, "I told Fred he was an embarrassment to the company. How can I bring my staff of people in here and tell them that you are a wonderful genius?"

Gale maintains Horner tried to get her out of the company at this point so he could become the company's president, and he doesn't deny it.

> I merely reacted to the fact that you couldn't run a meeting with her. None of us realized the amount of time they argued about bullshit. The fighting between them absolutely would have destroyed the company within a year. It was impeding our ability to do business. When she goes out to the trade and goes to St. Louis and tells David Farrell [May Company's CEO] that Fred doesn't understand how to run the business and she does, is that good for business?

Gale says she and Fred did not fight in public and Horner's assertion that she badmouthed Fred in front of retailers is outrageous and a "total lie."

> If we had an argument, it was in his office. I'm not saying people in close proximity didn't hear, but it was never in front of customers

in the store, never in front of retailers. If we had an argument in his office and someone was eavesdropping, it was their fault. They were building a case against me and David was helping to construct that case because David wanted to become the president of Giorgio.

Roth and Horner were not alone in their desire to see Gale harnessed. Kathy Franzen, the chief financial officer, and Katy Sweet, who headed public relations, joined them in drafting a list of complaints against Gale and presented them to Fred on February 11, 1985. There were fifteen charges against Gale, mostly involving her insubordination to Fred and her attempts to expand her role and image in the company. The first point stated that on three occasions Gale was asked to leave staff meetings by Fred and she refused, which "undoubtedly resulted in a loss of credibility for Mr. Hayman." The fight at the Louisville airport in front of Janet Block was the second point. Gale was said to have yelled and screamed at Fred, causing Fred considerable embarrassment in front of a department-store account.

The fourth charge involved a party Gale hosted in February at Mortimer's Restaurant in New York. It was a snowy night, but in the back room of this New York society enclave, Gale had gathered some of New York's important fashion and social names, including Giorgio di Sant'Angelo, Kenneth Jay Lane, Chanel's Kitty D'Alessio, Andy Warhol, Alfred Taubman, Carolina Herrera, Marian Javits, and Marvin Traub. Fred Hayman was not part of the affair and that stirred the caldron back in Beverly Hills.

Although Gale originally had told Kathy Franzen that the evening was a social function, she submitted a bill to Franzen for the party, now claiming it was a business function. The charge read:

At a party held in New York, which was purported to be for "personal friends," Mrs. Hayman invited Marvin Traub, chairman of the board at Bloomingdale's, and Mel Jacobs, chairman of the board at Saks Fifth Avenue. Mr. Hayman was not aware of this. Two days previous to this we encountered a major problem with one of the Bloomingdale's outlets, which may have required resolution by Mr. Traub. It was not beneficial to the overall situation for us to find that Mr. Traub was attending a social gathering with GH. Also on the date of this party, FJH had a meeting with Saks personnel to discuss the possibility of distributing with their chain, totally unaware that Mr. Jacobs would be seeing GH that evening. Members of the press were also invited to this party, such as Jane

Lane of *Women's Wear Daily*; Fay Rice of *Fortune* magazine and the *Newsweek* correspondent who wrote the story on Gale and Fred. It was also reported to Mr. Hayman that John Fairchild received extreme pressure to attend the event. Additionally many celebrities and other socialites not known to be close personal friends attended this gathering. FJH has an extensive list of particular individuals.

To those at the party, it was obvious what Gale was up to. She was simply trying to make her way in New York society. Jane Lane, who reported on Giorgio for *WWD* and became the newspaper's "Eye" column (society) editor, observed,

This was Gale's grand dame era and she was trying to make a social splash. She didn't want this party to be business. She was social climbing now, but I don't think Gale was being accepted. She was a good friend of Susan Gutfreund and she was using Kenny [Lane] as her social entrée, but those in New York society never really got it. Glen Birnbaum [owner of Mortimer's] would always complain about her and would ask why Kenny would go around with that woman.

The remaining ten charges accused Gale of exceeding her role as a product developer and embarrassing the company. Gale was errant because she was contacting senior executives among Giorgio's suppliers and media. One such executive was Richard Shortway, corporate vice president of Condé Nast, whom Gale contacted regarding the insertion of Night Treatment Cream samples in *Vogue* magazine. According to the memorandum to Fred, "She also insisted on having direct contact with the presidents of 3M, Arcade, and Webcraft to learn for herself that it is not possible to incorporate creams in scented strip form, a fact which was known by management of the perfume company and conveyed to GH."

Fred had asked Gale to stop working on a men's scented candle, yet she continued to contact a small cottage-industry supplier directly. Gale also was continuing on her own to develop products, such as a shampoo, that had not even been discussed at meetings. In the case of the night treatment cream, Gale sent the company on a "wild goose chase" to France to buy a product on which she had done no consumer testing, the four employees alleged in the document. They were also bothered by Gale's increasing insistence that she and she alone inspired and created the women's fragrance.

Gale was accused of sticking her nose into distribution, which was Fred's domain. "While visiting St. Louis, GH visited some Famous Barr stores and suggested that we open them. When discussing the matter with FJH she forgot the names of the stores she had seen. We subsequently learned that she had indicated to the management [of the stores] that she would take care of getting them opened."

The question of Gale's age irked the foursome. "GH insists on indicating to the press that she is 37 (sometimes 38). This has been questioned several times in light of the 20th anniversary party which took place in 1981. This would have made GH either 14 or 15 when she married FJH and either 12 or 13 when FJH hired her as a cocktail waitress."

The document portrayed Gale as a loose cannon, lacking diplomacy and distrustful of current management. Her product knowledge and understanding of the business was "that of a novice."

To outsiders reading about Giorgio in the consumer press, there were small hints that Fred and Gale were not getting along. *The New York Times* did a half-page story on the Haymans on February 1, 1985, which was reprinted nationally by many papers that carry the *Times'* syndication. The Haymans were interviewed and photographed in a suite at the Pierre. Gale, in a man's tie that hung well below her waist, stood above Fred, who was seated. Judy Klemesrud wrote that Fred jokingly called Gale, "the madam," a term Fred was using more in derision than in jest. Gale's age was given as thirty-eight, although she was forty-one at the time.

Klemesrud finished her article with a brief description of the Haymans' relationship:

> The Haymans seem to get along well, except that he has a tendency not to let his former wife finish her sentences. "That's because he's Swiss," she said with a laugh. Speaking of their decision to stay together, Mr. Hayman said, "Business is business and personal life is personal life. It is not easy, but neither is marriage. The bottom line is that it has worked so far."

Two weeks later, while Fred was in Dallas and Gale in New York, the *Dallas Morning News* did an interview with Fred in which he gave Gale credit for creating both the women's and men's fragrances. Fred described working with Gale "like being married, we fight. But we've made it a point to get along and be successful. And we are successful."

During several interviews with Jane Lane, the Haymans quarreled openly.

It got to the point where it would be like your parents arguing in front of you and it would make you feel uncomfortable. He would make snide remarks and there was just a lot of bitterness between them and it got progressively worse. While she was in the store working, she had a place and seemed so comfortable, there was no reason to argue. In that store she was the fashion person and knew exactly the look she wanted. She had a real fashion vision, right or wrong. When she got into her executive motif it wasn't so comfortable and she was a bit out of her league. She was trying so hard, seeing lawyers, going to seminars and reading books like *The One Minute Manager.* Fred was unhappy with her. She was becoming bigger than he wanted her to be.

Fred and Gale were approaching a showdown that would sever their business partnership. Fred met with Roth, Horner, Sweet, and Franzen on February 11 in his apartment and read the fifteen-point indictment they had written. This feedback from his employees "hit him like a ton of bricks" according to Marshall Grossman, Fred's attorney who helped draft a special resolution to remove Gale from the day-to-day fragrance operations. On Saturday, February 23, at 10 A.M., Fred called for a special meeting of Giorgio's board to discuss Gale's rights and duties as a vice president of the company. The Giorgio board included Fred, Gale, and Irene Fuhrmann, the controller who had been with Fred since his Hilton days and would remain loyal to him through the imbroglio. Gale, who would change her attorneys almost as often as her lipstick over the next two years, now had retained Richard Goldberg of the New York law firm Botein Hays & Sklar, founded in 1866. Goldberg would not last long. Grossman represented Fred throughout.

The meeting was held at the Century City offices of Gibson Dunn & Crutcher, where Leo Ziffren, the Giorgio corporate counsel, practiced. Fred made the opening speech, saying that he had received complaints about Gale from senior staffers alleging that she damaged morale, hindered management from performing its duties, and reflected an unfavorable image of the company. "These complaints have led me to the conclusion that the actions of Gale Hayman are no longer merely a personal matter between Gale and myself but have become so open and public and so disruptive of the operations of this corporation that they are affecting the future and the profitability of the corporation and therefore must be dealt with."

Fred then read a list of six general charges against Gale ranging from the refusal to coordinate public statements with the director of public relations to the refusal to implement product-development decisions. The first complaint was Gale's open refusal to follow "the directives of the president [Fred]."

Fred circulated the resolution, which severely limited Gale's authority and removed her from the day-to-day workings of Giorgio, Inc., around the room. Her new job was to develop a long-range strategic plan for fragrance development over a five-year period and present her plan to Fred by June 17. Grossman considered the resolution to be a "face-saving device" because she would still be receiving her full compensation and would still have a role to play. Before the resolution was voted on, Fred asked if there was any discussion. Gale promptly refuted each allegation and argued with Fred without shouting. She did not consider this a face-saving device at all, but saw it as her "ouster." If anything, Gale would be totally embarrassed by the implementation of the resolution and unable to face her colleagues in the company. A short recess cooled things briefly and after further discussion among the lawyers, the resolution was softened slightly by allowing Gale to hire outside consultants and chemists to help her come up with a plan. By 12:30 P.M. the second revised resolution was passed by a two-to-one vote, with Gale voting against and Fuhrmann siding with Fred.

The resolution clearly represented a demotion to Gale. She was to be exiled to an office and location specified by Fred. The resolution also barred her from hiring or firing any employees. It imposed a gag order curtailing Gale's speech. "Gale Hayman shall not be entitled to make any statement to the press, any public relations entity or the public with respect to any aspect of this Corporation which has not been approved in writing by the director of public relations and the president of this Corporation." In addition Gale maintains she was locked out of the Giorgio executive offices without Fred's permission to visit and was not allowed to discuss Giorgio's business with any suppliers or trade customers. If she failed to follow the resolution, the president would be authorized to fire her. The implementation of the resolution was held in abeyance pending a written notice from Fred to Gale.

The meeting and the resolution were, in part, scare tactics showing that Fred was ready to oust Gale but was giving her a chance to return to her former creative role and stay out of the company's fragrance business. However, Gale had come too far and was not prepared to step back into a supporting role that would allow Fred to hog the limelight. She wasted little time pushing Fred into firing her.

The final act of perceived insubordination came on February 28, at the party Fred and Michael Gould hosted for Robinson's employees at the Giorgio boutique on Rodeo Drive. The party was a first anniversary celebration of Robinson's success with Giorgio, and Gould had prepared an ad for that Sunday's *Los Angeles Times* thanking Fred for his friendship. Gale was not mentioned at all in the ad, which Gould unveiled at the gathering, and she confronted him demanding her inclusion. Gould was embarrassed and asked Horner for advice. Horner told him to do nothing and Gale left the party, shaken and angry. Fred stewed in his embarrassment. He described his version of what happened in his 1986 court deposition:

> For me, the straw that broke the camel's back was an incident on February 28, 1985, at a party we held at our store for over 100 employees of Robinson's, including the then chairman of the board, Michael Gould. When Gould was in the process or thanking me during his presentation to those assembled, Gale interrupted him. A few minutes later, while he was finishing up his speech, Gale walked up, grabbed the microphone out of Gould's hand, introduced herself and said that she wanted to say thank you, too. By the end of the evening, I was totally embarrassed. I reassured Gould that I was still very appreciative of Robinson's relationship with Giorgio and told him that there would be no problems from the incident.

There would be a host of problems for both Fred and Gale as a result of that incident. Fred left for vacation on March 2, but ordered the resolution sent to Gale while he was in Hawaii. He commanded Horner to have it delivered to Gale at her home, thereby implementing her ouster from the daily operations of the perfume company.

The letter was dropped on the doorstep of Gale's apartment that Sunday night. Inside, Gale was hosting cocktails for the owners of New York's Russian Tea Room restaurant, Sue Jacobs of *Newsweek* magazine, and Igor Stalew. After going to dinner in Santa Monica at Wolfgang Puck's Chinois, Gale discussed the letter with Igor, calling her attorney in New York the next morning. She was instructed not to go to the office and not to force a confrontation. Instead, she put her secretary to work in her library and began transforming her dining room into an office. Gale would never again enter the Giorgio offices.

The locks to the Giorgio offices were changed to keep Gale out, according to Gale and Stalew. "At that point Gale was stunned and in shock," Stalew recalls. "She was ousted because she dared to stand up to Fred and the publicity he was getting. I couldn't believe it; this was going from bad to worse. The lockout was a lowlife thing to do; then their strategy was to come up with a cover story with their attorneys to show how emotional Gale was. What kind of bullshit was that? Who made the company ninety-five percent of what it was?"

On March 5, Fred's attorneys filed a three-page legal complaint in

Los Angeles Superior Court, asking the court to declare the resolution adopted by the Giorgio board to be valid and enforceable. The suit claimed Gale was contending the resolution "is invalid and an actual controversy has arisen between the plaintiff and defendant relating to the legal rights and duties." This would be the first legal punch thrown and it took Gale by surprise. She would not legally fight back for another fourteen months. Her world had been hemlines and topnotes, but she would soon be consumed with depositions and injunctions.

Gale never expected Fred to actually implement the resolution. She refused to use the office Fred assigned her, the old Giorgio Perfume mail-order office at 9250 Wilshire, because it was too negative a working environment. Retreating to her apartment, Gale tried to come to terms with being ousted. She had lost more than a job of twenty years. Stripped of her niche, Gale was entering, "the worst time of my life." Instead of challenging Fred legally, a process that could have dragged on, she sought a quicker solution and attempted to buy him out.

On April 1, Gale sent Fred a letter on her personal stationery, making him an offer of $26 million for his 51 percent of Giorgio. He considered the offer insufficient; and it was, given Giorgio's hefty sales, profits, and luminous future. Salomon Brothers had become Gale's financial advisers through her friendship with shopping center magnate Al Taubman, whom she had met at the Giorgio boutique during the seventies.

"The twenty-six million was a low offer, but it was someplace to start. He didn't make a counteroffer. He didn't lift a finger. I was working away to resolve this problem and save this company. I felt that it was important that I get back into the company for its future. My preference was to get back into it. I knew the company needed me," said Gale.

Gale's ouster would have made juicy reading in the business pages of the newspapers, but the company kept it hushed up. Fred did not want to air Giorgio's dirty laundry in public. The future of Giorgio, Inc., was now in some doubt, given that the company's success had been based on the partnership of Gale and Fred. The business would not have reached this point without the Haymans' combined talents and personalities.

Only a teaser paragraph in the *Los Angeles Times'* View section "Listen" column of March 15 gave an indication of Giorgio's mounting troubles. After describing the party for Robinson's in the Giorgio boutique and printing a $12.8 million projection for Robinson's Giorgio volume, the column concluded,

> Hold on to your atomizers . . . there's more. Everything's not
> coming up gardenia and tuberose at Giorgio. Word from the inside
> is that a power shift is under way at Giorgio headquarters. The

official statement from Katy Sweet, the company's public relations director, is: "Fred will remain at the helm and Gale will continue as a vice president and co-owner or the company. But from now on, her responsibilities will focus on long range development projects related to fragrance." In other words, she will no longer be part of the boutique's daily operations. We'll be sniffing around for further developments.

Roth and Horner assumed that with Gale banished there would be no more impediments in taking Giorgio to $100 million in sales in 1985 and then to further heights and profits. They recognized the need for new products (primarily a second women's fragrance), and figured without Gale they would have the green light from Fred to get it on the market by fall 1986. Gale had begun working on a second women's fragrance with Fred, but that project was now on hold. Fred feared the original women's fragrance would not sustain the current growth pattern and wanted to have "an insurance policy." He told *WWD* on February 19, "We are exploring the possibility of a second fragrance because we never want to be caught with our pants down. I always buy insurance. Our fragrance has been enormously successful and we don't want to do anything to confuse the public."

The public was not confused by Giorgio. The scent had become almost inescapable. In addition to the millions of scent strips in magazines and the thousands of women who were wearing the fragrance, atomizers, called nebulizers, were installed above the revolving doors of Bloomingdale's to spritz the scent out into the street. The Rodeo Drive boutique also had an atomizer spraying pungent mists of Giorgio onto Rodeo Drive.

Whenever there was an opportunity to sample the fragrance, the Giorgio team took creative advantage. At the Boston Marathon, models in yellow-and-white striped bomber jackets sprayed Giorgio along the race route, alerting Bostonians that Bloomingdale's had opened its new store and carried Giorgio exclusively. On March 19, Beverly Hills held its first St. Patrick's Day Parade up Wilshire Boulevard and Rodeo Drive. Green shared the spotlight with yellow and white. Among the eleven floats was an eight-foot-high Giorgio perfume box on wheels and inside the wooden box was Will Ferguson, the company's vice president of operations, and his son, with Sears bug spray canisters filled with Giorgio perfume. Ferguson had become immune to the powerful fragrance after smelling it every day at the plant, and he had become the company's designated spritzer. The thin crowds along the parade route were hit with over two gallons of a very expensive, $150-an-ounce insecticide, Giorgio.

New York cabbies and hotel doormen got to know the scent and would yell out, "Giorgio," when good-looking women wearing it walked by. *The New York Times* said Farrah Fawcett, Jacqueline Bisset, and even Michael Jackson were wearing it. For some, the scent was too pervasive. Lavin's Restaurant in Manhattan banned Giorgio because owner Richard Lavin "didn't want his restaurant smelling like his mailbox," according to his son Steve, who works in the new American cuisine restaurant. Lavin's posted a sign in its front window: PLEASE NO CIGARS, PIPE SMOKING, CLOVE CIGARETTES, GIORGIO, OR PATCHOULI. Michael Coady, the senior editor at *WWD* and a long-time friend of Fred's, did not allow his editors to wear Giorgio at daily morning meetings because it made him woozy. A doctor at Cedars-Sinai Medical Center in Los Angeles hung a sign in his waiting room requesting that patients not wear the fragrance in his office. Steve Pinkowitz, an apparel sales representative based in Dallas, came up with an anti-Giorgio T-shirt showing the company's double horse crest and name with a big red slash running through it. Pinkowitz said, "There are as many of us who loathe the fragrance as those who love it. Every time you walk into certain unnamed department stores, you're either sprayed on the way in or spritzed on the way out. Personally, I try to stay upwind of it."

Positive or negative, Giorgio was smelling up America. The fragrance was still in great demand in 1985, and the new doors opening that year were having the same kind of explosive success enjoyed by existing doors in 1983. Wherever Giorgio opened, it quickly became the top-selling fragrance, a national phenomenon.

Kaufman's in Pittsburgh opened the fragrance in the downtown store in June 1984, and during 1985 added the suburban branches. Mike Ziegler, the divisional merchandise manager, gave the brand only a few cases; yet it quickly became the top seller with volume over $1 million in 1985. Ziegler said, "Initially, the first customers bought it because of the marketing. That caused all this pent-up demand and then it came to fruition in a landslide business. It was the repeat customer that made it so successful, and they came back because they really liked the scent. That was testimony to a good, acceptable but opinionated fragrance." Giorgio's success would help propel Ziegler's career; in 1987 he would become a senior vice president of Robinson's in Los Angeles, the largest Giorgio account.

Whether it was rigid Salt Lake City or ribald Las Vegas, Giorgio was number one. At ZCMI, the leading department store in Utah, owned by the Mormon Church, Giorgio accounted for 35 percent of the store's fragrance sales, according to Janine Coles, the store's buyer. In Vegas, Giorgio was carried exclusively at Bullock's Fashion Show Shopping Center store, located on the Strip across from the Desert Inn Hotel. In 1985, Giorgio achieved sales of $500,000 in the store, whose cosmetics department did $3 million overall, making Giorgio not just the top-volume fragrance but top cosmetics vendor, according to Jack McCarley, the store's general manager at the time. Although Bullock's had the scent in just two of its Phoenix area stores and Las Vegas, Giorgio was among the three top-selling scents in the entire twenty-two-store chain.

Fred grudgingly allowed distribution to grow, and by Mother's Day Giorgio was in 260 doors, including some prestigious new ones such as Saks Fifth Avenue. Horner was trying to convince Fred that the big profits in the cosmetics industry were generated not on Fifth Avenue, but on Tobacco Road, in the dominant stores of more rural markets. Belk's, the giant in the Carolinas, and Dillards, the powerhouse in Arkansas and the Southwest, were among the stores in which Giorgio did exceptionally well. Advertising and promotional costs in these markets are well below those in major markets such as New York, Chicago, and Los Angeles.

Giorgio, Inc., was not soliciting any new accounts. Instead, retailers called, asked, and, in some cases, begged for the fragrance. Ron Chavers, the vice president of sales, had an unusual task. In a typical fragrance company he would be visiting stores and making presentations to convince the retailer to take his line. At Giorgio, his job was to canvas America and report back to Fred and Horner which of the stores requesting the fragrance actually had the makings of Giorgio accounts. For once in the industry, a manufacturer was dictating terms to retailers; and Giorgio, Inc., was smart enough not to abuse its clout. Chavers said,

> We knew we only had eight to twelve stockkeeping units [SKUS] in the line and we didn't want to go wild and were intelligent about the way we got space and location. We didn't become spacemongers. If a store had eight cases, and the best-selling fragrance at that point had one full case, then we wanted two full cases. We knew we were going to be number one and we wanted to look like it. We never went into a store and said, "We need a full bay," even though in some stores we were doing more business than Lauder and we deserved a lot of space.

Fred demanded that Chavers visit every store Giorgio opened to ensure they were quality stores and fit the Giorgio image.

Fred was worried we were going to be in too many department stores and get too widely spread and become a mass fragrance and I don't blame him for that. It's a credit to him that he kept us from only looking at the dollars, and the image of Giorgio lasted longer because of Fred Hayman. David was looking at the P and L [profit and loss] and there was a good balance between the two. Fred may have been too conservative and David too liberal, and that is where the checks and balances come in. David realized we needed to be in more cities.

Horner did not want to travel with Fred any longer, after spending many days and nights on the road with him in 1984; and Chavers accompanied Fred to several major store openings. Chavers considered Fred good-hearted and well-meaning, but even after long business days on the road, Fred incessantly talked about business. "He was constantly writing notes at dinner about new ways to improve our business. His other real interest was about family and he was interested in my relationship with my father. He appreciated people who had strong feelings about their families."

Chavers said Fred constantly read business magazines (*Forbes, Fortune*) but never books. Despite the time he spent touring major department stores, Fred still had much to learn. According to Chavers, Fred couldn't understand why the in-store models who sprayed and sold the fragrance at Burdine's in Miami weren't all cover girls and couldn't tell the customers everything there was to know about Giorgio. Fred controlled his little Beverly Hills store, where beautiful, intelligent women served his customers. He expected big-time retailers throughout America to be as customer driven and detail-oriented as he—an impossibility, given the minimum wages and rampant turnover inherent in most big retail operations.

Horner and Chavers convinced Fred to open in two branches of Belk's and were pressuring him to open in more outlets of this important southern speciality-store chain, whose overall sales recently topped $1 billion. When a journalist in Atlanta told Fred that Belk's was the J. C. Penney of the South, Fred took her word for it and got the company into an embarrassing situation, Chavers said:

They came down to pick us up in Atlanta in their corporate jet, and Tom Nipper, the senior vice president and an extension of Tom Belk's right arm, greets us and says, "We are happy to have you here."

Fred says, "I'm not sure about this. I'm really worried our business is getting away from us. We are in too many stores that I don't know what they look like, and I don't want my image to be destroyed and I understand your stores are very much like J. C. Penney." Tom and I are sitting behind Fred and I could tell Tom was mad, because the veins in the back of his neck were popping out of the side. He was very diplomatic and he explained he had some smaller stores in backwoods cities but they were the top of the line. He relayed that story to Tom Belk and they never invited Fred back again, but they were happy to have Fred as a celebrity and all the socialites showed up at the Belks' private country club and it was a pleasant experience. They treated us very well.

The private party hosted by the store's president was part of the Giorgio launch formula. The publicity hype also included the delivery of the fragrance to the store in a Brink's truck, with armed guards unloading it as if it were liquid gold. This ploy received television coverage in Charlotte and other cities.

Although Fred could be pompous and haughty, he was also tanned, charming and dimpled. To socialites and the young women who sold and modeled Giorgio, Fred epitomized Beverly Hills and Hollywood. Some even thought he looked like Merv Griffin. Fred was now the personification and living image of the fragrance, and he did not have to share the spotlight with Gale.

Retailers were eagerly rolling out the yellow-and-white carpet for this emperor of perfume, because the Giorgio exclusive allowed their stores to gain not only millions of dollars in new business but visibility in their market. In hotly competitive markets, having the Giorgio exclusive was the automatic market-share turning point.

Los Angeles was the most obvious example. Giorgio's power enabled Robinson's, which had been the smallest of the four major Southern California stores, to quickly become the fastest growing and most exciting fragrance store in the city. Hitting $11 million in sales with Giorgio in 1985, Robinson's quickly overtook Bullock's, which was doing only around $8 million in its entire fragrance department. Robinson's, on the strength of its $3 million Giorgio Christmas business, overtook Bloomingdale's in December 1985 to become Giorgio's number-one account; yet the store had only had the scent for two Christmas seasons, whereas Bloomingdale's had had it for four.

Giorgio's exclusive with Bloomingdale's in the New York market ended in 1984 with the entry into Macy's. A year later, in May 1985, the first signs of slippage appeared when the fragrance debuted at Saks, Bloomingdale's archrival. In 1984, Giorgio had accounted for 18 percent of Bloomie's women's fragrance business. Sales volume had been over $9 million, with 20 percent coming through mail order. The 59th Street flagship alone had done $1.7 million; but once Saks and Macy's had Giorgio, the growth at Bloomingdale's started to ease.

Management there was not happy. Arline Friedman, who succeeded Mike Blumenfeld as the cosmetics divisional, hated to lose the exclusive and had a savvy argument for not expanding:

> With our Giorgio exclusive, it was unheard of what we did. When a vendor [Giorgio] has to expand distribution, it has to expand promotional money and expenditures. Which would you rather do? Ten million dollars in one store or one million in ten stores? [Giorgio] didn't need the other stores. They broke the exclusive and I didn't feel it was okay. I would have loved to have kept it. We tried to keep the exclusive as long as we could and were prepared to invest in space and hopefully grow the business.

Giorgio's figures at Bloomingdale's would dwindle from almost $10 million in 1985 to less than $3 million over the next three years.

Fred did not exactly help the morale on the Bloomingdale's selling floor. After a *New York Times* article on Diana Romanello, the Giorgio fragrance-counter manager at Bloomingdale's flagship, revealed that she was making $100,000 in salary and commissions to become the highest-paid saleswoman in the industry, Fred ordered her salary cut. He was furious. The sales managers of his Giorgio boutique in Beverly Hills did not earn close to $100,000, so how could the Giorgio fragrance-counter manager at Bloomingdale's make that kind of money? Romanello, at Giorgio's peak growing period in 1984, had a staff of seventy-two employees to man the Giorgio outposts in the 59th Street store. Her original deal with Roth and Horner called for her to receive a 5 percent commission on every bottle of Giorgio sold in the store. Regardless of who recorded those sales, Romanello got the commission.

Fred wanted to hire two additional counter managers and cut Romanello's salary in half. She became bitter. No other saleswoman in the history of the industry had ever made so much money. Romanello was a success story to which the other fragrance salespeople, earning a meager $25,000, could aspire. Chavers tried to smooth over the situation, but he thought the Bloomingdale's system had gotten out of whack and that one person should not get all the commissions. Though Chavers felt it was hard to change the policy midstream, Fred ruled; later in 1986 two additional counter managers split the commissions.

Bloomingdale's was discovering that not everything Giorgio marketed turned to green. The night treatment cream, which was launched at Bloomingdale's early in 1985, was doing poorly and Friedman decided to discontinue it. With Gale out of Giorgio she didn't get much pressure to keep it in the store. The cream was also dropped from the Rodeo Drive boutique. Fragrance is an impulse item, but a woman thinks twice about putting a cream on her face to improve her appearance. Gale's cream didn't stand a chance sitting in a case in Bloomingdale's competing against Lauder, Clinique, and Lancôme, with their batteries of experienced sales help who could explain the scientific efficacy of their products. Beverly Hills meant glitz and glamour; it had nothing to do with scientific breakthroughs. The failure of the treatment cream was the company's first major product failure and an ominous, albeit quiet, hint of things to come.

Going into Saks had been Fred's dream from the start. Fred saw Saks senior executives Burt Tansky and Mel Jacobs at the Paris fall collections in March 1985, and he told Horner to invite them to his suite at the Plaza Athenée. Horner, who did not want to go into Saks, was furious. Horner recalls:

We didn't want to open Saks. We were giving a five percent commission to all the stores and with their special Saks plan they wanted ten percent. With Tansky and Jacobs in his suite, Fred literally, in the middle of breakfast while I went to the bathroom, made a deal with them. Tansky made a little joke and said, "We ought to keep you out of these meetings more often." I thought if we didn't hold our ground and stand by our policies we would have lost credibility and by keeping Fred out of most meetings we were able to do it. Fred would have compromised to get into the stores that he wanted.

Giorgio was launched at Saks not with Brink's trucks, but with a parade down Fifth Avenue of a fleet of hansom cabs decked with yellow flowers. It was from one of the horse-drawn buggies that Fred made his grand entry into the store. Giorgio's launch at Saks turned out to be a not totally joyous occasion for the store. Oscar de la Renta was Saks' best-selling fragrance and Saks was Oscar's top-volume account. Milton Stern feared the Giorgio entry; he did not want the scent knocking him from the top spot. When Stern heard Giorgio was coming into Saks with advantageous terms and space allocations he demanded to renegotiate his package with the store. Margaret Hayes, the store's veteran cosmetics merchandiser, had watched Bloomingdale's score with Giorgio in 1982 after Saks senior brass failed to return Fred's calls. She was not about to compromise this Giorgio deal. Saks refused to renegotiate with Stern. Although Oscar was the store's top brand, there was no reason to give Oscar the same amount of space and perquisites as Giorgio, which had piled up huge volume figures around the country.

Muriel Gonzales, the divisional merchandise manager under Hayes, said, "There was no point in making them equal. Giorgio did business that Oscar never dreamed of. It wouldn't make sense philosophically to start renegotiating all your arrangements with every company, so we decided to part with Oscar. Giorgio more than filled the void."

Giorgio became Saks' top seller by the end of 1985 in only nine of the chain's forty-plus doors. The fragrance was at its peak and the company was unraveling.

CHAPTER THIRTEEN

Estée Lauder to the Rescue?

The success of the fragrance created bickering at Saks, but it was mild compared to the ongoing tempest within Giorgio, Inc. With Gale banished, Roth and Horner assumed Fred would continue to allow them to run the daily operations of the perfume company without his getting involved in the inner workings. They were wrong.

According to Horner,

> After Gale left, Fred became worse and worse. When she was there she would occupy him for four hours a day and when she left he was going to show her that he could do all these things. Her departure gave him four hours a day to go do something else and he increased his mavenistic tendencies. He believed he knew the secret of being successful and would say he didn't want to grow anymore. He wanted to maintain or lessen the volume and keep the same profit. Bigness terrified him. The problem with our bigness, he wasn't growing with the company.

Roth urged Fred to play up the fragrance over his own personality in the many press interviews he was giving. The fragrance should have gotten more ink and Fred less, but Roth realized Fred was locked in a battle with Gale over the company and he was going to take the lion's share of the credit.

"Fred was a very good outside guy until he started to believe his own press clippings. When he believed what was in those scrapbooks, we had our biggest problems," says Horner, adding that Fred did change his corporate philosophy. "I couldn't remember the last time I saw a customer. When I worked in the big cosmetic companies, I was up there on the forty-seventh-floor pontificating, and I wouldn't know a customer if it ran me over in a truck. What Fred did for me was make me pay attention to the customer."

Roth and Horner envisioned Giorgio reaching around $300 million before hitting its peak. Despite the sensational growth of the women's fragrance and the strong start of the men's (about 20 percent of the women's volume by the second half of 1985), they were not content with existing marketing strategies and wanted to push in new directions to avoid peaking. The business was quickly reaching a plateau and would need something new to exceed $100 million and fend off the new fragrances that were coming out in 1985.

The competition had awakened to the profit potential of a powerful fragrance advertised via scent strips. The 1985 launches appeared formidable, especially Calvin Klein's Obsession, which had a gaudy, $13 million launch budget. Calvin Klein Cosmetics, a division of Minnesota's Minnetonka, Inc., had been one of the industry's laggards, whose first Calvin Klein signature fragrance was mediocre. The company was losing money on volume of only $6 million before the launch of Obsession. Under new management led by Robin Burns, who had left Bloomingdale's in 1983, Minnetonka decided to roll the dice behind Obsession. The big advertising budget was a signal to retailers that the company was trying to become a serious player.

Burns had studied the industry's blockbusters, Opium and Giorgio, during her Bloomingdale's tenure. She wanted to combine the controversy of Opium with the marketing techniques of Giorgio. Obsession, a sweet, cloying scent, was presold through magazine scent strips. On top of that, Klein was spending $7 million of its budget for national television advertising, the first time a manufacturer of a limited distribution (eight hundred doors) fragrance had ever invested that heavily in television.

Burns's plan worked and Obsession quickly became the top fragrance in non-Giorgio stores and the number-two fragrance in many of the stores that did carry Giorgio. Obsession was not the only new competition. In September, Estée Lauder was due to launch Beautiful, her first new fragrance after a seven-year launch hiatus. Christian Dior's new scent, Poison, already was doing well in Europe and was targeted for the U.S. market. Giorgio, Inc., had to do something if the company wanted to grow an already huge business in its existing accounts. As number one, Giorgio had the most to lose to the new fragrances. In an industry whose overall growth was at a plateau, Giorgio's market share was in jeopardy.

Roth and Horner's growth plan for the company revolved around the creation of a second Giorgio women's fragrance to be launched in spring 1986. The new scent would be limited to the original Giorgio three hundred doors to give those retailers new incentive and reinforce the original fragrance. That original Giorgio women's fragrance then would be expanded to another six hundred or seven hundred doors that were still clamoring for it. Development had begun on the new fragrance, which Fred wanted to call 273 North, the address of the Rodeo boutique. Horner thought 273 North was a great title for a restaurant or an Alfred Hitchcock movie but the wrong name for a women's fragrance. Although they were receiving submissions, little progress was being made because Fred was not being decisive, according to Horner.

Fred wanted to step up the mail-order campaign, but Roth was convinced that Giorgio had saturated its mail-order universe and more Giorgio scent strips would be overkill. There is a point at which a fragrance can become overexposed. Despite its limited distribution, through heavy sales, in-store sampling, and scent-strip advertising, Giorgio rapidly was reaching that point. When a woman in a fur coat gets in a cab on Manhattan's Upper West Side and the cabdriver compliments her fragrance, saying his wife also wears it, the woman in the fur coat often starts looking for a new fragrance.

Instead of mail order, Roth and Horner wanted to put Giorgio on television, a departure for the company, which had never used a second of television time. Fred balked, saying television advertising was for the masses and mass products such as tires.

The merchandising differences between Roth, Horner, and Hayman reflected their growing personality clash. Horner did not want to lose control of Giorgio's daily operations to Fred. He was tired of being Fred's puppet. Horner had been uncomfortable in subservient roles in large companies such as Helena Rubinstein and Max Factor, and a clash with Fred was inevitable. Horner enjoys a fight, and he was past the feisty stage in his relationship with Fred. It would seem, from Fred's perspective, that Gale's sniping and criticism were replaced by Horner's second-guessing and badgering. He began calling Horner the "king of schlock" and Horner, in response, labeled Fred "the dwarf." After frustrating meetings with Fred, Horner would sit at his desk and write poems about

Fred. They were not exactly love sonnets. One was entitled, "Travels of a Head Waiter."

There once was a waiter named Fred
Who must have been dropped on his head
He bought a bazaar
And an old Rolls-Royce Car
And here are the things that he said
My name is worth ten million bucks
And I won't deal with fly-by-night fucks
They're shysters and crooks
I can tell by their looks
And the deal that they offered me sucks
When I want cash I'll get it by phone
As a waiter I'm very well known
I'll invite them to dinner
And show them my winner
Or I'll put up the bucks all alone
When Freddy returned to the ground
The trouble began to abound
The bottles were broken
And Roth was a token
And Horner had skipped out of town
So Freddy went out in the street
And stomped with his size seven feet
While Leo the Ziff
Jumped off of a cliff
The fragrance was gone in a whiff
So Fred has returned to the past
He knew that it just couldn't last
He's given up fables
He now waits on tables
And people are truly aghast.

The bickering was becoming a threat to the future growth of Giorgio, Inc. Horner almost slugged Fred over a dinner table at the Fragrance Foundation Awards in New York in early June at Lincoln Center's Avery Fisher Hall. According to Horner, Fred came to the table and ordered him to get Ramlösa water, the Swedish version of Perrier, for the two tables the company had taken for the night.

"I'm not the banquet manager of this company," I said and when he said something demeaning I pulled my hand back, ready to slug him. My wife, Katrine, had to hold me. All through dinner I sat there, glaring. Every time he would try and start a conversation with me he would ask me what I thought and I said he would find out later. I later pointed a finger at him and said, "Don't ever do that again to me. I'm not the maître d' here."

While tempers were flaring in Beverly Hills and Lincoln Center, Gale was trying to figure out a way to extricate herself from Fred and get her 49 percent out of Giorgio. She was spending most of her time in New York, where she had taken an apartment in a modern high-rise overlooking the East River on East 52nd Street. As a child she had lived in a cheap, small apartment nearby; but now she had ascended to an apartment with a view of the river and the Empire State Building. In neighboring buildings lived Greta Garbo, Henry Kissinger, and John and Susan Gutfreund. Gale's passion for leopard was evident throughout the apartment. Leopard rugs, a leopard slipcover on the sofa, and a large leopard-print steamer trunk dominated the living room. The walls featured a Greta Garbo blowup and a *La Dolce Vita* movie poster.

Costume jewelry designer Kenneth Jay Lane became a close friend and her New York sounding board. Lane found Gale to be "an attractive extra woman" and took her to parties where they fox trotted and he attempted to distract her from her problem. He also was introducing her to powerful and social New Yorkers and they went to Europe together where he provided Gale with social entrée to the elite of Paris. Lane said the Europeans found Gale refreshing because she was candid and would enthusiastically praise their outfits and accessories.

Lane describes Gale as being stressed. "She didn't realize how vulnerable she was. Giorgio was her life and it was almost like having your child taken away for no reason and being called an unfit mother. She hadn't done anything; she may have rubbed Fred the wrong way, but usually that kind of thing can be ironed out."

Gale was at a crossroads. "I was reevaluating my life," she recalls.

Maybe it was time to become a jet setter and travel and have a home in Paris and in New York. Being born in New York, I had always loved it and maybe I should move back. I was like a college student when she is out of school. What should I do? Where should I live? I was seriously searching inside myself to see what makes me tick. It was the first opportunity in my life to do that since I was nineteen. It became very clear to me that I desperately love the cosmetics business.

Gale was obsessed with her career problem and it dominated her personal life. Her boyfriend, Igor Stalew, was sympathetic and supportive and tried to help her find a solution. The next eighteen months would test and strain their relationship. Gale circa 1985 was not the same woman Stalew fell in love with in the late 1970s. Her earthy and robust laugh was less forthcoming now. Gale's moodiness tested Igor's patience and he would give her pep talks. "I told her she had no choice but to fight and make a comeback. She was beginning to get tougher but she would get battered and she was not in the greatest shape."

Stalew and Gale had enjoyed traveling together and had visited Mexico several times, Spain, and the Orient in the early 1980s. The couple was frugal; Igor found the best airline rates. On a trip to Puerto Vallarta, they stayed at the posh Garza Blanca for one hundred thirty-five dollars a night, but also spent a few days in a simple but romantic eight-dollar-a-night hotel in the nearby but isolated village of Jalapa. Stalew wanted Gale to be pampered but also wanted to show her the real Mexico. With her ouster from Giorgio, however, Gale lost interest in adventure travel, preferring to visit New York in an attempt to solve her problems.

Gale began to turn to religion for support. Although she had attended an Episcopalian Sunday school every week as a child in New York, she became an agnostic after moving to Los Angeles. While Fred was still working at the Ambassador he was curious about the teachings of Dr. Norman Vincent Peale and once took Gale to the Founder's Church in Los Angeles. Hedda Hopper had given Fred a Science of Mind textbook by the group's founder, Dr. Ernest Holmes, which he kept in the foyer library of the Charleville apartment. In the mid-1970s Gale started reading it, and when Dani Janssen walked into Giorgio carrying the same book her curiosity was further sparked. Janssen invited Gale to hear Dr. Carlo Di Giovanna, "Dr. Carlo," the minister of the Church of Religious Science in North Hollywood.

Before becoming a minister in 1971, Dr. Carlo had been a hairdresser in Grand Rapids, Michigan. He felt a "great rapport" with Gale because she was in the beauty business. "She was trying to beautify the world and make it smell good, but unless you change the interior of people, no matter what essence you put on them or how lovely you dress their hair, there is no substance," Dr. Carlo says.

Most of Dr. Carlo's six-hundred-member congregation had come seeking help for various problems (drugs, divorce, job loss), and his simplistic Sunday service begins with a rollicking tune that echoes the philosophy of the religion, i.e., "The Best Things in Life Are Free."

Dr. Carlo recognized Gale was trying to hold on to her business and build an empire:

> The bottom-line message I had for her was, "God is not choosing you not to succeed. In spite of all the problems, difficulties, and frustrations in trying to build an empire"—which is what she was doing—"the larger the project, the more faith you have to have." That was my message to her. This is not a blind faith; you build on the past successes you have had. I told her to bear in mind that "the mind you used to create the Giorgio fragrance is the same mind you are using now. The mind that Estée Lauder used is the mind that you are using now. Use the same mind that you used to create Giorgio to just create again."

Gale found "plugging into the universal energy" of the church important. In 1978, when her personal relationship with Fred was deteriorating, and again in 1983, when her business relationship with Fred was coming apart, she sought Dr. Carlo's counsel. Gale faithfully attended the church's Wednesday night group "healing services," during which members give Dr. Carlo "a prayer request" (a list of problems they would like aired). Per Dr. Carlo, "We let the amplification of our faith work on everybody's request. It's not a question of big or little. I'm convinced this is for the person who comes for their kid to pass a grade and is equally important for someone building a business empire. We generate enough faith to heal the cancer, or the corporation. Sometimes there is cancer in the corporation."

Explaining her attraction to the faith, Gale says, "It's basically a philosophy of life, if you think good thoughts, good things happen; if you think negative thoughts, negative things happen. It's not esoteric, it's not cultish; but when I was going through my divorce I would go almost every Wednesday and it gave me strength and it got me over a hurdle." After her ouster from Giorgio, Gale went back to the small chapel on Whitsett Avenue and prayed. "I prayed the problems would be resolved for everybody's good. I wasn't trying to do anybody out of anything and I was praying for Fred as well, which is something he didn't understand. I wasn't trying to injure anybody."

While Gale was finding solace in religious meditations, Fred was seeking peace of mind in his Malibu retreat. Renting a small apartment at the north end of the Malibu Colony, Fred was hopeful the ocean and long beach would provide a safe and healthy haven from the increasing hostilities in Beverly Hills. Although the apartment was modest by his

Beverly Hills living standards, it had a wide ocean view and steps leading down to the beach where he could walk with his girlfriend, Betty Endo, and his two dogs, Giorgio, a dachshund, and Fawn, his German shepherd and loyal companion.

His relationships with Betty and Fawn had become protective and nurturing for Fred. After Gale left Fred in 1978, he dated glamorous women such as Beverly Sassoon and Kathryn Klinger; but it was simple, unsophisticated Betty with whom Fred chose to live. She was the kind of listener to whom Fred could pour out his problems both day and night. When he talked in his sleep, Betty reassuringly talked back. When Fred awoke at 5:30 A.M., Betty walked with him. His back was hurting from thirty years of jogging, and Betty massaged it—his feet, too—often in front of guests at the beach house.

Betty was not simply Fred's geisha. Fred was shaping her, transforming a mousy-looking girl into a stylish and increasingly traveled woman who carried Vuitton luggage and wore Jean Louis Scherrer gowns. To her credit, Betty was unaffected by the social exposure at the many events to which Fred dragged her. She truly enjoyed the beach house, Fred's dogs, and her cats—more than being with movie stars or affluent socialites. Fred's children were not a threat to her and she was a gracious companion for Fred, who remained the majordomo.

Fred's friends and customers understood the relationship and thought it made a lot of sense. Jean Kasem, a buxom television actress (*Cheers*), the wife of Casey Kasem, and a solid Giorgio charge customer, observed, "Betty knows how to be the good, strong, intelligent woman behind the ultimately successful man. There is nothing wrong with that. A lot of modern women can't do that in this town. Egos get out of control and it's difficult to make a marriage or a relationship grow. I have seen women take credit for their men's success but you don't see that with Betty." Betty was protective of Fred, and as their relationship solidified she was able to became a buffer between Fred and his ongoing problem with Gale. Betty encouraged him to spend more time in Malibu and less time at work.

Fred was robbed at gunpoint in broad daylight in the alleyway off his Charleville garage in 1983. After that, Fawn became his constant companion, walking to and from work with him. The sleek, muscular dog became part of Fred's image; they were photographed together during interviews. Fred valued Fawn's unfaltering loyalty, a quality that had disappeared from his business.

Gale had become a hindrance and Fred wanted to sever their business relationship. Gale was desperately looking for a way to get back into the cosmetics industry and the obvious way was to sell Giorgio, Inc., to a third party with herself as part of the package. Gale had begun working with Salomon Brothers, the prestigious New York investment banking house run by John Gutfreund. Although Estée Lauder, Inc., had never made a corporate acquisition, the company was a logical candidate to acquire Giorgio. The Lauder corporate philosophy dictated the creation of new companies from within to attack new market segments. Clinique had been created to capture market share in skin care and Aramis had been introduced to make inroads in the men's toiletries business. Both were brillant successes, created in Lauder's understated, tasteful style.

These spin-off companies under the Lauder umbrella enabled Estée Lauder, Inc., to become the country's preeminent prestige cosmetics company. During the 1980s, however, Lauder's momentum had slowed, allowing Cosmair's Lancôme division to cut into the company's market share by attracting a more youthful, career-oriented customer. Although the Giorgio fragrance was too unrefined, bold, and jazzy for the Lauder psyche, it was doing the kind of volume that Leonard Lauder envied. Thus, when Al Taubman called Leonard Lauder and told him Gale Hayman was trying to orchestrate the sale of Giorgio, Lauder was ready to listen.

Taubman is one of the biggest shopping-center developers in America and among the country's richest men. In the time since he had met Gale in the Giorgio Rodeo Drive boutique, he had bought a controlling interest in Sotheby's. He was not interested in owning Giorgio, but he called his friend, Leonard Lauder, on Gale's behalf. A meeting was set up with Gale, and Lauder was impressed with her ambition. He went to California and had dinner with Fred to evaluate the other half of the equation. What made Gale and Fred collide immediately was evident to Lauder. Neither wanted to be the backroom expert while the other became the company's public persona. Both wanted to be on the front page, but there was not room in Giorgio, Inc., for two superstars. Fred and Gale had become the movie star couple who break up because they fear they will be overshadowed by each other. Gale and Fred were fast becoming the fragrance industry's version of Taylor and Burton or Sonny and Cher.

Fred and Gale had agreed to almost nothing since the resolution was passed, but a minor breakthrough occurred in April 1985, when both sides agreed to retain Salomon Brothers as their investment bankers. Marshall Grossman considered this a major breakthrough because it was the first time Gale was willing to sell Giorgio to a third party. Gale's new high-profile attorney, Marty Lipton, of Wachtell, Lipton, Rosen & Katz, was gaining notoriety as the father of the poison-pill antitakeover defense. Major companies trying to repel unwanted suitors often called Lipton, who saw megadeals and mergers as economic doom, although his firm profited handsomely from them. Lipton came recommended by Taubman and knew Grossman. Their firms had shared Salomon Brothers as a client in the past, and Grossman did not look upon Lipton as an adversary, thinking instead that he would facilitate matters.

Michael Zimmerman, managing director of mergers and acquisitions for Salomon, and Rikki Rothman, the vice president of mergers, met with Fred at the Pierre Hotel to assess Fred's desire to sell Giorgio. No financial questions were asked. It was more a get-acquainted session. Rothman recalls,

> When I walked into his suite, I understood that I should stay quiet and let Michael, who had the title and was a man, handle the meeting; and that's exactly what he did. Either I or Michael asked Fred why the business was a success and he said it was due to him. He was a little bit arrogant and pretty much of an egomaniac, but at the same time a nice, polite, and bright man. Over a period of time I got the feeling Fred was taking credit for the fragrance's success and felt largely responsible for the success of Giorgio; and I think he did give Gale credit for creating the fragrance, but not for the marketing or the final success of the perfume.

Rothman did not get a strong feeling from Fred that he was ready to sell Giorgio. Salomon Brothers would not get paid if a deal were not consummated. Although a Giorgio, Inc., prospectus was being prepared, Lauder wanted to make a preemptive bid to take the company off the market.

As acquisitions go, this one was messy from Salomon Brothers' point of view. There were two different sellers, Gale and Fred, whose relationship was strained; both loved Giorgio and neither wanted to be separated from the company they had built. Fred wanted badly to sever his business relationship with Gale and if it meant selling Giorgio to another company he would do it grudgingly and at lucrative terms. Further complicating the prospective deal were all the representatives involved at the bargaining table. Grossman, a tough litigator and not especially conciliatory negotiator, was in Fred's corner. Gale's new lawyer, Lipton, didn't know her well, but he at least had a working relationship with Grossman and Salomon Brothers personnel. Ira Wender was negotiating for Lauder, and Leo Ziffren, the Giorgio, Inc., counsel, also was involved.

The initial Lauder offer came on July 15. Fred and Gale would split the $150 million according to their 51 and 49 percent stock ownerships. Leonard Lauder, in a letter to Fred and Gale, said he would keep Giorgio, Inc., a separate operating company in Beverly Hills and would not merge it with Estée Lauder, Inc., in New York. He would retain all the present employees. However, it was up to the Haymans to cancel the arrangement with IMG (Roth and Horner) and the costs for doing so were to be borne by them. Lauder told Fred he did not want Giorgio's distribution expanded and Fred agreed, further slowing the company's momentum. Fred tried to keep the negotiations a secret within the company, but Horner found out about them and became increasingly uneasy after Fred was spotted in Lauder's executive suite.

Wender thought he had a gentleman's agreement on the July 15 offer, but when he flew to Los Angeles for a further negotiating session, the stakes were higher. Grossman came back to the table with Fred's increased demands, although he refused to give Wender a specific number. Grossman describes the morning portion of the negotiations:

> He made an offer and I said it wasn't enough. I told him I had received authority from Fred to accept a number but I couldn't say what it was. Wender kept pushing me to find out what the number was. He came up another five million and it still was not enough. He kept asking what was my proposal and I asked him what his best offer was and he came up another five million. At that point I told him I had an important lunch date and he went into a modified rage and said I wasn't being fair to him. He said he had been making offers and come up with many millions, yet I hadn't given him our number. Nobody had ever put that kind of money on the table as far as I was concerned, and I wanted a little break to enjoy the dynamics of the situation.

After lunch, Wender kept raising the ante and Fred's magic number finally came into play—$110 million for his share of the business. By this time, Wender had loosened his tie, taken off his jacket, and been on the phone to Lauder asking him for authority to press forward. It appeared he was there to do the deal, come hell or high price. Grossman threw up his hands when Wender offered $110 million and then they started negotiating the nuances of the deal. The most critical side issue for Fred was that he retain the Rodeo Drive boutique. Salomon Brothers valued the boutique at $10 million and Lauder had no interest in keeping it.

To meet Fred's demands and capture Giorgio, Inc., Lauder came up with a creative, albeit complex, package that in effect would have Gale financing the deal. Fred would get his $110 million in cash plus a $10 million non-interest-bearing note. At the closing of the transaction, Fred could buy back the boutique for $10 million, payable by cancellation of the note. Gale's deal was much more complicated. She would receive $50 million, but only $10 million would be paid in cash at the closing. The balance would be paid annually in installments of $10 million, and

Gale would retain a 20 percent interest in Giorgio's total equity. In addition, she would remain an employee of the company and receive an annual royalty of 2 percent of Giorgio's net sales. If she were to leave the company, her royalty would drop to 1 percent.

Leonard Lauder wanted to keep Gale in the business and felt she could be the "engine" to drive Giorgio forward. The new offer to Fred was presented in Los Angeles on August 9 and an agreement in principle was reached between Fred's attorney, Gerald Kagan, and Wender. Kagan had taken over the negotiations from Grossman, with whom Wender refused to negotiate. However, the terms of Lauder's separate agreement with Gale were not revealed at the session as they had not been agreed upon at that point. As far as Fred was concerned, he didn't care what arrangement Gale had with Lauder and didn't have to know.

Although Gale was eager to solve her problem and get on with her career, she did not understand Lauder's new offer, which, on the surface, appeared to give Fred much more cash than it gave her. Rothman tried to explain to her that the true value of her arrangement could not be calculated for at least five years. If Giorgio were successful and continued to grow rapidly, Gale's stock option and royalties would be worth considerable millions. Rothman said:

> After the meeting [when Fred's attorney agreed in principle], I took her into a conference room and started to explain to her what it meant. She didn't really understand it. She asked the right questions and intrinsically is a very sharp lady, but it took a period of four to five months for her to know exactly what you were talking about. When we started with her, though, she understood perfumes and cosmetics but had no understanding of financials.

The deal did not move along. Estée Lauder, Inc., was supposed to supply formal agreements to both Fred and Gale; but it took weeks for the expected documents to arrive at Grossman's and Kagan's offices. When papers finally arrived in November, Grossman suspected two reasons for the delays: Lauder was sitting back monitoring the Giorgio business for performance in the important fall season, and Gale and Lauder were having problems coming to terms.

The executives at Salomon Brothers were growing frustrated with Gale. They were spending considerable hours on this relatively small acquisition, which Gutfreund had taken on partially because of his friendship with Al Taubman. To complicate matters, Gutfreund's socialite wife, Susan, had become friendly with Gale. Gale was summoned to Salomon's stately offices in New York. Rothman describes the stir Gale caused the day she walked onto the Salomon Brothers trading floor on her way to John Gutfreund's office:

> There are about a thousand guys sitting at their desks on the trading floor and Gale comes in wearing a leopard dress, her hair pulled back, leopard hoop earings, ballet shoes, and little white ankle socks. She goes into John's office with Marty Lipton, Al Taubman, Michael Zimmerman, and they were all trying to explain to her what the deal and stock options meant. After two hours John got to the point where he was getting frustrated because Gale wasn't enthusiastic about the deal and didn't really understand it. He said, "I don't care how long it takes, but you are staying in these offices until you understand it. You will go upstairs with Rikki and will sit with her until you understand it." So the big meeting broke up and, as we walk out of the office, the whole trading floor turns around and is watching us. Gale is totally oblivious and gets on tiptoes and kisses John and Al Taubman on the cheek. I started to crack up and all the traders just watched and had no idea what was going on. All they knew was that there were a lot of heavy hitters in that room and this woman in a leopard dress was kissing them good-bye.
>
> We went upstairs and she started getting the hang of it. She got excited when she understood that her deal was not worse than Fred's, just different. A lot of the value depended on her performance and when she realized Leonard wanted her badly and she would be important to the company, she got excited about the whole thing. Not only was this a way out from the mess she was in, but it was her future. After another hour with her she could understand that her deal was not undervalued, but I don't think she could have repeated the deal to somebody.

While Gale was creating a scene on Wall Street, Fred was trying to make Giorgio a sensation on the Champs-Elysées. Fred's dream was for Giorgio to be the number-one fragrance in Paris. No American fragrance had ever held that position, but Fred wanted to try. Giorgio had had an overwhelmingly successful introduction in London at Harvey Nichols in late 1984, quickly becoming that store's top seller, a feat that encouraged Fred to try to conquer Paris. He said, in a September 13, 1985, feature in *WWD*: "I would like to be the number-one-selling fragrance in Paris. I haven't figured out what volume it would take, it's just a wonderful dream. It will take us a year and I know it's a big order, but we will be the number-one fragrance there. To have our own boutique in Paris would be the ultimate." French tourists in Beverly Hills were buying his heavy scent. "I know the French love it and right now in Europe, America has a cachet. America is very in and Beverly Hills is totally in."

Fred, too, recognized the plateau Giorgio was about to hit in the U.S. and he was pushing to expand in Europe. He hired Mike Martin, a former Revlon International executive, to head his European operation. The plan was to grow slowly there with no more than 150 doors and retail volume of $30 million by 1986.

The Paris launch was critical to the European success and, after two years of negotiations, Giorgio had an arrangement with Galeries Lafayette, the largest department store in Paris. The store had agreed to give Giorgio windows, outposts, and a large counter in a key spot in the cosmetics department. Fred planned to make the launch party as flamboyant as the Rodeo Drive bash in 1981 and sought a unique venue. Mary Lou Luther, the fashion editor at the *Los Angeles Times*, suggested to Fred that he hold the party at the American embassy. Geoffrey Beene had set the precedent with a fashion show there, and Luther called the designer for Fred and found out how it could be done.

The party was held on Sunday night, October 20, at the embassy, which at the time was in a state of semisiege. Security was straitjacket-tight following the attack on the American military compound in Beirut and frequent terrorist attacks in Paris. Fred hired Patrick Terrail to orchestrate the party and supervise the fourteen cooks, twelve wine tasters, and sixty waiters, while he was busy that week attending the Paris fashion collections and buying clothing for the Giorgio boutique. For Terrail, the Paris party was a logistical nightmare, much more difficult than the Beverly Hills Giorgio party. Terrail, who was suffering from a double hernia, recalls:

> There were two problems with the embassy: one, it was too small for us; and the security was so tight, they wouldn't let us build a tent outside because they were afraid terrorists would throw bombs. We had an elevator to work with the size of two chairs and we had to move a party for four hundred through that elevator. The security didn't allow any cars to park outside for more than fifteen minutes and every box that came in had to be checked by the U.S. Marines. Every guest had to pass through a metal detector, but once they got in it was very festive.

The black-tie affair was a celebration of American food and music and established Fred as an American impresario in Paris. A jazz quartet, strolling violins, and harp music were not enough. Fred had his minions scour Paris for a mariachi band and they found two bands who agreed to combine forces and guitars for the party. The food included Virginia ham, New England crabs, cheesecake shipped from New York and, of course, apple pie. A special Statute of Liberty ice-cream cake was created to reinforce the theme. Claude Philippe, Fred's French mentor during his Waldorf years, would have been proud.

Fred was sparing no expense and expected perfection, even on foreign turf. Upon entering the embassy shortly before the guests arrived, the impresario was far from happy. Luther said, "Five minutes before the violins were to start, he changes the tables because they were too big. They were set up for twelve, but he wanted six at a table. When he saw the Statute of Liberty cake, he hated it and threw it out. It was yellow and green and so corny."

Although the party competed head-on with Sonia Rykiel's fashion show and party that night, the Giorgio party was unusual enough to draw enough counts, countesses, ambassadors, socialites, designers, and movie stars to make the European newspapers and television broadcasts. The fragrance launch at Galeries Lafayette was successful, and Fred's European campaign was off to an auspicious start. Lauder negotiations or no, Fred was not ready to make Paris his last hurrah.

CHAPTER FOURTEEN

Lawsuits and Lost Market Share

Coming into the 1985 Christmas season, Giorgio was still blazing new volume trails and the expectations were for it to continue the torrid streak despite new competition and an overall lackluster retail climate. The fragrance industry was showing little growth and retailers were putting their dollars behind proven winners such as Giorgio and the exciting new lines, Calvin Klein's Obsession, Chanel's Coco, and Lauder's Beautiful. Following Giorgio, virtually every major fragrance house was using scent strips in magazines. Well-stocked corner newsstands and sundries shops selling magazines were now almost as pungent as the fragrance departments of major department stores.

While Giorgio was able to meet most retailers' lofty sales objectives, there were signs the scent had reached its zenith. At Robinson's, executives hoped to finish the year with Giorgio at $14 million, but the brand fell short. It reached $11 million, an incredible figure, nevertheless. Bloomingdale's business also fell short of its sales projection for Giorgio, partially because distribution had expanded in New York (Saks). Industry insiders were starting to hope and whisper that Giorgio had peaked.

Leonard Lauder was watching Giorgio's fourth-quarter performance carefully, and as the selling season grew closer to Christmas Day he noticed considerable overstocking in department stores. He was afraid if he acquired the company just then there would be very little inventory on hand to propel the business into 1986 and he would have to invest heavily in producing fresh merchandise. On December 12, Lauder made a new offer that Fred rejected on December 20. Lauder still was offering Fred $110 million, but he now wanted one-half of all the Giorgio profits from July 1, 1985, to the closing of the deal. Those dollars would represent well over half the year's profits and would cost Fred several million. Marshall Grossman and Fred were wary of Lauder's "moving target" presentation. Another onerous condition was Lauder's insistence that at least $15 million in saleable finished-goods inventory be on hand when Lauder took control. Fred knew the inventory levels were low and rejected the offer.

A final offer to Fred was sent to Salomon Brothers, Inc., by Ira Wender on December 26. This offer dropped the inventory and profit stipulations, putting $100 million in Fred's pocket—60 percent at the closing and $10 million over the following four years. Fred thought the deal was fair and a meeting was set in Los Angeles in January to document the transaction. Salomon Brothers sent its team to Los Angeles thinking the deal would be consummated without any foreseeable hitches. Gale's deal hadn't changed materially and she was ready to sell her portion of her stock and remain with the company while taking considerably less cash up front than Fred.

Wender came to the table at the Gibson, Dunn & Crutcher offices with several new hitches. Leonard Lauder wanted to change the deal from a sale of Giorgio's stock to its assets, a change that would have major negative tax implications for Fred. Also, Lauder renewed the inventory demand. These modifications were important to Lauder because they would have allowed him to pay out the Giorgio acquisition over a six- or seven-year period based on the company's sales and profits. Without the modifications, the payout would be eight to nine years, too risky for Lauder. He doubted the fragrance would be able to sustain itself that long.

After two days of haggling and negotiating, Fred spent forty-five minutes in a private room with Kagan and Leo Ziffren and decided to walk away from the deal. Rothman and Fred Goldstein, who now represented Gale, tried to salvage it; but Fred had made up his mind. Rothman recalled:

His response to us, he was getting sixty to seventy million after taxes plus the store, so why should he sell his company when he could make that money in three years if he kept the company? There was no way to convince him and he was growing indifferent to it. He never brought up Gale's involvement with Lauder, but

I suspected it. He just walked out. He didn't stop by the conference room to say anything to the Lauder people, to thank them or shake their hand and say, "I'm sorry but it just didn't work out." They were all in the glass conference room and they could see him walk by and everybody was a little shocked.

Rothman thought the Lauder demands were not unreasonable and could have been surmounted if Fred wanted a deal and was willing to negotiate. The inventory and tax liability changes would have taken approximately $25 million away from Fred. Although that was reason enough for him to walk away from it, he also considered the change in tactics at the last minute a breach of good faith, which made him walk away faster.

Gale was more than a little disappointed by the failure of the Lauder deal:

Leonard and I were both almost in tears, we were both very upset. He called me from a restaurant and told me how sad he was, that he was not a drinking man but he had already had two drinks before dinner. I was starting to lose my patience. Fred was playing a game and he had no intention of selling. It became extremely clear that Fred was happy with the status quo. He was in control and was part of a very successful company.

If the deal had been consummated, Gale would have been able to sever her professional and financial umbilical cord to Fred in addition to getting her old job back. Now all she had was the cord and no immediate way out. Gale sought Dr. Carlo's counsel over the setback. She was trying not to be overcome by hostile feelings for Fred, according to Dr. Carlo.

It was a marvelous achievement not to feel hate. When she felt herself slipping into [hate] then we had talks. At no time ever did I pray for Fred's demise or for Fred to fumble. I would say, "Let's not get angry with him, let's do nothing but send him blessings and love." I told her not to pray for Fred, "I'll do it." I prayed for Fred to find the level that would make him feel fulfilled and successful. I didn't treat Fred and Gale as the devil and the divine. They were both divine; but it's like saying, "I like sugar and I like salt, but I don't like salt and sugar in my coffee."

Gale had a legal option. She could put some pressure on Fred with a lawsuit, a solution she had rejected earlier as being too time-consuming, costly, and painful. Her career option was to start a cosmetics company under her own name; that, too, would be costly and risky. She decided early in 1986 to pursue both options, and she started shopping for a lawyer and a cosmetics-industry pro who could help her get her new venture off the ground.

With offices still in her apartment, Gale began to develop a leopard-print cosmetics line and it helped take her mind off the Giorgio situation. Her depression deepened after the failed Lauder deal and she called her friends, among them actress Linda Evans and local NBC television news anchor Kelly Lange, for advice and solace. Susanna Hoffman said, "When she got fired and her foundation [was] wiped out, she almost transported into another world, a world out of reality. The Lauder deal was a real roller coaster. All she could see were the issues and was becoming obsessed by them and not with herself. Her humor, her lightness, the giggly part of Gale was gone."

Fred started mapping a plan to take Giorgio to new heights. He refused to comment to the press on the failed Lauder deal, but in early February 1986, he told *WWD* that the company was no longer for sale and he was not considering taking the company public. Instead of being the acquiree, Fred expressed an interest in being the acquirer. "We are looking to buy a treatment company. We have started to look because we feel it has great potential for us. We want to buy a small, advanced treatment company that has a great product but has been unable to merchandise itself." Fred had freely given volume figures in the past but now he was reticent. "Last year we hit one hundred million dollars and that was part of the phenomenon. Now we don't have to brag anymore and we won't be giving our volume. We are looking for substantial increases, mostly coming out of international markets. We plan to stay small in the U.S. and then perhaps grow with new products." Six new products were being developed, including a day and night cream. Fred was also talking about going into the catalogue business and trying to double the mail-order business. Increased distribution in department stores was still anathema to him; he wanted to expand distribution in the U.S. to only twenty outlets in geographic areas such as Beaumont, Texas, where the brand had not been available.

Fred was much more generous in distributing Giorgio's cash than he was in distributing the fragrance. A multitude of local and national charities were the beneficiaries of Fred's generosity. Earlier in his career Fred gained the respect of his coworkers with his largesse and now he was earning the respect of the community. His frequent contributions to the Maple Center, a Beverly Hills mental-health outpatient facility, had earned him that group's Man of the Year honors in 1982 and in early March, Fred was named Citizen of the Year by the Beverly Hills Chamber of Commerce at a black-tie dinner at the Beverly Hilton Hotel. Charlton Heston also was honored that night and Fred Hayman stories were swapped at the various tables.

Michael Gould, Robinson's chairman, recalled setting up a lunch between Hayman and Michael Newton, president of the Performing Arts Council, at the Music Center's Founder's Room:

> There we were, the three of us alone in this colossal room. It was like having a private lunch in the U.S. Capitol. Newton gave a speech about donating money to the Music Center and with a fifty-thousand-dollar contribution, Fred could be a founder. Without batting an eye, Fred pulled a check out of his wallet and wrote the fifty-thousand-dollar check. Newton just looked at me because no one had given in such a way. Fred didn't want any big thank yous.

Between October 1984, and September 1985, at Fred's behest Giorgio, Inc., donated $217,298.11 to over eighty different groups and charity organizations. The contributions ranged from as little as $50 to Easter Seals to $16,666 to Federated Department Stores. Among the contributions were $10,000 for a Rudi Gernreich Retrospective, $10,000 to the Partnership for the Homeless and $6,000 for the Princess Grace Foundation, headquartered in Monaco. The Partnership for the Homeless was to be become Fred's pet charity and he would donate $500,000 to the group in 1987 after selling out of Giorgio. "I founded [the homeless campaign] and gave it the seed money to get it rolling. These people need help. They get sick and lonely, just like we do and it's really a terrible problem," Fred said. Los Angeles in 1987 had an estimated thirty thousand homeless people, and Beverly Hills its share of street people —few, if any, as lucky as the Nick Nolte character in *Down and Out in Beverly Hills*. The Partnership for the Homeless was raising funds to build a shelter for the city's homeless.

Fred's charity began at home, in his own organization. Earlier in the 1980s, Fred paid the tuition of a young black shipping clerk at the boutique, Kim Taylor, to attend the Fashion Institute of Design and Merchandising, an education she otherwise couldn't have afforded. She would graduate and later get a job with Creative Artists Agency, among the top Hollywood agencies representing actors.

Part of Fred's plan for Giorgio in early 1986 was to find a new president. Fred had identified the candidate, Michael Gould, and started making overtures late in January 1986. There was an eager candidate within the Giorgio house, David Horner, but Fred chose to look outside.

Horner was not bashful about asking for the job, nor was he diplomatic when, in February 1986, he asked Fred over lunch at The Bistro to step aside and name a new president from within the company.

> We had a big blowup when I told him, "Gale was right. You can't manage the business. You can't go to Europe and have parties and just open one door in France." I asked him to make me or Jimmy president and for him to step back. I was upset because people who were reporting to me would go right around me. He told the guy who manages England and who I hired that he could call Fred anytime although he reported to me. He didn't want anybody in the company to have a power base.

Horner was frustrated with Fred's reluctance to expand the business, and he browbeat him over his indecision. In October 1985, Fred had given Roth and Horner the okay to step on the accelerator and double the distribution in 1986, putting the scent in seven hundred total doors. Production orders were placed to fill the pipeline, while at the same time money was being spent to order molds for the new fragrance, which was supposed to launch in spring 1986.

There were stipulations with the Lauder negotiations that Fred not expand distribution. If Fred were seriously considering the Lauder offer, it made no sense to have a new fragrance that, when bottled, would become Lauder's property. Roth and Horner's marketing plan made sense but remained in limbo as the negotiations continued. Fred not only blocked the distributions plan, but he also dragged his heels on the new fragrance, and then the Lauder deal collapsed.

The combination of the failed Lauder deal and Gale's estrangement caused a malaise to settle over Giorgio, Inc., during the second half of 1985; and it grew worse in 1986 when Roth's and Horner's hands were shackled. Their compensation package was part of their undoing and a major reason for Fred to look elsewhere for new management. Roth and Horner were being compensated on a percentage of Giorgio's pretax profits. Based on escalating percentages of $50,000 increments, the duo would receive the maximum percentage on any profits over $400,000. In 1985 when the fragrance's volume soared and pretax profits hit $39 million Roth and Horner's slice was $6,135,000. Fred haggled with them over the amount, saying, according to Roth, he didn't understand the contract. Roth and Horner demanded to see the accounting and in late 1985 were on the eve of arbitration and a legal action before they received their payment. Fred did sign the hefty check with a note saying they deserved every cent.

The IMG contract was expiring on September 30, 1986, and Fred could find new talent for far less then he was paying Roth and Horner. Realizing their windfall compensation was excessive, Roth and Horner were willing to renegotiate their deal to make it more acceptable to Fred, but they were not given the chance.

Fred did not have to engage an executive recruiter to conduct a nationwide search for the next Giorgio president. Gould, Robinson's chief executive officer, impressed Fred with his rough-and-tumble style and results. Robinson's had surpassed Bloomingdale's as Giorgio's number-one account in 1985 and Gould was to a large degree responsible. He had made sure Giorgio was given top billing from a space, location, and visual standpoint in Robinson's fragrance departments. When Fred called Gould in January to see if he were interested in the job, Gould thought Fred was calling to "bitch" about Robinson's small and frumpy Palm Springs branch.

Gould had just come back from New York and a meeting of the Associated Dry Goods, Inc., (ADG) board, on which he served as a junior member. The meeting had not gone well as far as Gould was concerned because Associated's CEO, Joe Johnson, did not respond to a board member's query about December sales results. Gould says,

> This meeting blew my mind. One of the board members asked for the December results and Joe Johnson said, "We can't figure out the end of the year until we have inventory results." I said what a bunch of bullshit. They hadn't figured out how to get the per share earnings to match their overall earnings and I couldn't believe it. I said to myself, "This is never going to work out," and I called Fred back and we had lunch at The Bistro.

By the last week of January, Gould was offered the job and said he would consider it. As bad as things were becoming at Robinson's and though he knew he should start considering his options, Gould was not eager to leave the corporate big leagues. Over the last eighteen months he had gone from the ADG wunderkind to the organization's Colonel Kurtz, the Marlon Brando character in *Apocalypse Now*, who abandons his command to go up a Vietnamese river and carve out his own fiefdom in the bush. Joe Johnson would terminate Gould's command and throw him into the middle of the Giorgio jungle.

Gould was a talented anomaly who was a step away from the presidency of conservative and stagnating ADG in March 1984. Gould's mentor, Bill Arnold, ADG's CEO, was stepping down for health reasons and Johnson was succeeding him. The likely candidate to succeed Johnson as president was Gould, who had turned Robinson's around and was making the store the most exciting within the conglomerate. ADG's other stores included Lord & Taylor, Goldwater's, Horne's (Pittsburgh), the Denver Dry Goods, and Caldor. Gould's crusade against Bullock's to win the upper moderate and better apparel business was succeeding; Robinson's was showing the most sales growth within ADG. Gould was named Robinson's CEO in 1981 when the store's sales were under $300 million and the chain had nineteen stores. In four years Gould had nearly doubled the volume, and Robinson's was on the verge of achieving more volume than Bullock's in Southern California.

In March 1984, Gould was offered the vice chairmanship of ADG by Johnson; but he wanted the presidency, a job that was not going to be filled right away. Instead of swallowing his pride and accepting the job, Gould asked for some time to think it over. He took too much time; Johnson called and withdrew the offer a forty-one-year-old executive should have jumped at.

Gould's days at Robinson's were numbered, growing fewer as the profits started to dwindle in 1985. While the other CEOs of ADG divisions were watching their budgets carefully and pursuing relatively low-key marketing programs, Gould had gone Hollywood. A splashy billboard campaign along Southern California's freeways coupled with a heavy television and newspaper advertising campaign created high visibility for the chain, but sales promotion expenses were ballooning. Robinson's missed its 1985 profit plan by $5 million, although Gould claims the store still made over $20 million pretax profits that year.

The relationship between Johnson and Gould deteriorated in early 1986. Gould felt ADG's corporate office under Johnson lacked leadership and merchandising direction. Johnson, on the other hand, was starting to get pressure from his colleagues to harness Gould because of his lack of humility and shrinking profits. The gentlemanly Johnson, who was about to retire, flew to Los Angeles to meet with Gould about budgets. The question of humility came up and Gould told Johnson he and his staff were upset about not making the plan. A terse exchange followed with Gould telling Johnson, "It was nice knowing you."

Fred Hayman and Leo Ziffren knew about Gould's forced resignation before the staffers at Robinson's. Fred, who was in Switzerland visiting his aged mother, had called Gould in Boston, where he was visiting his parents. According to Gould, Hayman, in response to the news of Gould's demise, said, "Those corporate bastards, don't they understand what a good store is all about?" Fred now wanted Gould as Giorgio's president even more. When Gould returned to Los Angeles and announced his resignation at the store on March 24, a long line of employees waited outside his office to say good-bye. He had built incredible loyalty with his open-door policy and encouragement of debate and experimentation. Gould's photo was pinned to a cash register in the Beverly Hills store by a sales associate in the rug department who was touched by Gould's interest and compassion for the people in the branches. Many in the line were weeping. An era at Robinson's was passing and the store was heading into a traumatic tailspin. Gould was going to Giorgio.

On Tuesday, April 15, Gould's appointment as Giorgio's president and chief operating officer was announced. Fred was relinquishing his president's title and taking the titles of chairman and chief executive officer, new positions. Fred supposedly also was relinquishing day-to-day control of the business. Gould's duties included overseeing the $100 million fragrance company and the retail boutiques on Rodeo Drive and Madison Avenue. With Gould shouldering the day-to-day load, Fred would be free to spend time on the creative and conceptual side of the business and would become more visible on the promotional end. Retailers had visions of Fred visiting their stores with a blonde on each arm, effusing Beverly Hills style and sex appeal as he would sell his fragrance.

Gale's role on the creative side had never been filled and now Fred would try to become the company's resident "nose." "We needed someone like Mike. There is a lot to be done, and we have expansion ahead of us to become a major force in the industry," Fred told *WWD*. He was smitten, and he thought he and Gould would make a splendid team. "Mike and I will have a ball," said Fred the day Gould's hiring was announced. It would be more like a brawl.

For someone who had no experience running a fragrance company, and who had just been forced to resign over eroding profitability at Robinson's, Gould was offered a lucrative compensation package by Giorgio, Inc. On April 17, the Giorgio board approved a three-year contract for Gould, despite Gale's vote against hiring him. She cast that vote at the same time she tried to have the February 1985 resolution ousting her rescinded. She was outvoted two to one; the board approved Gould's contract. Salary the first year was $1.35 million and $1.55 million the second year, escalating to $1.75 million in the third year. In addition, he would receive 2 percent of the net income in excess of $20 million. Gould's golden parachute was $1 million in severance compensation, half payable after thirty days notice. Giorgio, Inc., also agreed to loan Gould $650,000 over a ten-year term and to provide him with a company car, which turned out to be a sleek Jaguar. No number-two executive in the fragrance industry was making that kind of salary. Giorgio, Inc., could have had a president with manufacturing experience for considerably less.

Fred may have been happy to have Gould join the team, but the yellow-and-white welcome mat was not exactly out on May 5 when Gould arrived at the perfume company's Santa Monica headquarters at 1725

Stewart Street for his first day of work. Roth and Horner had set up the company and now were being unceremoniously demoted by Fred. Gould was sensitive to the situation and tried to soften the news of his arrival but to no avail.

> When I decided to take the job, Fred was going to have a meeting with Jim and David and the three people who ran the store for him, the managers of the shoe, men's, and women's department. I told Fred, "Don't do that. We should just meet with Jim and David to tell them about me. You don't understand how they are going to feel." Well, he didn't and we had them all together in the little conference room at 9595 Wilshire. I walked in a few minutes later and it was less than pleasant. Jim and David couldn't believe the insensitivity that they weren't at least told before. They were disappointed, and some time later Jim told me he never thought he would be president, but at least he would be treated with dignity.

Roth and Horner maintain they did not get a dignified reception when they first met with Gould. Roth describes his first meeting with Gould on the Giorgio premises, "Gould comes into the room and says, 'You guys will have jobs forever.' I said 'Mike, we are not looking for jobs,' and he said, 'We will evaluate your roles,' and I said, 'No, Mike, we are going to evaluate your role and we will get back to you.' Within ten minutes we went up to our lawyer's office."

On April 22, Roth and Horner announced they would not renew their contract with Giorgio, Inc., when it was up on September 30. Horner told the *Los Angeles Times*, "We're all very friendly, we introduced Mike Gould to Fred Hayman in 1984." Off the record, Roth and Horner thought Hayman had made a terrible choice. They felt Gould lacked experience and knew about his messy track record at Robinson's. It would take Gould months to learn the manufacturing side of the fragrance business and Giorgio, Inc., needed immediate attention and direction. They also were hurt and angry with Fred over the demotion, even though he had helped make them millionaires. Roth wanted to spend the rest of his career at Giorgio, but "it wasn't in the cards." In a May 16 article in *WWD* about the coming of Gould, Fred was quoted, "Jim and David are part of a very good team and they will be a loss; however, everybody is replaceable, even myself." Fred had gotten rid of Gale and now had put Roth and Horner out to pasture. Giorgio, Inc., the company that clicked with four cylinders, was now running on one.

Roth and Horner played a pivotal role in the fragrance marketing coup of the 1980s—no prestige fragrance had ever achieved so much volume in so few doors in so short a time—yet during their five-year run, they received little recognition from Fred or Gale. Their combined forty-three years of experience in the industry would be missed at Giorgio, Inc. The advice from their attorney was to honor the rest of the contract and remain on the Giorgio premises until September 30, unless Fred specified otherwise. Fred wanted them to stay until their contract expired. Gould thought they would clear out thirty to forty-five days after his arrival and let him run the show.

Gould came to work on May 5 suffering from a bronchial infection he had been fighting since February. He would be sick either physically or emotionally over the next twelve months. Taking a new job in a new industry is always difficult, but there were extenuating circumstances at Giorgio, Inc. The company's momentum had dramatically slowed. The fragrance was softening and retailers had not placed the expected reorders following the Christmas season. Stocks were bloated and without large reorders Giorgio suddenly found itself with a cash-flow problem. Huge profits had been pulled out of Giorgio, Inc., by the Haymans (Gale alone received a lump-sum payment of $7 million in December 1985) and not reinvested in the business. Their animosity toward each other encouraged the Haymans to build up their personal war chests rather than the company's. In addition, there had been expenditures to build up inventory in late 1985 when Roth and Horner expected to increase distribution.

In early 1986, the company went to the bank and established a $5 million credit line, actually taking a series of short-term loans at the prime rate to finance operations, marking the first time since the perfume company was started that outside financing was required. City National Bank provided the loans and Bram Goldsmith, an old friend of Fred's, helped in arranging the financing.

Gould came into Giorgio with an ambitious agenda he and Fred agreed upon. As a retailer, Gould wanted to push the opening of other Giorgio boutiques around the U.S. and to license the Giorgio logo. He was unhappy with Giorgio's advertising, which had changed only slightly over the preceding three years, continuing to rely on the "best selling fragrance in Beverly Hills" line. The need for new products was obvious, and retailers were growing increasingly critical of the painstaking pace of Giorgio's new product development. Horner had promised the stores increased distribution and a new women's scent in 1986, but the company did not deliver.

Fred acknowledged there was no "super nose" at Giorgio, but he was now carrying vials of samples with him every day and testing them on associates and acquaintances. He established a fragrance-testing panel, composed of an odd assortment of his "elite" Beverly Hills friends whose taste level he valued. The panel included Linday Gray, Merv Griffin, the

Robert Culps, the George Peppards, local television news anchor Tawni Little, John and Maureen Dean, and Murray Schwartz, publisher of the *Beverly Hills Courier*. People outside Giorgio had always influenced Fred, a fact that angered Roth and Horner. Gould, too, would be infuriated when Fred would allow nonprofessionals to provide input.

As far as Gale was concerned, Gould's arrival would do nothing to fill the creative void. Gale was ready to emerge from her fourteen-month press exile and harped to *WWD* about Gould's appointment in a May 16 article. "Giorgio will never achieve its full potential with me not in the company. My strength was I was unrelenting until I was satisfied with the Giorgio products and that creative hole was never filled when I left. I've got nothing against Michael Gould. He is a strong manager and the company needed that, but it also needs a creative force such as myself."

Gale's printed critique of Giorgio, Inc., included second-guessing the wisdom of launching a second women's fragrance in November: the timing was bad and the company should have been introducing a cosmetics line instead. Gale had announced earlier in May that she was beginning work on her own cosmetics line, Gale Hayman, Inc., to be launched in 1987. She hired Red Weiss as a consultant, assigning him the tasks of creating a business plan, hiring people, and organizing the company. Weiss was a veteran cosmetics marketer who had done time at Max Factor and Revlon. He liked the entrepreneurial nature of this start-up venture. Weiss's office was Gale's kitchen; Gale worked in the living room.

Gale also hired attorney Arthur Crowley, who was preparing a $75 million civil suit against Giorgio, Inc., and Fred Hayman. The well-timed suit would be filed within days. Giorgio, Inc., was in disarray, with Gould trying to establish himself in an organization that was loyal to the previous management.

The suit was filed May 19 in Los Angeles Superior Court, and named Fred, Leo Ziffren, Irene Fuhrmann, and Giorgio, Inc., as defendants. In legal terms, the accusations were standard for a civil suit involving business partners. Breach of contract, breach of fiduciary duties, unfair business practices, and intentional infliction of emotional distress were Gale's complaints; but in layman's terms it was simply a power struggle between Gale and Fred over Giorgio, Inc. Gale was asking the court for an injunction forcing Fred to allow her back into the company, nullifying the February 23 resolution that ousted her. She claimed the resolution violated the Haymans' divorce settlement, which she interpreted to guarantee her an active role in the company.

Gale's contract to develop the long-range fragrance plan ended in October 1985, and was not renewed. She never submitted a plan to the company and from October on was supposed to have been serving Giorgio as a consultant. However, the bills she submitted to the company in December 1985 were not being paid. For all intents and purposes Gale had not worked in the company since March 1985.

Ziffren and Fuhrmann were dragged into the suit because they "acted at the direct command of Fred Hayman and didn't exercise independent judgment in the best interests of Giorgio." As the third voting member on the Giorgio board, Fuhrmann was the critical swing vote and, having worked with Fred since his Hilton days, she was supportive of Fred's efforts.

Gale's original lawsuit was almost impossible to win. It was undermined by the 1983 divorce settlement agreement when she agreed to give Fred 51 percent control of Giorgio, Inc., despite the advice of her independent legal counsel at the time. It would take compelling evidence to convince a judge that Gale should now be reinstated in the company as an equal partner. Her return was an unrealistic dream and the last thing Giorgio, Inc., needed after Gould's shaky arrival. Gale's ouster had not been Fred's doing alone; it was supported by Giorgio's senior management, who would not be eager to take Gale back. Her request for $75 million in damages was hard to justify. After all, Gale had taken $20 million out of the company over the last three years by virtue of her 49 percent stock ownership and compensation package.

Gale's complaint charged Giorgio, Inc., had slipped badly since she was ousted and Fred's mismanagement was causing the "precipitous decline" in profits and a 25 percent drop in sales during Gale's inactive period. Gale listed a dozen examples of improper conduct to illustrate Fred's breach of his fiduciary duties. They were a combination of gossipy tidbits aimed at Fred and more serious accusations about mismanaging the business. Little or no substantiation for the charges was included in her court papers. These accusations included:

- The introduction of a new women's scent, which is of inadequate smell and standard
- Intention to launch this new fragrance in November at Giorgio's twenty-fifth anniversary party in both New York and Beverly Hills
- The extravagant [$350,000], poorly conceived launch of the women's fragrance in Paris
- Nepotism of putting Fred Hayman's son Robert in charge of the 57th Street store. Robert was twenty-three and has no retail experience
- Selling Giorgio perfume to known retail outlets who are known diverters, i.e., Brigade

- Improper testing of the new fragrance on girls in the office and wives of the Giorgio staff
- Oversupply of Giorgio fragrance at numerous charities
- Reneging on promotional promises to retail stores, causing bad relations between them and Giorgio, Inc.
- Excessive charitable contributions of $217,289.11 from October 1984 to September 1985
- Excessive expenditures for payment of Fred Hayman's personal expenses, including his chef at a rate of $20,000
- Hiring of Michael Gould, a man who has no experience in wholesale, manufacturing, or fragrance as president and chief operating officer at a vastly excessive salary while Fred Hayman delegates his responsibility to Gould while continuing to be paid millions in compensation.

A hearing date was set for July 18, and Judge Warren Deering was assigned the case. After a year of remaining backstage while the spotlight was on Fred, Gale was making a comeback in the national press and it was not good news for Giorgio, Inc. On June 9, *Fortune* magazine headlined its story about the spat THE ROMANCE TURNS GOTHIC AT GIORGIO and indicated that the business was losing some of its allure because of the turmoil. The article by Fay Rice had a quote from Fred on the controversy. It was the last on-the-record quote he would give a journalist regarding the conflict. Fred said, "Gale and I were going in different directions. It became an obstacle course which you cannot have when you lead a big company." The loss of Roth and Horner would not help the company's prospects, Rice wrote.

Newsweek's headline on June 23, A WHIFF OF TROUBLE included a caption reading "Sweet smell of success gone sour" and showed photos of a smiling Fred and a staring Gale. "Fred wanted Giorgio to be an expression of Fred Hayman alone," Gale was quoted. "He thought I'd just step aside, collect my dividends, and be a socialite. Fred misjudged me; money isn't everything." *Newsweek* called the power struggle between Fred and Gale, "the Giorgio potboiler" and put a light ending on the story by quoting Lester Gribetz of Bloomingdale's, "It might even help sales, if the perfume becomes notorious."

New products and creative advertising can help a fragrance, a lawsuit diverts management's attention. In Giorgio's case, the lawsuit was causing a siege mentality to develop. Gale had focused the spotlight on Fred's ability to manage a $100 million fragrance company and he was hurt by the accusation that he was a poor and wasteful manager. The grand parties he enjoyed hosting were now a legal issue. Fred may not have considered spending $200,000 excessive for a publicity-generating party, but he was also a tight-fisted manager who would question the necessity of adding another six-dollar-an-hour shipping clerk. His entrepreneurial nature was well suited to the fragrance industry, where advertising and hype are critical. The pending lawsuit cramped Fred's style. He had to curtail the lavish affairs he loved to host. Fred wanted to have a gala on November 23, to both celebrate the twenty-fifth anniversary of the store and to launch the next Giorgio women's scent. Plans for the party had been announced in July, but the party was scrapped and the new management team never selected the fragrance. Gale's suit was making Fred paranoid about all costs to the company, and for Fred the party was over. Giorgio, Inc., was becoming much less fun.

Flamboyant Fred was being transformed into Silas Marner watching every nickel for fear a fiscal misstep would add fuel to Gale's fire. With Fred's increasing vigilance, Gould never had a chance to run the company with the autonomy Fred had promised. Gould said,

> Fred got those papers [the lawsuit] on a Friday [May 16] and that changed everything in the company. There were decisions made in this company over the next year or not made because of the lawsuit. "Don't spent money because she will say you are spending money." I was here for a month and a half and we had stores here for meetings and we were eating deli food. We weren't taking them to The Bistro, but ordering in from Sy's Deli and eating off paper plates and plastic forks. I thought it was hardly the image of the number-one fragrance company. I wasn't hung up on some fancy executive dining room. I wasn't asking for sterling silver and china. I sent some of our people to By Design in the Beverly Center to buy some nice plates. I didn't send them to David Orgell in Beverly Hills. I don't know who told Fred, but you can guess, and when he heard about it he got hysterical and we almost had to take the stuff back because it would look bad because Gale would say we were wasting the company's assets.

Horner was the snitch who was reporting to Fred on Gould's operating procedures and would be a nagging pain in Gould's back until he left at the end of September. As angry as Horner was with Fred, Hayman still held the purse strings and Horner's 1986 compensation was tied into the profit performance that Gould could influence. Profits were deteriorating as Gale alleged partially because of a slowdown in orders but also because operating costs were escalating. Among the additional overhead costs were the salaries of the executive team Gould brought into the company from Robinson's. Just prior to the lawsuit, Gould hired two Robinson's executives, John Funck and Barry Erdos, at generous six-figure salaries (Funck had a three-year contract starting with a base salary of $350,000).

Funck had engineered Robinson's advertising and sales promotion; he was instrumental in forging a trendy image for the store. Red glasses, beard, and European double-breasted suits made Funck a chic contrast to the conservative Gould. Funck is a health nut, eschewing red meat, wine, and coffee and has his own exercise trainer. Gould was fond of Funck, and at his urging started taking vitamins. Some jokingly said Funck had become Gould's guru. Erdos had been Robinson's chief financial officer, a dubious distinction, considering the 41 percent profit decline reported by ADG in late May that the company blamed on Robinson's performance.

Gould hired Funck to head Giorgio's marketing department and to oversee new product development, both areas in which he had no experience. Funck also would have control over the advertising—in effect, filling Jim Roth's role. Erdos was to be the chief financial officer and also handle operations. Kathy Franzen was Giorgio's chief financial officer and her contract said she reported to Fred, not anyone else. She was not prepared to be demoted and report to Erdos, at least not without a fight.

The arrival of Funck and Erdos in late May made it obvious to the company's employees that Fred had hired not merely Michael Gould, but had bought a package deal. Roth and Horner were not happy about being supplanted by Gould; now they were further being replaced by Funck and Erdos. Horner, soon after the trio's arrival, began calling them "the Robinson's wrecking crew."

Roth tried to work with Funck and went to New York to sample fragrances. Their relationship was strained and they stopped talking midway through the summer. Roth recalls, "I found Funck to be an art director of moderate taste level, the kind of guy I would have hired in the seventy-five-thousand- maybe eighty-thousand-dollar range; but I would never have put him in an advisory capacity. John was all façade."

Franzen didn't mince words either. There was no way Erdos was going to usurp her spot. "I said, 'Fred, you made this commitment to me and I have done the job for five years and I don't want to stop doing it. I don't have a problem reporting to Mike Gould, the president, but I don't want to report to an executive vice president. You signed the contract with me; you figure it out.' Soon thereafter Fred reassigned Barry to work in international."

Gould and Fred were on a collision course from the day he started and it didn't take long for their relationship to begin deteriorating. Retailers who knew about Gould's rambunctious style and Fred's ego were predicting a clash, and it occurred within a month of Gould's arrival. At ADG, a billion-dollar retail company, Gould had not been bashful about speaking up and staking out his territory. He spent $150 million of ADG's capital budget over a four-year period. He had come up through the pit of retailing, being schooled at A & S in Brooklyn, whereas Fred was a Rodeo Drive gentleman retailer, trained at the Waldorf-Astoria Hotel on Park Avenue. If a public corporation such as ADG couldn't control Gould, how could Fred Hayman, who in his store's biggest year never did more than $15 million? Gould had built Robinson's into a $500 million company and there was no reason for him to suddenly become submissive at Giorgio, Inc., especially with his guaranteed contract. Fred got more of a president and chief operating officer than he bargained for.

Franzen, the only senior Giorgio, Inc., executive to bridge the start-up years and the Avon acquisition, said Gould and Fred were tense with each other from the beginning and the employees were confused over who was leading the company. Roth and Horner had a group loyal to them, Gould and his Robinson's minions were trying to win acceptance, while Fred was grappling with Gale's lawsuit and Gould's personality. Franzen said, "Fred in all honesty and sincerity hired Mike and made the commitment to let him run the business and he meant it; but he had never done that, to let loose, and it was difficult. He had David constantly calling him about this and that. Fragrances were not being created and the you-know-what was being stirred. It was a traumatic time for the company, but we survived."

The company desperately needed a burst of excitement during the fall 1986 season, to stem the erosion of the original women's fragrance; but the new team could not deliver the new scent. "No one could agree on anything, the bottle, the packaging. It was sniffed and sniffed forever," Gould recalls. "Nobody could make a decision, it didn't make any difference what the idea was. Fred had strong opinions on the way it ought to be, even if nobody in the company thought that way."

Without a new scent to present to retailers, Gould went on the road visiting Giorgio's top accounts and tried to be a convincing pitchman and keep the stores excited about Giorgio. Unlike Fred, who would be content to maintain distribution at the cost of having sales drop, Gould was concerned about growing the market share. If it meant investing in sparkles and fireworks and whatever industry promotion was available, he was ready to try it. As former CEO of Giorgio's top retail account, Robinson's, Gould knew the stores loved selling Giorgio but did not especially care to do business with Giorgio, Inc. The company had a haughty reputation with a dictatorial, take-it-or-leave-it attitude. Horner, Hayman, and Ron Chavers were able to dictate terms to the powerful stores when the fragrance was exclusive and the hottest scent in America; but Gould did not have the same bargaining power. He was faced with trying to prop up a fragrance that was falling by as much as 40 percent annually in some key doors such as Bloomingdale's.

Gould was the little Dutch boy who had to put his finger in the dike to stop the yellow-and-white bleeding at retail. The virtual free ride Giorgio had enjoyed between 1982 and 1986 was over. Giorgio was no longer a phenomenon. The company had to start spending co-op advertising dollars and giving retailers previously unthinkable promotional concessions. Giorgio was joining other fragrance manufacturers in having to placate the stores to reach the consumer, although the scent still was far and away the top seller in the stores that carried it.

Chavers was heading the sales department when Gould arrived and was loyal to Roth and Horner. Gould would fire him early in 1987, but Chavers gives Gould some credit for trying to arrest the slide:

> We never paid for the in-store transparencies and the hoopla, but Gould did. Now, whenever Bloomingdale's wants to change the case pads and the lettering they charge Giorgio for it and they pay it. We never paid for that stuff in the beginning, but Gould started paying for it and he wasn't totally wrong. We weren't doing the business and somebody had to grip the business and say we are willing to do this and investment spend. We must spend to prime the business. Fred didn't want to run the business this way. He wanted the old days. Now it wasn't fun. He had to be tough with people. He enjoyed being in the room with a bunch of retailers, and he just wanted to be friends, one of the guys. It was not in his nature to haggle out a deal.

The only way for Giorgio to maintain its volume in the U.S. was to expand distribution; and Gould was able to convince Fred to add another one hundred fifty doors during the balance of the year, expanding the fragrance to five hundred accounts. The Giorgio explosiveness was still there in new markets where the scent had never been distributed. Bakersfield, California, had not been touched because the market lacked a prestige store; and when the Broadway got the scent in 1986, the store was able to do $400,000 the first full year.

Giorgio's lack of growth in existing accounts was due in part to competition from Giorgio imitations. The scent's success, coupled with its parsimonious distribution, encouraged knockoff fragrance companies to come out with their own versions of Giorgio. Primo, Juliano, and Dessini Uno were all cheap Giorgio imitations that smelled similar to

Giorgio out of the bottle and usually cost less than $10. There was nothing subtle about these knockoffs, with Primo's box declaring, "If you love Giorgio, you will love Primo." Fred was furious about the knockoffs and recognized their damaging impact on the prestige industry. Not only did the knockoffs ridicule the $150-an-ounce bona fide fragrances, but they took a slice of the overall fragrance pie. In 1986, the copycat-fragrance industry accounted for an estimated $150 million in retail sales. Primo was the most aggressive and successful of any copycat scent and was marketed by Parfums de Coeur, a company run by Mark Laracy, considered a turncoat by the fragrance industry for making Parfums de Coeur the copycat market leader with about 66 percent of the total business. Laracy had been a bright young marketing star at Charles of the Ritz and was part of the team that launched Opium and Enjoli. His strategy was to make Primo and his other knockoffs part of the mainstream of the industry with aggressive advertising. When the Fragrance Foundation nominated Primo as one of the most successful introductions for 1985, Fred withdrew Giorgio's membership from the foundation in March 1986. Although Primo did not win the award, it would rack up sales of around $45 million, taking business away from Giorgio. In 1987, Giorgio would sue Parfums de Coeur and successfully knock its Primo television commercial off the air.

Fred had feared another part of the industry, the duty-free market, because of possible diversion. Gould convinced Fred to open in duty-free shops in Honolulu, Anchorage, and Singapore. The results were surprisingly disappointing, the first time Giorgio failed to meet a retailer's launch expectations. Duty Free Shoppers Ltd., the largest duty-free operators in the world, with 1987 sales of $1.8 billion, had wooed Hayman and Horner for two years and, when they finally got the brand in the second half of 1986, took a major position with Giorgio. No American fragrance had ever been given the visual and space allocation that Giorgio received in the downtown Honolulu Duty Free Shoppers outlet. The hordes of Japanese consumers who move through that store prefer French fragrances, but Chevza Musbay Zerkel, vice president of fragrances for Duty Free Shoppers, hoped Giorgio would alter the French dominance and appeal to her Japanese clientele. Despite the dramatic displays and a special promotion, Giorgio was running 15 to 20 percent below expectations. Zerkel said Giorgio's low recognition among the Japanese was the reason the scent did not sell. In the Anchorage Duty Free shop, Giorgio did so poorly it was discontinued after nine months. However, in Singapore, a duty-free outlet frequented by many Europeans and Americans, Giorgio was a star and ranked among the top ten fragrances, Zerkel said.

The big-city U.S. retailers who had had Giorgio for two years had marveled at how quickly the fragrance dominated their departments.

Now they were almost equally astounded at how quickly the fragrance had peaked and they were becoming wary of Giorgio. Giorgio was part of a new breed of meteor fragrances; unlike the old days, when it took five to ten years for a scent to reach its peak, Giorgio could get there in two. That was the good news. The bad news was that it was disintegrating and coming back to earth quickly, and the stores who were dependent on the brand for as much as 30 percent of their total sales were vulnerable.

The impact of Giorgio's rapid rise and fall was exemplified at Rich's in Atlanta. The scent peaked in 1985 at $5 million, and by fall 1986, the women's scent was dropping at least 15 percent per month. By 1987, the store was getting clobbered with 30 percent decreases. Although it still maintained its number-one ranking, sales of Giorgio dwindled to a little over $2 million by the end of the year, causing a decline in Rich's overall fragrance business that did not look good to senior management.

Manny Roth, Rich's divisional merchandise manager, watched the scenario and partially blamed Giorgio, Inc., management for not being creative. He also took some blame; he had depended on Giorgio and failed to pay as much attention as he should have to other fragrances. "We have learned a lesson, that when forty percent of your entire fragrance business is being done in one brand, you better have a backup plan in place and be ready to implement it when the growth of that one fragrance ceases," Roth said.

Gould hoped if Giorgio could grab more space it could maintain its sales in cities where the exclusive was being maintained. More space was not the answer, as Gould quickly saw in Southern California. After arriving at Giorgio, Gould started twisting arms at his alma mater, Robinson's, to get more space, and the store built Giorgio huge bays in several key locations such as downtown Los Angeles. These bays were on a par with the space to which Estée Lauder was accustomed, but Lauder had much more than fragrance to put in those cases. The Giorgio cases were jammed with just the Giorgio women's and men's scents. The Giorgio bays were labeled "Giorgio shrines," by people in the industry. The additional Giorgio space at Robinson's did not stop the slide, according to Hank Schubert, Robinson's divisional merchandise manager at the time.

You reach a point where you max out and we may have reached the Giorgio maximum very early in its life cycle. Because of the huge success, how much further could you go? Anything is possible, but to take Giorgio from eleven million to twenty million dollars is inconceivable. How much legitimately could we expect? It's a rhetorical question because no one had ever been at eleven million and I don't think anyone ever will, but I don't want to say never. But it will be a long time before anything hits the cosmetics industry like Giorgio.

On July 11, 1986, at a meeting of Giorgio's board of directors, Fred tried to push Gale over the edge. As long as Gale had her salary and dividends from Giorgio she could afford to meet her corporate tax obligations while pursuing the increasingly expensive lawsuit. Fred had been receiving 9 percent of Giorgio's annual sales and Gale 6 percent of sales since 1980. In the fiscal year ending September 30, 1986, Fred's salary was a monstrous $8,996,000, while Gale's was just excessive at $5,997,000. The salaries of captains of industries far larger than the cosmetics business did not come close to the compensation of Fred and Gale Hayman. With the Giorgio business slowing in 1986, it was estimated Fred's salary would be reduced to a mere $8,725,000 and Gale's to $4,877,000.

At the board meeting, Gale, accompanied by her attorney, Nick Cuneo, read from a prepared statement and at one point made a motion to extend Fred's employment contract for another year at the familiar 9 percent of gross sales as long as her consultant agreement with Giorgio was also extended at 6 percent. After reading the motion, Gale asked if anybody would second the motion. There was silence.

Fred had his own motion and a plan for his new contract. He would be paid 5 percent of Giorgio's annual sales. In addition, the board voted not to distribute dividends to its shareholders (Fred and Gale) in the next fiscal year. It also was proposed that since Gale was no longer performing any services for Giorgio, her consulting arrangement with the company would end along with her 6 percent of sales compensation. Fred's plan was approved by the familiar two-to-one vote split, with Gale vociferously objecting. The board also approved a resolution authorizing the company to pay the defense costs of Fred, Ziffren, and Fuhrmann in the case Gale had filed against them. Gale, with a 49 percent ownership in the company, was now having to pay to defend the people she was battling.

Although Gale essentially was cut off from all future income, as a 49 percent owner of the company she still was responsible for 49 percent of Giorgio's federal tax liability, which was considerable. She had been paid over $20 million by the company over the previous three years, and she would have to use those funds to continue the struggle against Fred, pay her taxes, and finance her fledgling cosmetics company.

Fred's aggressive move would trigger further litigation. It was designed to silence Gale and knock her out, but it came eighteen months too late. Gale already had her $20 million war chest and, like an irritated queen bee, was going to pursue Fred until she got her share of the honey.

CHAPTER FIFTEEN

Avon Calling

Lawsuits are often played out like the dueling scene in Stanley Kubrick's film *Barry Lyndon*. In the English period piece, each duelist carries a rickety, questionably accurate pistol. After they walk away from each other back to back, a coin is flipped. The winner of the coin toss gets to shoot first while the loser stands there, hands at his side, hoping the bullet will miss. If the shot misses or only wounds, then the other side gets a chance to kill the first shooter.

Gale fired the first shot when she filed her lawsuit in May, and she grazed Fred, drawing a little blood. Her suit may have rattled Fred and affected his management style, but it failed to scare him into asking Gale to come back into Giorgio or selling his controlling interest to her or a third party. Now it was Fred's chance to shoot back. The July resolution cutting off Gale's salary and dividends was on target, wounding Gale, and had the potential to kill her suit if her money ran out. Fred, through his attorney, Marshall Grossman, took some more potshots at Gale in August during five days of depositions.

Grossman gained his reputation for aggressive courtroom tactics and actually forced a settlement in a 1979 case involving sports agent Michael Trope, after putting Trope through the deposition ringer for three days. By calling for Gale's deposition, Grossman could lock her up in a courtroom atmosphere. There was a chance she would fold under hard questioning and settle out of court.

Gale's deposition began on August 20, 1986. It was taken in a large room at Gibson, Dunn & Crutcher's office in Century City, a five-minute walk from the new offices of Gale Hayman Beverly Hills, Inc. The question-and-answer session lasted twenty-seven hours stretching over five days and provided the only face-to-face courtroom drama during the almost year-long legal tussle. John Swenson, of Gibson, Dunn, the law firm representing Giorgio, Inc., was the interrogator. Grossman, accompanied by his associate, Karen Kaplowitz, could interrupt the proceedings at any time to challenge Gale's testimony and attempt to have it struck from the record. Gale's latest counsel was Arthur Crowley, a portly forty-year-veteran Los Angeles litigator whose white mustache provided a stark contrast to Grossman's black mustache and rock-solid figure. Crowley and his associate, Nick Cuneo, were in the room trying to keep Grossman from ripping Gale to shreds. Fred Hayman, dressed in a funereal black suit and nervously chomping on gum, was present; he silently attended the proceedings every day. A video camera focused on Gale for the entire twenty-seven hours and a court reporter, Ben Newlander, recorded her testimony for the Los Angeles Superior Court.

Visibly uncomfortable and nervous, Gale was wearing a demure, double-breasted blazer and white blouse and appeared feminine. She had discarded her tough and kooky look for a conservative, ladylike appearance and when the video camera started to roll, Gale's voice was strained and tense. After solemnly swearing to tell the truth, she was asked the first question by Swenson. It was the most basic, her full name. She answered, "Gale Elizabeth Ann Miller Hayman," and before Swenson could finish his next question, Grossman jumped in and asked, "Could we have that name again, please?" Gale had forgotten her maiden name, Gardner, and promptly corrected the record. Grossman was not going to give Gale much slack.

Gale appeared to have little patience for the proceedings and when, during the first five minutes, Swenson asked what type of market research she used to develop new products she replied merely, "My brain."

The first of many Grossman-Crowley clashes came ten minutes into the deposition. Gale described the February meeting where the resolution was passed to oust her a "rigged" board of director's meeting, which set off Grossman and then Crowley:

> Mr. Grossman: I move to strike the last comment of the witness
> on the ground that it is not responsive to the pending question and
> was impertinent and intemperate.

Mr. Crowley: Don't characterize my client's testimony in those pejorative terms, please. All right?

Mr. Grossman: I shall make whatever statements I deem appropriate to the proceedings, Mr. Crowley, not withstanding your attempt to instruct or obstruct otherwise.

Mr. Crowley: Don't make comments that I am obstructing. That is unprofessional as well as being discourteous.

Mr. Grossman: It is also factual.

Mr. Crowley: It is not factual. You should know better.

Mr. Grossman: The record will reflect—

Mr. Crowley: I realize it seems to be an effort for you to be courteous to me, but I would appreciate it if you would make it.

The next hour was spent discussing Gale's background, schooling, and work experience prior to Giorgio. Under oath, Gale had to provide her proper birthdate, admitting she was born on September 1, 1943. Gale testified she never graduated from Hollywood High, but obtained her high-school diploma by going to night school at Hollywood High. She could not remember the year she received the diploma.

Swenson pressed Gale to find out what her special talents were as a product developer in an effort to discredit her contention that she created the fragrance. Gale told the court her talent was innate and she had the ability to interpret submissions from perfumers.

I'm able to translate the concept of the fragrance that you see in your head, which is how I did it with the Giorgio fragrance and translate that to a living breathing liquid in a bottle. That takes a combination of a creative skill, a very strong discipline, it takes a lot of patience, it's arduous, it's gut wrenching, it's frustrating. It takes a lot of tenacity because you're told continually, "This is great, this is great, take this, take this," and I couldn't be sold and it took me two and a half years to develop the fragrance.

Swenson, a calm Minnesotan who grew up on a farm, knew little about the fashion/fragrance business. He blew up when Gale refused to discuss the specifics of the Giorgio creation. Gale didn't want to reveal her trade secrets with Fred in the room. "We have heard ad nauseam that her creative genius developed this perfume, yet we are now told that we aren't going to hear a word how it was done or why so that we can evaluate the actual role that she played," Swenson complained.

Crowley convinced Gale during a recess to spell out the creation story and she spent the rest of the afternoon detailing the development of the scent. Fred, Horner, and Roth deserved no credit for the development of the scent she testified, although she gave Fred credit for the marketing philosophy.

Grossman wanted to extend the daily sessions to 5 P.M. and complained about the shortened sessions that ended at 4 P.M. Gale brought her own Evian water and a leopard pillow to the proceedings. She became more self-assured as the days ground on, although during the third day, while discussing the embarrassment of being fired from Giorgio, she lost her composure and cried, necessitating a recess. The depositions ended on August 28 and produced almost a thousand pages of Gale's testimony. Giorgio's attorneys would use only twenty pages as exhibits to bolster their defense in November. Gale's acknowledgement that she did not perform any service to the corporation between February 1985 and June 1985 was a point that could justify cutting off her salary. The other portion of testimony submitted to the court was more germane and involved Gale's giving Fred control of the company in 1983. Gale testified she willingly gave control to Fred to placate his ego and admitted her attorney advised her that there existed the possibility a disagreement with Fred could lead to her firing.

The July 11 Giorgio board meeting and the deposition were held behind closed doors. Neither the press nor the fragrance industry had been aware of Gale's deteriorating situation. The reasons for her lockout were never explained to Giorgio employees, leading to speculation within the company and the industry of her misdeeds. The lawsuit let the public in on her losing power struggle.

The strain of the legal imbroglio was affecting Gale's health and relationship with Stalew. "It was a bad time; I don't want to say how bad, but let me tell you it was bad," Stalew says.

> Gale's smile was not there anymore. She didn't sleep well, she was not in good shape, and I began to worry about her. You can't take that much emotional shock and negativity for too long. The religious studies helped—maybe it kept her from snapping. She did some positive thinking and listened to positive tapes and maybe that's what held it together, because I was worried she would snap. She had temporary things where she would give up for a night or a weekend, but she fought and came back.

Stalew was frustrated and powerless. He saw Gale slipping away from him; she was withdrawing and becoming less communicative. Igor tried to help Gale by researching law firms and corporate compensation packages to compare Fred's salary with those of executives in much larger corporations. He also took Gale out to meet and befriend influential politicians. Stalew saw Gale's problem as a power play, with Fred having the advantage of political connections. He set out to court Congressman Anthony Bielenson and District Attorney Ira Reiner. Lieutenant Governor Leo McCarthy also became part of Gale's circle; she would host a dinner for him when he ran unsuccessfully for the U.S. Senate in 1988.

Igor considered himself a computer whiz and could spend hours trying to cure computer viruses. Unfortunately, his computer expertise backfired when he overruled Red Weiss and Angela Arensman, whom Weiss brought in as controller, on choosing a computer system for Gale Hayman, Inc. On Igor's recommendation, the fledgling company put in an Apple computer; but when Stalew accidentally erased some of the work in the system, Gale went into a rage and had Weiss call him to say he was barred from the office and to turn in his key.

Says Stalew,

> I was angry and frustrated by this whole thing. Here is this monster, power politics and ego. All I could do with this absurd stuff was to be as positive as possible and think about strategic things that Gale or her lawyers may not have thought about. Then Gale got more and more withdrawn. Finally it reached a point where it was tough for us. She couldn't be receptive to love, but you stay with a person who is in that situation. You don't abandon them.

The industry knew the company's momentum had slowed primarily because the women's scent had peaked. Retailers knew that without a new fragrance, Gould would not be able to pull a miracle and stop the slide during the Christmas season, and they sensed the relationship between Gould and Hayman was less than perfect. Horner on his travels kept the retailers well informed of the "Robinson's wrecking crew" progress. In September, Fred told *WWD* the second Giorgio's women's fragrance would not be ready in November and the party to commemorate the twenty-fifth anniversary would not be held. "We are not ready and will keep working on it. We will launch in the spring if we have a really extraordinary fragrance. We didn't want to cut off development work until we had something great. There will be no compromise. I'm disappointed we can't launch this November but there is no urgent need for a second fragrance."

There was an urgent need for a second fragrance in November to spark the Giorgio business. Fragrance-industry growth was at a standstill and only the manufacturers who were aggressively advertising, promoting, and putting new product into an already stuffed pipeline would grab the consumer's attention. The exciting new scent was Christian Dior's Poison, which launched exclusively at Bloomingdale's and almost instantly became the top brand at the 59th Street flagship. Though it was not the only new scent of the fall 1986 season, Poison clearly had the most cachet. Other new brands, including Liz Claiborne, Decadence, and Scherrer 2, failed to take off in September.

Had Giorgio been able to come up with its second fragrance, there was a good chance of success against the other new brands, especially given Giorgio's excellent space, location, and reputation. As Jim Roth would later say with a touch of bitterness, "Giorgio needed a new fragrance, and with a new fragrance and innovative plans we could have had another blockbuster. Calvin Klein had Obsession and then he had Eternity. Giorgio never got its Eternity, instead it got the Robinson's Wrecking Crew. Instead of Eternity, it got Oblivion." Finally in 1989, long after Horner and Roth's departure from Giorgio, Inc., a second scent, called Red, was successfully launched.

The only major new wrinkle Giorgio was preparing for retailers and consumers for Christmas 1986 was its first attempt at television advertising. The commercial featured an exploding champagne bottle and looked more like a spot for soap suds. It was conceived by Funck and Giorgio's Los Angeles–based agency, Eisaman, Johns & Laws Advertising, Inc. Fred was not included in the creative process and never approved the spot. Neither retailers nor consumers reacted enthusiastically to the commercial.

Roth and Horner packed up their bag of tricks and left Giorgio, Inc., at the end of September, allowing Gould to cement his organization. Roth and Horner opened a new IMG office at 9100 Wilshire Boulevard in Beverly Hills and started entertaining new fragrance ventures. Soon they would hook up with Caesars World Merchandising, a division of the gambling and resort operation, to launch a Caesars Woman and Caesars Man fragrance. They left Giorgio, Inc., without hard feelings on the surface and still were owed one large cash payment based on the fall season's profits. They accepted Fred Hayman's weekly invitations to lunch at The Bistro. "We became Fred's sounding board and had lunch once a week with him when he was in town," Horner said. " 'I regret it didn't work out. I'm sorry; we should all remain friends,' he told us. Fred probably realized sixty days into his deal with Gould that he had probably made the biggest mistake in his life."

In mid-October, Gale accidentally came face to face with Fred at a cocktail party at the Westwood Marquis Hotel. She used the occasion to try to make peace.

I shook his hand and said, "Why don't we try to work this out; only the lawyers are getting rich," and he said, "Sure, Gale, I agree." I felt really good. Gee, isn't that great that we will probably be able to work it out between the two of us. "What is the next step?" I asked, and he said he would tell his lawyer to work it out tomorrow. His idea of working it out was to give me almost nothing, and that is what made me really mad. It was demeaning; it was insulting.

Fred's offer was for less than $10 million, Gale said, and was so low because the company was not doing well. She did not give the offer much consideration.

Grossman denies Fred made such a low offer and maintains the offer was $50 million:

Any suggestion that Fred tried to buy Gale out for a song is insanity. Fred was adamant that if Giorgio was sold, it had to be for a fair price and if an attempt was made to buy his stock or if he tried to buy her stock it had to be fair. From a practical point of view neither could afford to buy the other out. It would not have been a good business decision for either to assume a debt of between fifty and one hundred million to buy each other out. It would have required mortgaging their entire fortunes and risking everything on the continued success of a fairy tale.

Fred's attorneys were planning a cross-complaint against Gale, and Roth and Horner agreed to testify. Before Fred could file for his cross-complaint, on October 23, Gale's attorneys filed an amended lawsuit against Fred and Giorgio asking the court to fasten a constructive trust on Fred's new salary which was estimated at between $5 million and $6 million. In addition, Gale asked for an extra $50 million in damages because of "wrongful acts." She had asked for $75 million in the May filing.

The new complaint alleged Fred's salary was a disguised dividend to him while Gale had been cut off from salary and dividends at the July 11 board meeting. Due to the company's Subchapter S tax status, Gale was exposed to 49 percent of Giorgio's federal tax liabilities and without compensation had been put in a "supine position." Gale charged that Fred's new compensation package was a plan to force her to sell her 49 percent of the company to Fred for a fraction of its true value.

Fred's salary was "grossly and vastly excessive," the complaint charged, contending senior executives of Southern California's leading companies have salaries rarely exceeding .1 percent of gross sales, whereas Fred was receiving 5 percent. Gould's hiring reduced Fred to "part-time" services, making his $5 million salary all the more excessive. Fred breached his fiduciary duties when he nixed the Lauder deal, the suit further alleged. A court date of December 4 was set before Judge Warren Deering.

Fred's feisty court defense began on November 24 when his attorneys filed opposition papers to Gale's suits. The papers included Fred's deposition and recounted his version of Gale's 1985 ouster. The defense attempted to justify Fred's salary and pointed out Gale was not in immediate harm, given the $20 million she had received from the company. "They [Giorgio, Inc.] have put more than $20 million in plaintiff's pocket in the past three years. Only a mind as Machiavellian as plaintiff's could even imagine such a scheme, let alone prove it," the defense document read.

The document compared other privately held companies such as Aaron Spelling Productions and Reebok, Inc., whose founders were taking salaries comparable to or larger than Fred's. The document downscaled Gale's contributions and gave Roth, Horner, and Fred equal credit in selecting the women's scent. Fred's involvement since Gould's arrival had not been diminished, the defense asserted, as he continued to work nine hours a day, six days a week with responsibilities for running the Rodeo store, merchandise buying and promotional work for the fragrance. In addition, he had taken a new office in the Santa Monica fragrance division headquarters. Fred's deposition took exception to Gale's assertion that he was spending time on a yacht. "I remain committed on more than a full-time basis to the leadership of Giorgio, and I believe we are poised for dramatic new growth. I do not own a yacht, or even a dinghy."

On December 1, Fred tried to sink Gale when he filed a $13,711,000 countersuit, claiming she had breached her contract and fiduciary duties. The $13 million damage figure represented Gale's salary from 1983 throughout 1986. The countersuit alleged Gale did not fulfill her contract and was disloyal to the company. "She has used and continues to use Giorgio trade secrets and other proprietary and business information confidential to Giorgio for her own purposes and without authorization (particularly in connection with her own company, Gale Hayman, Inc.)." The document failed to provide specific evidence of the use of trade secrets.

Hayman vs. *Hayman* certainly did not have the makings of a precedent-setting legal case. What started out as a tiff for control of a fragrance company was being blown into a complicated legal battle by some of Los Angeles's most expensive lawyers. Although she initiated the suit, Gale loathed spending time and money with lawyers, realizing they were the prime beneficiaries. Judge Deering put the matter in proper legal perspective on December 4, when he held a brief hearing in his chambers in downtown Los Angeles Superior Court. His courtroom is several floors above the room where Fred and Gale had been married twenty years before (November 21, 1966), but this day neither Fred nor Gale came to court. Deering was asked to adjudicate the Haymans' corporate divorce.

Gale was in New York on December 4. Fred remained in Beverly Hills. Crowley and Cuneo had not made much progress and Gale added Ed Rosenfeld of Patterson Belknap to her legal team. Rosenfeld specialized in corporate matters and was recommended by Ira Wender, the attorney, who had represented Lauder during the Giorgio negotiations. Rosenfeld's contention that Gale was in a "supine position" because she was unable to meet her $5 million income-tax liability was heard by Deering against Grossman's claim that Gale could easily afford to pay the taxes because of the $20 million she had received. Rosenfeld charged Fred's salary was unreasonable compared to the $2.5 million salary of the president of Walt Disney Studios. Grossman countered by saying it's impossible to put a price on "creative genius."

Judge Deering issued his decision on December 12 and shot down Gale's attempt to restrain Fred's salary. He refused to grant a preliminary injunction blocking Fred's compensation and wrote in his two-page decision that Fred was the dominant force in the company's success. Deering noted Gale failed to demonstrate that her assets couldn't meet her tax obligations, citing her $20 million salary and dividends of the three prior years.

Gale lost on all counts. If it had been a football game, she would have gone down 56–0 and been carried off the field on a stretcher. Grossman exercised bragging rights by telling *WWD* that Fred had been fully vindicated and was not going to settle the dispute out of court. "If Gale Hayman expects any money to pass to settle her claims, she will have to pay."

Rosenfeld said the court applied the wrong standards and he would appeal Deering's decision. While Rosenfeld prepared papers and filed an appeal, Gale started shopping for a new lawyer. Rosenfeld had failed to produce results and his bills were mounting. During the Christmas holidays she averaged two to three daily interviews with prospective attorneys, quizzing them about their proposed strategies for her case.

Gale gave her employees sweaters from The Limited for Christmas. She was investing around $1.5 million to get her company going, and she was worried about money. After failing to convince Linda Wachner, the former Max Factor chief executive officer who had connections with Alder & Shaykin, to invest, Gale was financing the start-up on her own.

By December 30 Gale had dismissed Rosenfeld. Red Weiss called *WWD* to say Rosenfeld was out and a new legal contact would be named shortly. The attorney most highly recommended to Gale by her tax attorney and her contacts in law enforcement was Hillel Chodos, who, unlike her other lawyers, was a tough litigator and could be crude. Unfortunately for Gale, Chodos's secretary told her he was not accepting any new clients. Gale was depressed by her situation and approaching desperation. She got out the phone book and looked up Chodos. His address was 9595 Wilshire Boulevard, in Beverly Hills, the same as Giorgio, Inc. The coincidence was meaningful for Gale, who believes in karma, and she sent Chodos the court documents with a note. Chodos called Gale at her home at 9:30 that night and said that although he couldn't take the case, he thought she was being treated unfairly.

For fifteen years, Chodos, fifty-three, had specialized in complex business litigation in his one-man law firm. Although he tried to stay out of the press as much as possible, Chodos had several high-profile clients and in 1980 served on the state commission for judicial performance, which held televised hearings that year. At six-feet-two and three hundred pounds, Chodos looked mean and had developed a reputation for never bluffing. In his current office is a bronze of classical Greek wrestlers, adversaries tearing each other's head off. A colorful, built-in aquarium is filled with predatory fish Chodos watches intently, explaining that often the larger fish swallow the smaller ones.

Ironically, from his sixth-floor office he could see Gale's old office on the fifth floor. Over the years, Chodos had seen a dapper, gray-haired gentleman in the elevator accompanied by his dog. Eventually he learned the man was Fred Hayman, the successful entrepreneur of Giorgio, Inc., but the two never exchanged pleasantries. As well-tailored as Hayman is, Chodos is the opposite, seldom dressing in a suit unless he has to make a court appearance. He frequently wears casual slacks and a mismatched shirt to the office and is fond of working in his stocking feet. However, like Fred he works incredibly long hours, a habit with which Gale Hayman could identify.

After three phone calls from Gale, Chodos agreed to take her case and Gale returned to 9595 Wilshire. She knew she had to change the direction of the suit, and in early January 1987, Chodos provided her with a radical new tactic. It was obvious to Chodos that Gale's original suit to get back into the company was an uphill fight. According to Chodos, she had "a gorilla in the living room." Her giving Fred the 51 percent control made her original complaint and amended suit a tough case and a waste to pursue. A better strategy was to try to dissolve the company. Gale realized she would never go back to the office she could see from Chodos's window, but she was not willing to capitulate to Fred. If liquidating Giorgio, Inc., was a viable solution to her dilemma, she was ready to explore it.

With his big court victory in December, Fred became less concerned with legal issues; he was trying to focus on the business and maintain Giorgio's number-one position. On January 5, over lunch at the Bistro Garden, Fred's ego appeared bruised over the brand's slippage in some key accounts and he was threatening to pull the line. "We are number one now; I'm too proud to be number three," Hayman said while eying the table next to him, where Barbara Walters was hosting a prewedding luncheon for Alexis Mass, soon to become the new Mrs. Johnny Carson.

Carson was now Fred's neighbor in the Point Dume section of Malibu. Fred had bought a small, unspectacular house that he planned to rebuild about eight miles north of the Malibu Colony. The house sat on a bluff and from the large front yard, Fred could watch the waves rolling into Paradise Cove carrying surfers and dolphins. Fred and Betty followed a rickety stairway down to the beach where they walked every weekend. As he had entertained at Charleville for many years, Fred now enjoyed the more relaxed and athletic atmosphere at the beach. Guests invited for Sunday lunch were first offered a chance to bicycle around the Point Dume area, with its share of steep hills that Fred easily could handle. Next, there was Ping-Pong in the driveway, with Fred allowing Peter Jaram, the manager of the Giorgio men's store, to represent him and the store against the most athletic guest. Then, before lunch, a long walk on the beach. Finally, a simple buffet luncheon was served by a white-coated butler at 4 P.M.

At The Bistro Garden, Fred was trying to impress the press and scare a few retailers. "We may limit the fragrance to those who understand us. We are prestige, we are class and must be treated like a star or otherwise the fragrance will suffer. To me this business is more than just money, it's staying power and style." Fred thought Giorgio was overdistributed although it was in only five hundred doors, still the tightest distribution of any major fragrance in the industry.

Fred's legal problems were about to flare up and give him indigestion. He went to Smoke Enders to kick his cigarette habit, but with the added stress of Gale's new litigation could not quit. California state law allows a shareholder with at least a 33 percent stock ownership in a company the legal right to dissolve that firm. If that stockholder has between 33 and 49 percent of the shares, the majority stockholder can avoid dissolution by either buying out the minority shareholder at an appraised value or selling to a third party. Chodos planned to use this statute and wanted to show that Gale owned more than her 49 percent of the stock. The 2 percent trust that gave Fred control would shift to Gale when Fred died, but Chodos was preparing an argument that Gale had a piece of that 2 percent. He was going to use the almost twenty-year age difference between Gale and Fred to ask the court to reconsider. The age gap gave Gale fairly good odds on gaining control of Giorgio at some point in her lifetime.

Chodos said, "Whether the court would have accepted that Gale had better than 50 percent of the company based on her age, I don't know, but it was something to make Fred and Marshall Grossman run down for Rolaids." At the very least, a dissolution suit could force Fred to buy Gale out. Or it could force him to sell to a third party. There was also the risk that he would be stubborn and let the company be liquidated and nobody would get very much.

On January 16, 1987, Chodos filed a complaint for involuntary dissolution, asking the Superior Court to force the company to be sold to a third party for cash. If such a sale could not be accomplished then the corporation should be liquidated. The suit asked the court to appoint a receiver to take over Giorgio and manage it pending a hearing and determination of the complaint.

Gale's intention was not to liquidate Giorgio, but to force the sale of Giorgio to a third party and cash out. Chodos explained to Gale, "If you start out to blow up the company, you have to be prepared that if you blow it up nobody gets anything. You are playing chicken and you have to be prepared for a head-on collision. You have to be emotionally ready for total destruction. It's not likely, but it's possible. If Fred toughs it out, you blow it up and nobody gets a dime." Gale was prepared to take the chance; at this point she was getting no dimes out of Giorgio anyway.

In his eight-page dissolution complaint, Chodos pointed out the Haymans' age discrepancy and charged Fred with allowing the business to slip. Due to "wastefully caused" administrative and operating expenses, Giorgio's net profits dropped 46 percent in fiscal 1986. Sales and gross profits increased 10 percent for the year. Operating expenses were 41 percent higher for the fiscal year. The suit said Giorgio accountants were the source for the figures.

Grossman had a confident reaction to the new suit. He told the *Los Angeles Times*, "Gale Hayman has not been a part of Giorgio's management for better than a year now, and this lawsuit is significant because it's an admission on her part of the reality that she will not be rejoining the management of Giorgio." To *WWD* he said, "This new suit is nothing but the same old charges that were rejected last month in court, only dressed up in a new package. The fact that she has lost with a full airing of her charges is likely to have an influence on any judge who hears the same charges over again. The courts don't take lightly to those who try to take two bites out of the same apple." Grossman added that Giorgio was not on the auction block and there would be no settlement with Gale.

Privately, Grossman and Fred both knew that as a 49 percent shareholder in Giorgio, Inc., Gale was entitled to substantial stockholder rights. A permanent separation between Gale and Fred was the only way out. Grossman and Fred were afraid Gale's new legal challenge would further "pollute" the image of Giorgio and lessen the company's value.

The public face Fred adopted was that Giorgio, Inc., was not for sale and he was content with the status quo. Fred could cloak his misery from most of his friends and business acquaintances. He never answered Gale's challenge in the press, which gained him additional respect among his friends. Mr. Blackwell, the designer and creator of the ten best- and worst-dressed lists, knew Fred from the Hilton days and acquired a dislike bordering on hatred for Gale. "I began to feel terribly sorry for Fred because I saw him being demolished emotionally by her very assy attitude. He was taking it hard but in a conservative, quiet way. He learned the class way and never let it show, he had a lot of class and he covered up very well and never publicly stood up to her."

In reality, according to Grossman, Fred was eager to unload both Gale and Giorgio, Inc., but he figured if that eagerness were known in the industry it would reduce the price of an already tarnished company. His apparent reluctance also would make Gale more pliable in negotiations, should a third party come along and make an offer. Gale would have to find that buyer; Salomon Brothers did not want to represent the company any longer and Fred was not in a position to go looking for a suitor given his sensitive position in the company. Grossman and Fred hoped Gale could find a buyer who would offer at least $150 million, which would put $75 million in Fred's pocket.

Chodos called Grossman and began to talk in tough language Grossman could understand.

I said, "Look, Marshall, figure it out, you have outdone yourselves, you have taken everything away from her and she has nothing to lose—she has half the company and no salary, no dividends, no office, no typewriter, and she is being vilified in the press. Fred and his people are running the company into the ground, expenses are up, profits have gone to hell, their market is degenerating and it's turning to shit. Gale has made up her mind, she is taking it right to the wall. Don't even speculate that she may be joking about dissolving the company." Marshall then starts telling me that Fred is stubborn and won't agree to this or that and I said, "Well, fuck him then, if he can't take a joke."

Chodos said Grossman told him Gale would not be able to find a buyer for Giorgio, Inc. " 'Don't be so sure,' I told him. The basic position that emanated from Fred and Marshall was that Gale is just a woman, a housewife."

Convinced the dissolution complaint had put her in the driver's seat, Gale went to New York in mid-February and decided not to return to California until she found a buyer. She had confidence in Chodos and started believing they could rally and win. Gale saw Chodos as the hammer and herself as the nail. Together they would make some major alterations on the house of Giorgio. Fred would be hard pressed to reject an offer on a par with the Lauder deal, if it could be found.

Working out of her New York apartment on 52nd Street overlooking the East River, Gale started calling major cosmetics companies to ascertain if there was any interest in Giorgio, Inc. If anyone expressed an interest, she turned him over to Chodos, who would supply Giorgio's financial data and talk terms. She wasn't employing investment bankers now. Estée Lauder, Inc., was a natural starting point, as they had been close to a deal in 1986; but Leonard Lauder was no longer interested. Revlon was about to embark on its acquisition binge and Gale approached Ronald Perelman, Revlon's new owner. He made a perfunctory low bid. She also contacted Cosmair, the owner of Lancôme, and The Limited, the national specialty-store chain run by Leslie Wexner. It began to appear as if Giorgio were not high on anyone's list. Sales had softened and there was the unresolved legal imbroglio. Gale grew increasingly uptight.

Avon Products, Inc., was on Gale's list and she found Jim Preston, president of Avon's beauty division, to have more than cordial curiosity about Giorgio, Inc. Avon was a cash-rich company in transition, eager for an acquisition that would allow entry into the high-priced retail fragrance business.

Increased numbers of women in the work force meant Avon representatives were finding fewer women answering the doorbell and, during a six-year period in the late 1970s and early 1980s, Avon's sales were flat and earnings were on the decline in the U.S. Although Avon's sales had improved 16 percent in 1986, to over $2.8 billion, Avon's management had been planning since 1983 to become less reliant on door-to-door direct selling. The company wanted to enter retail distribution through a combination of acquisitions and internally generated startup ventures.

Avon, which celebrated its one hundredth anniversary in 1986, had originally been called the California Perfume Company. Over the years it had developed the most prodigious product-development department in the industry. Avon annually churned out over three hundred new products for the U.S. market, at least twice as many new items as the other industry giants. Management wanted to turn that force loose on the retail market. Avon's research showed it was missing out on 85 percent of all the fragrance and cosmetics business done in America.

Avon had a twofold retail strategy. First, the company started its own retail fragrance division called Parfums Phenix, through which it was planning the launch of a Catherine Deneuve fragrance in the late spring. Avon also got involved in a joint venture with Liz Claiborne, Inc., to market the designer's first fragrance. The second element was acquisitions, and in 1986 Avon made a strong bid to acquire Charles of the Ritz/Yves St. Laurent from the Squibb Corporation. St. Laurent's Opium fragrance was the key attraction for Avon, but St. Laurent and his business partner, Pierre Bergé, wanted to buy back the YSL fragrance franchise from Squibb and outbid Avon, paying $635 million. Avon, a careful, methodical company, bowed out of the Ritz bidding after Bergé played hardball. He told Avon officials if Avon were successful in acquiring the Ritz/YSL brands, there would be very little cooperation in the future from the YSL camp. Squibb could not promise Avon the Parisians would cooperate if Avon owned the brand. YSL would later sell off the Ritz part of the business to Revlon.

Elizabeth Arden was also for sale in 1987 and Avon started sniffing around, but Eli Lilly's asking price—over $700 million—was much too high, Avon's executives reasoned.

On Friday, March 13, Jules Zimmerman, Avon's chief financial officer, got a call from Gale Hayman. Zimmerman called Preston to gauge his interest level in a meeting with Gale. Preston didn't mince words:

> You bet your sweet bippy we were interested. We knew from the press accounts of the Lauder/Giorgio negotiations, a deal that didn't go through at the last moment, and we thought Gale and Fred wouldn't sell and it was a dead issue. When we got the call we were quite surprised and excited about the opportunity. Giorgio may have peaked in 1985, but it was a dynamite brand with strong loyalty in the marketplace, with tremendous international potential and was totally underdeveloped. There were no product extensions worth a damn, except in the bath area; and in the men's area they just had a spray.

Gale was invited to Avon's boardroom on Wednesday, March 18, to meet Preston, Zimmerman, and Bill Henn, a senior vice president of strategic planning and development. The room is dominated by a sleek, thirty-foot wooden table, a large video screen, and eighteen leather chairs. An anteroom with Oriental rugs and vases softens the businesslike atmosphere. An array of Avon cosmetics and fragrances was displayed on the table, as Preston wanted to impress Gale with Avon's product capability. He also wanted to use the first meeting to test the chemistry between Gale and Avon. It may have been Beverly Hills meets the Heartland, but it was an almost perfect match. Avon could rescue Gale from purgatory by acquiring Giorgio, and Giorgio could help Avon establish itself overnight in the retail fragrance world.

Avon's officials had done their homework and knew the strengths and weaknesses of Giorgio; but Preston, with his friendly, colloquial style, did not come off as if he were an expert on the prestige fragrance market. He complimented Gale on the great job she had done for the company and told a short story about a secretary at Avon who was wearing a strong fragrance on the elevator one day. When Preston asked what she was wearing, she said Giorgio. He was impressed that the woman paid retail for Giorgio, as Avon employees get Avon fragrances for free. The secretary looked a little guilty, but Preston assured her it was okay because Giorgio was a great fragrance. During the meeting with Gale, Preston explained Avon's evolution and desire to crack the retail fragrance field and how important Giorgio could be to that strategy. Gale told the Avon officials about her input at Giorgio and how she envisioned the company going forward. The meeting lasted two hours and money was not discussed. A second meeting was planned for early the next week. Gale conferred with Kenneth Jay Lane, who had a contract with Avon to design costume jewelry pieces for the door-to-door market, and he assured her Avon was honorable, a fine company to do business with.

At the second meeting, more substantive issues were discussed. The price Avon was willing to pay for Giorgio, Inc., was of primary concern; but of almost equal importance was Fred's willingness to sell the company. "Gale said there was a probability Fred would sell to the right company at the right price, so at that point we started to talk about price. Based upon what she knew, the price we came up with was reasonable, but obviously it had to meet the test of Fred and his lawyers," Preston said. Taking into account the Lauder offers and where Giorgio stood now, Avon was preparing to make an all-cash offer of $185 million.

Chodos went to New York to negotiate with Preston and his executives, and after three days, the price of $185 million was set. Gale was eager to take the offer, but the deal hinged on Fred's willingness to go along. The lengthy and failed Lauder negotiations were still fresh and

Gale did not want the scenario repeated. Chodos called Grossman, told him there was an offer, and then clamped on the final squeeze:

> Grossman asked me, "How do I know the offer is real?" I said, "Trust me, Marshall, it's real. You can take it or leave it, but here is the deal. If you don't take the deal, I'm going down to court tomorrow to get a summary judgment for dissolution." I had the papers in my hand and I delivered them to Marshall. The summary judgment papers had financial statements, had the stupid contract with Gould. It was all there and essentially laid out why Gale wanted to dissolve the company. The press would have jumped on it like a duck on a june bug.
>
> Marshall said, "If you file this, you will kill the opportunity to get this price [$185 million]." I said, "Yeah, but I got an offer now. You can take the offer now or you can take the risk that your client bears the entire decline when I file this." I didn't give him any time—Marshall doesn't give you any slack—and he understood our strategy perfectly. I said, "Look, Marshall, I'm holding the pistol now. If you had it, you would put it to my head. There are no hard feelings." I don't know what he said to Fred, but he came back in one day and said, "We will do business."

Predictably, Grossman's account of the Avon deal differs substantially from Chodos's: "Chodos's threat of filing for a summary judgment was no more weighty than the several ounces of the papers he had. He had been threatening to file those papers for weeks, months, and each time I told him, 'Go ahead, file your damn papers.' Those charges were so shopworn and had been made previously by Gale. Chodos's papers had zero impact on the Avon deal." Grossman went on,

> Hillel called me and said Avon was prepared to pay one hundred eighty-five million. I asked how would the money be divided he said fifty-fifty and after consulting with Fred, we decided one hundred eighty-five million is more money than anybody could expect to see in a lifetime. I told Hillel Fred was interested in the Avon deal but really wanted to keep the store. He didn't know if that was possible nor did he care. I told Chodos I would call Avon separately and I called Jules Zimmerman. After thirty seconds we were on a first-name basis and I asked him how important was it for Avon to own the store. He asked, "How much is Fred willing

to pay for it?" and I said, "Five million." He called back within one hour and said, "The store is Fred's for five million," and I said, "Then we have a deal."

On April 7, 1986, Avon Products, Inc., announced it had reached an agreement in principle to purchase Giorgio, Inc., for $185 million in cash. The deal had been approved by Avon's board and was scheduled for closing May 7. The most amazing parts of the announcement were the sale back to Fred of the Rodeo Drive Giorgio boutique and Avon's discussion with Gale of the possibility of her remaining creatively involved with Giorgio. Avon was considering bringing back Gale, who had been in exile for over two years. If it happened, Gale would be involved in the Giorgio fragrance business and Fred would be on the outside. Both would be considerably richer, splitting the $185 million.

News of the negotiations had not been leaked to the press, and it came as a shock to Giorgio employees at the perfume company in Santa Monica and the store on Rodeo Drive. There were tears from the women who had worked in the store with Fred and Gale from the start. What would Avon do with Giorgio? The first assumption was that the fragrance company would be moved to New York, but these fears were unfounded. Fred showed up at a backyard cocktail party at Gould's home the night before the announcement and seemed preoccupied the whole night, not his normal charming self. The next day Gould was conducting a national sales meeting in Giorgio's small upstairs conference room and Fred interrupted the meeting, summoning Gould to tell him about the Avon deal.

"The first words out of my mouth were, 'Are you happy?' " Gould recalls asking Fred:

He said he didn't know and I said, "More important than you being happy, you will be a lot healthier," and I said mazeltov. I watched that man and saw what the lawsuit was doing to his health. I don't think Fred was mean or vituperative or vindictive, but that lawsuit made him such a different person, it was criminal. I don't think one person [Gale] had the right to do that to another person.

I said to myself this was the greatest thing that could happen to the company and the best thing that could happen to Fred. Not because he was going to walk away with all the money but from his health point of view. He was in a no-win situation. He was preoccupied with the lawsuit—in his phrase, he was "expending negative energy."

On April 8, Jim Preston and Fred Hayman met for the first time, when Fred took Preston to dinner at The Bistro. Using a conciliatory approach, Preston told Fred he understood how difficult it must be for both Fred and Gale to have put so much creative energy into a business and now having those energies diverted by the litigation. He promised Fred if Avon bought the company it would be nourished and would grow. Fred told Preston that because of the struggle with Gale, it might be easier for Giorgio to grow in the hands of a third party. Preston had spent much of his career working in the field with Avon's sales force. Fred and Gale represented glamour and he was more than impressed. "Fred is one of the world's great people, he is a gentleman—urbane, intelligent," says Preston. "He knows the market as Gale does, too. I can see why the two were so successful. They understand the Beverly Hills market and the cachet. They know how to talk it, they know how to build on it, and they know how to live it."

By taking the Avon deal, Fred was off the hot seat. He had been squeezed by Gale on the outside and by Gould on the inside, and it was no longer fun to lead Giorgio, Inc. Fred's relationship with Gould had deteriorated badly and he accused Gould of not keeping him informed of decisions in the company, both major and minor. When Gould gave a speech to women cosmetics executives in New York, Fred had a fit because he wasn't told. He felt he was losing control of his company, and was "out of the loop." Fred fell into a managerial trap that perplexes and frustrates many successful entrepreneurs. After hiring high-priced talent, he could not give up the reins; and tension over his broken promises wrought havoc with employee morale.

Fred stopped using his Santa Monica office and remained in Beverly Hills, avoiding face-to-face confrontations with Gould. He communicated his displeasure through Katy Sweet or other people in the company with whom he was comfortable. They, in turn, would let Gould know the chairman was not happy.

Gould never could adjust to Fred's style. He refused to mimic the Fred Hayman personalized touches of sending thank you notes, explaining that returning all his phone calls should be enough to qualify him for "mensch" status. Fred's consensus decision-making further frustrated Gould. Toward the end, Fred's attorney, Leo Ziffren, was frequently in attendance during meetings with Gould. Despite his fat contract, by early 1987 Gould was unhappy enough to consider leaving Giorgio, Inc.

Fred could no longer wear two crowns—the king of Rodeo Drive and the emperor of perfume. He had to give something up and he chose to keep the store, which he repurchased from Avon for a bargain-basement price. The Rodeo Drive real estate alone would be worth $5

million. Avon was taking the New York Giorgio boutique. Fred was allowed to keep the Giorgio logo on the Rodeo store until January 1, 1989,
when, in addition to losing the Giorgio logo, he would have to bid adieu
to his yellow-and-white stripes. The famous boutique at 273 North Rodeo
Drive would have to be outfitted with new awnings as well as a new
name.

Fred declined comments to the press on April 7, but Grossman told
WWD, "Fred Hayman is delighted with the agreement and is pleased
Giorgio, Inc., will be in the good hands of Avon. Fred is also pleased he
will continue the sole ownership and management of the boutique and
he will continue to have a presence in the industry." Grossman refuted
the contention that Fred sold out because of the legal pressure. "There
certainly was no pressure from the litigation. The court vindicated Fred
and Giorgio, Inc., in every major hearing, including Gale's effort to
preclude Fred's right to draw his annual compensation. This sale to Avon
buries the hatchet between them."

The sale to Avon may have ended the litigation, but the lawyers were
the clear-cut winners. The combined legal fees of Fred, Gale, and Giorgio,
Inc., during the debacle were in excess of $3 million.

Gale was in New York, hard at work on her new cosmetics line and,
although she did not boast to the press, considered the Avon deal to be
her victory. After being thrown out of the company and cut off financially
from Giorgio, Gale now stood to pocket well over $50 million from the
deal. Further, Avon was interested in keeping her involved in Giorgio in
the capacity of consultant. She celebrated the sale with a quiet dinner
at Le Cirque with Kenneth Jay Lane. The Avon deal was almost anticli-
mactic after the last two years. Gale told *WWD* on April 8,

> I'm extremely enthusiastic about the sale. It finally resolves all
> the negativity. I'm impressed how quickly Avon moved for such
> a large company and how professionally they think. Giorgio is still
> number one in the U.S. and Avon has great plans for its future.
> I'm still president and chief executive officer of Gale Hayman Bev-
> erly Hills and I'm in the midst of launching my new line in Sep-
> tember. I wish Fred well and I'm happy to get on with my life.

Privately, Gale was pleased she had forced a solution and found a
deal that was good for all parties, Fred included.

> I remember what Al Taubman told me: "The only good deal is a
> deal that is good for everyone." I repeat that often to people that
> I negotiate with now. This was a deal that was great for everyone

and I was very happy to see it happen. Do I think I won? I think we all won. I brought a second fabulous deal to Fred and Fred never did anything. I think I did a pretty terrific job, and he still hasn't sent me flowers.

Although they were not being quoted in the press, Roth and Horner had their own observations about the deal. They maintained Fred sold because he was clamped in an untenable vise between Gale, Gould, and the fragrance business, which was stagnating domestically. Horner said, with a few sour grapes in his mouth:

Eighteen months ago, someone [Lauder] offered $185 million and, in my mind, greed and ego caused that deal to not go through. After that deal he lost me and Jimmy and got new management and the profits were down fifty percent. Avon then came to him and dramatically overpaid for the company and gave him a magnificent opportunity to save face in his lawsuit. I would hope Fred would take between eight to ten percent of the proceeds from the sale and distribute them amongst the people in the company who have been there for more than two or three years and have had to endure the Robinson's wrecking crew. Fred should make some people comfortable who have been loyal to him.

Despite all the talk, the deal was not final when the May 7 closing deadline passed. A logjam had been created by new demands from Avon and the deal was in jeopardy of blowing up. Avon's accountants pored over the Giorgio books and examined the operation in their late April due diligence review. The contracts Fred had given the Robinson's crew, especially Gould's, were not acceptable to Avon. Gould's salary was higher than Preston's and Avon could not allow him to continue working for Giorgio with his seven-figure contract. Fred would have to buy out the remaining two years of Gould's contract. The Giorgio figures showed the company's sales had been slightly under $100 million in 1985, going slightly over $100 million in 1986; profits, however, had gone from $39 million to $29 million in 1986. The figures were not what the Avon executives had expected and they were also alarmed at the heavy inventories in the retail accounts. Avon would pay $165 million for Giorgio, Inc., and not a cent more.

Fred went to New York to host his last Giorgio fragrance launch party. A new men's fragrance, Giorgio VIP Reserve, was being launched nationally with Saks. VIP Reserve was actually a stronger, long-lasting version of the original Giorgio men's fragrance. Ironically, it was at Saks Fifth Avenue that Fred had hoped to launch the women's fragrance back in 1982, when he was snubbed. Nobody was snubbing him now, and the New York socialites (Judy Peabody, Nina Griscom, Kimberly Farkas) showed up at Mortimer's on April 22 to celebrate the new cologne and toast Fred on the impending Avon deal.

Fred was cornered by a *WWD* reporter and said, "Giorgio will always be mine emotionally. It feels sad but it also feels very good. We're leaving something very positive." The reporter asked what had pushed Hayman to sell. "It was a good offer to very good people who also understand the importance of Giorgio. I felt that by selling, I was not selling out."

Fred was willing to take the $165 million, although he did not believe anything warranted the price reduction. Gale would accept the $165 million offer only if Fred made up the $20 million difference and paid her $10 million. She took the position that the deal was being diminished because of Fred's poor management, which she had nothing to do with, as she was out of the company. She also was complaining bitterly about the sweet $5 million deal Fred was getting for the store and wanted part of that $10 million to reflect her interest in the store. Avon was eager to proceed with the deal but Chodos, Grossman, and their clients were at a stalemate.

Chodos attempted to break the impasse with a bullying legal tactic, again threatening to file a summary judgment for dissolution, including many of the old charges and some new ones. Grossman called Zimmerman at Avon and asked him what effect these papers would have on the deal:

> He said if those papers are filed Avon would no longer be the buyer. I called Chodos and said, "If you file those papers, be my guest; but Gale doesn't get her ten million and Gale doesn't get anything, because the deal with Avon is off." By the end of the week, Chodos called me back and it looked like the deal was not going forward. By now Fred wanted out. He was sick and tired of the craziness. He had within his grasp more money and independence than anyone could realize in his lifetime, but it was being threatened by his copartner, who was trying to get even more from the deal.

Chodos agreed to meet Grossman for Sunday brunch at the Beverly Hills Hotel. Fred had told Grossman to offer Gale $10 million if he had to, but he wanted to close the transaction. Over brunch Grossman offered Chodos $5 million, which he rejected. Grossman tried another approach.

Take the Avon deal now for $165 million before it slips away, and then go to arbitration and let an independent judge decide who gets the $10 million. Chodos agreed and on May 18 Avon announced that a definitive agreement had been reached and Giorgio would be acquired for $165 million in cash.

Charles Vogel, a judge in Los Angeles Superior Court between 1969 and 1977, was now a Century City litigator respected by both Chodos and Grossman. They hired him to arbitrate the dispute. In a high-stakes, $10 million crapshoot, Chodos and Grossman submitted to Vogel the volumes of court papers and affidavits that had previously been submitted to the courts. If *Hayman* vs. *Hayman* had gone to trial in the state courts, it would have been drawn out over a five- to six-year period. Vogel took four hours to hear the arguments by Chodos and Grossman. That evening, the respective attorneys received the verdict. Gale was awarded just $2.5 million. Fred was thrilled with the decision. Grossman said, "As soon as the deal with Avon was closed, Fred called and said he appreciated what we did for him. He said, 'You offered her five million; she turned it down and got two and a half million. There will be a two-and-a-half-million-dollar bonus check for your law firm.' "

Fred, in effect, bought back the store for $7.5 million, including the $5 million he paid Avon and the $2.5 million he paid Gale. Although Gale received more money than Fred in the transaction, both were winners, having pocketed over $50 million each for a business they had started with considerably less than $1 million.

After the sale closed, Fred took Betty Endo on a vacation to Acapulco. He was in a jocular mood. "I'm twenty years younger with all this money and I'm much more attractive. I don't have a blonde on both arms, but if you know of any, let me know," he joked in June. Actually, Fred was content to be with Betty. After three marriages and one messy business divorce, Fred had decided he would never remarry. Betty was not pressuring him for a ring and she attended to his needs at home, though he wasn't planning to spend much time there. Instead of relaxing over the summer, Fred plotted his future. At sixty-three, he was not going to wind down his operation. Expansion was on Fred's horizon; he was looking for bigger offices and new worlds to conquer.

Gale was putting in ten- to twelve-hour days preparing to launch her mail-order cosmetics catalogue in November 1987. She hired New York publicist Samantha Drake to stage her return to the cosmetics-industry spotlight.

Drake had been a publicist for Vidal Sassoon, Inc., where she saw the Vidal and Beverly Sassoon husband-and-wife team self-destruct. "Gale was now on the second drive for success and was driven to make up for the hurt that she felt from having been ignored and thrown out of

Giorgio," Drake said. She spent hours with Gale, tape-recording her life story to prepare a bio. Drake observed, "Gale's biggest problem is how to trust people. The disappointments have made it difficult for her to trust. She had been burned by her husbands."

The Giorgio fairy-tale/nightmare was over for Gale and Fred. Gould would stay on as president of Giorgio, Inc., in Santa Monica; the company would not be moved to New York. Avon's market research and manufacturing capabilities would bolster Giorgio's new product capacity, but Preston assured Gould that Giorgio would retain its creative autonomy. The Avon-Giorgio deal was not one of the blockbuster buyouts of the 1980s, but was among the top two hundred corporate acquisitions (*Business Week* ranked it 190) in America in 1987.

After over twenty years, Fred and Gale Hayman's business ties had been severed, making them richer than most of the spoiled people over whom they had fawned while building their boutique. Two Cinderellas from Beverly Hills, the Haymans waltzed into the fragrance industry in 1981. They were lucky enough to have more than one dance; together they consumed a few magnums of champagne and got to split $165 million. Yet despite their new wealth, neither Hayman would be content to slink back to Beverly Hills to enjoy it quietly. Both were restless and had something left to prove: to do it all over again, but on their own.

EPILOGUE

Although the pain in his back was intense, the short man in the charcoal suit was walking briskly through the snow in Central Park on his way up to the Metropolitan Museum of Art. Venturing out from the warmth of his thirtieth-floor Pierre Hotel suite overlooking the park, Fred Hayman was taking his weekly Sunday jaunt—no matter that it was mid-January in New York and he had chipped disks in his lower back. He was feeling energetic and, with his boyish dimples and unlined skin, hardly looked sixty-three. Fred was doing the thing entrepreneurs enjoy most, starting fresh, building a new business.

The Avon deal made Fred a multimillionaire. He bought a new home with a tennis court in Malibu to use while his original Point Dume house was being remodeled; but, far from spending all his wealth and time on his ocean-view retirement palace, Fred was spending heavily on his new endeavor.

He closed the old office at 9595 Wilshire and in early January 1988 moved his company, Fred Hayman Beverly Hills, Inc., into ten thousand square feet of office space in Don Tronstein's new building on Rodeo Drive. The building housed Rodeo's latest and most opulent new boutiques, Giorgio Armani and Ralph Lauren/Polo. Fred proudly conducted tours of the new offices, with a balcony overlooking Rodeo Drive and Beverly Hills. He invited friends to lunch in his private dining room, where he employed a corporate chef, replete with starched toque. The new digs were befitting Fred's unofficial standing as mayor of Rodeo Drive, a position he had maintained throughout his foray into the fragrance industry. The enlarged quarters also would accommodate additional staffers he was hiring for his new fragrance and leather lines.

The reason for Fred's trip to New York in mid-January was not merely to buy for the Giorgio boutique, but also to meet with executive recruiters to help find a chief financial officer for his new company. Fred had learned a lesson from his problems at Giorgio with Gale, Roth, Horner, and Gould. He was tired of looking over his shoulder for demons, be they real or imaginary; loyalty was the prerequisite for the new team. Both Fred and Gale had been angered by comments Horner and Roth had made to the press after the Avon deal about the history of their fragrance business and who was most responsible for its success. The Haymans felt Roth and Horner had inflated their importance and were trying to grab too much credit for Giorgio's success.

Fred and Katy Sweet wanted to set the record straight and in an interview with *WWD* on November 21, 1988, he claimed credit for all the Giorgio marketing innovations—direct mail, exclusive distribution, scent strips, and the in-store hoopla. "I must say that the entire marketing, whether you want to believe it or not, was totally Fred Hayman, all the way through. I can tell you right now, Jim and David were never brought in for marketing. They were brought in simply to implement a fragrance business," Fred said.

Roth and Horner did not agree with Fred's assessment. *WWD*'s Mike Marlow called Roth for a response and Horner commented, "I feel sorry for a guy who has to shoot down a couple of guys who helped him walk away from a business that went from five million dollars to one hundred sixty-five million. After participating in the greatest fragrance and outdoing Revson and Lauder he still couldn't be gracious enough to afford a modicum of credit for those involved."

Fred does not like to look back on the past, but allowed himself, on that January walk through Central Park, to reminisce about his Waldorf, Beverly Hilton, and early Giorgio years. He saved none of the elaborate menus from the Waldorf and Hilton heydays; the celebrity photo wall at Giorgio is Fred Hayman's scrapbook. He has made a career out of providing luxury service and products with flair. Capitalizing on his ability to pamper the public, he catered to the new American dream of the 1980s, when it went from merely owning a home in the suburbs to building an estate in Beverly Hills. Fred Hayman made his customers, from Biloxi to Bel-Air, feel rich and spoiled.

The success brought celebrity to Fred. Tourists would walk into the Giorgio store and ask for him. Although the store had become his main business after the Avon deal, Fred did not spend much time there—partially to avoid the autograph seekers. The media was interested in him now more as a personality than as an entrepreneur. *Millionaire* magazine did a full-page profile in February 1988, and the author, Mr. Blackwell, labeled Fred as a "visionary in fashion, a genius in merchandising, and a perfectionist. . . ." Fred also had become grist for the other end of the media mill. The *National Enquirer* featured Fred in its "Success without College" series on July 26, 1988. Less sycophantic than *Millionaire*, the *Enquirer* headlined its story, HIGH SCHOOL DROPOUT TURNS HIS FAILING STORE INTO $165-MILLION JACKPOT WITH GIORGIO PERFUME. The bitingly irreverent *Spy* magazine, in its first California issue in September 1988, listed Fred on its "Has-Beens" list along with celebrities Barry Manilow, Olivia Newton-John, Ed McMahon, and Robin Leach. Fred was the lone nonentertainment figure to make the dubious list.

While Giorgio's phenomenal success made Fred a personality, it also forced him to change the way he liked doing business, and this made him uncomfortable. His beloved boutique and small fragrance company were forced to grow faster than he would have liked. To take Giorgio beyond $100 million and challenge Lauder and Cosmair, Fred would have had to build an efficient, bureaucratic machine and delegate effectively. He did not have a corporate mentality; he loathed even small meetings. Fred's major regret with Giorgio was that he allowed Horner and later Gould to convince him to expand the fragrance beyond three hundred doors. "I preach all the time, 'Let's be the master of our destiny.' There are two ways of doing business, one with sheer volume, which can be very profitable, and the other is small volume, but great productivity, small overhead and greater control," he said.

There was no heir apparent on the Giorgio horizon. Robert Hayman would have been the obvious choice, but he was suffering "please my father" burnout and was not interested in working for Fred. After his stint at the Giorgio boutique in New York, Robert held various posts with Giorgio in London and in Santa Monica. He stayed at his marketing post after the Avon acquisition until March 4, 1988, when he left to start his own contemporary sportswear business. His vibrant Russian-theme T-shirts, called Red Square Wear, were prominently featured in the windows of his father's boutique in early 1989.

Charles continued to build his unusual art-transport business in New York, while Nicole was pursuing her singing career. Fred had hosted her coming-out party in June 1987, at a nightclub in Santa Monica. Barbara Sziraki and Betty Endo were among the guests applauding Nicole's renditions of "Night and Day," "Take a Chance," and "Mister Not So Nice Guy."

Fred underwent three hours of spinal surgery on January 26, 1988, and the chipped disks were successfully removed. Although unable to sit in a chair, much less get to the office, he made business calls from his hospital bed and held meetings at his Charleville home. The new business strategy was set and Fred was eager to implement it, whether standing or lying down per doctor's orders. The plan was to create new fragrances and prestige leather accessories for his about-to-be remodeled boutique. Fearing the dated store was on the verge of being called venerable, a word he hated, Fred revamped the store over the summer with new lighting, shelving, and dressing rooms. He had a new bar built, but the original pool table remained. After twenty-seven years, Giorgio was given a facelift.

Fred wanted the boutique to be contemporary when the Giorgio name came off the door. On January 1, 1989, 273 North Rodeo Drive officially became Fred Hayman Beverly Hills, and twelve days later the yellow-and-white stripes and Giorgio crest were replaced with bright solid yellow and a red Fred Hayman signature logo in Fred's own script. Fred's new gardenia dominated perfume, 273, replaced the Giorgio fragrance. The numbers had great meaning to Fred, "Two seventy-three is a famous address on a famous store on a famous street." He predicted 273 would be another blockbuster and planned to do $1 million in sales of the long-lasting scent the first year in just his boutique.

Fred held another gala party to kick off the new fragrance and celebrate the renaming of the store, this one even bigger and brassier than the original Giorgio bash. As more than nine hundred guests arrived at Universal Studios sound stage 24, they were serenaded by the University of Southern California Trojan marching band. Inside, on the cavernous *Phantom of the Opera* set, seventy-five mariachis, fifty pounds of Beluga caviar, six hundred forty-two yellow balloons, and food from six top chefs in Los Angeles awaited. Spago's Wolfgang Puck personally served his ginger lobster, but the crush of television cameras and spotlights was on Fred and his celebrity guests, Vanna White, Connie Selleca, Valerie Perrine, Charlton Heston, Maureen Reagan, Charles Bronson, and George Peppard. The night had its disappointments for Fred. His "good luck" charm and intended master of ceremonies, Merv Griffin, came down with the flu and Marilyn McCoo had to pinch hit. Michael Coady, Fred's friend and senior executive of Fairchild Publications, left the party early when he couldn't find a table, and Fred's photo was not among the eleven run by *Women's Wear Daily* in its coverage of the party. The party generated plenty of positive publicity; 273 reached $250,000 in sales during its first two months.

Fred planned to launch 273 at Saks Fifth Avenue in New York in September 1989. In addition to the scent, Fred is marketing a line of leather goods he hopes will be the first prestige American line to achieve the status of a Vuitton, Hermès, Gucci, Bottega Veneta, or Fendi. To that end, he hired several former Gucci sales and creative people and launched his leather handbags, wallets, and luggage in May 1989. If successful on Rodeo Drive, Fred will take the concept wholesale. However difficult the task, he wants the new venture to be another Giorgio-like success, "a breakthrough in exclusivity, something almost historical." This time, though, he will restrict distribution to only the best stores. His modus operandi will not change: start small, build exclusivity, create consumer demand, establish a classic, and make a lot of money along the way. Within two years of the leather line and fragrance introductions Fred wants the boutique's volume to increase from $13 million to $20 million. If the new items are successful he would like to open a small boutique in New York.

Gale Hayman's plans are more ambitious. She wants her fledgling business to become the premier cosmetics company of the 1990s. Cosmair's Lancôme had emerged to challenge Lauder for dominance of the U.S. market in the 1980s and Gale remains determined that she and her company will be the next major force in the industry. "I intend to be the breakthrough color company of the 1990s. Although this is a start-up company, it's an extension and mental continuation of the work I always did at Giorgio. I'm ambitious and I would like this to be a major company—not in ten years, but as quickly as I can with the proper planning," says Gale.

The millions from the Avon deal allowed Gale to pour assets into her new company and her wardrobe. She began to travel extensively and took a lavish new apartment in New York. Following the Avon deal she spent on average between $4,000 and $7,000 a month shopping at the best stores in New York and Los Angeles. At Bullocks Wilshire's Christian Lacroix fashion show in June 1988, Gale treated herself to a $4,200 short black double-breasted coatdress, an $800 leopard hat, and a $500 leopard belt. She kept her thirteen-year old red Mercedes, although she bought a second car, a Jeep, in late 1987. Escorted by Kenny Lane, she purchased a Chanel belt for $4,675 from Diana Vreeland's costume jewelry collection auctioned at Sotheby's in October 1987.

In the summer of 1988 Gale ended her ten-year relationship with Igor Stalew, and she started dating Kirk Douglas's son, Peter. The legal battle with Fred had taken its toll. "Being there, associated with a certain negative time in her life, obviously didn't help our relationship," Stalew said some months later. He and Gale remain friends. "I will always have a place in my heart for her."

Gale wanted to be a maverick in business. "I don't want to hear how it has been done in the past. I'm not interested. I want to break ground every time. That is exciting to me and keeps me interested in my business. I don't want to do it the typical cosmetics-industry way because I think that is antiquated. It's time for a change in an industry that has become dull and uncreative."

Posing in a Norma Kamali fake leopard coat and bright red gloves, Gale brazenly dominated the cover of her first mail-order catalogue, sent to over a million consumers in November 1987. The headline read, I GAVE THE FRAGRANCE, GIORGIO, TO THE WORLD. AND NOW HERE'S MY BEST MAKE-UP SECRET FOR YOU.

Gale feels she never received proper credit for the Giorgio fragrance. Her name is boldly emblazoned in giant letters on everything to do with her new company, from catalogues to stationery and mailing labels. Customers ordering by phone are instructed to call 1-800-FOR GALE. Having grown up without a father, in Fred Hayman she had found a mentor who ultimately stifled her. Now, with her ego still unsated, her creative juices unbridled, and her capital flowing, she is looking for recognition.

Gale hired and fired several publicists on both coasts within a twelve-month period following the Avon deal, but she got a lot of press. Mentions of Gale and her new line appeared in *Vogue, Glamour, The Hollywood Reporter, Bazaar, Woman's Day, Advertising Age, The New York Times* and *The New York Times Magazine, Los Angeles Times, Cosmopolitan, Self*, and *Forbes*, among others. *Los Angeles Magazine* in February 1989 proclaimed Gale L.A.'s most eligible woman. Press releases were created to chronicle almost every move she made. In October 1988, Gale went to the Paris collections for the first time in three years and publicist Philip Minges III of Solters Roskin and Friedman tried to make it news: COSMETICS ENTREPRENEUR GALE HAYMAN, CREATOR OF GIORGIO FRAGRANCE, CONCORDES TO PARIS TO VIEW SPRING COLLECTIONS OCT 20–24. Despite the effort, Solters Roskin no longer handles Gale Hayman.

Leopard, an endangered species, was Gale's passion. It covered her furniture at home and at work, to say nothing of her letterhead. When she told the packaging companies in New York that she wanted to imprint leopard spots on her metal lipstick bullets and plastic compacts, she was told it would be difficult; no cosmetics company had ever done a totally patterned cosmetics line. Gale challenged them to find a way. They did.

No major cosmetics company had ever tried to sell color entirely by mail, either. Cosmetics are impulse items and women like to try them on in a store before buying. Gale broke ground when she introduced seventeen mail-order cosmetics, including lipsticks, eyeshadows, eyeliners, and self-sharpening pencils. Most of the products were small to fit into a woman's handbag. Gale's concept was based on the customer's eye color. There were palettes for each of four groups, blue/gray, hazel green, brown, and dark brown. For evening, she offered rhinestone beauty marks, 14K Glitter Gel, and 14K gold powder highlighter. Gale saw these as fun flash, not trash. "The point is makeup should be fun. It shouldn't be frightening to women. They shouldn't be afraid to try a new color, and I have made it easy for them with my new system," she said.

The accessories portion of the line included a $45 leopard pin called Lucky, designed for Gale by Kenneth Jay Lane, along with matching leopard half-hoop earrings and leopard bangles. A $2,200 hand-jeweled leopard-print minaudière made by Judith Leiber was the most exclusive item in the collection and four were sold the first year. The pièce de résistance was a $4,500 Beverly Hills black lacquer dressing table complete with makeup lights and Ultrasuede leopard-print stool. Gale was thrilled to sell three tables and four stools in the first six months.

Sensing she needed a stronger executive to run the business side of the company, Gale fired Red Weiss and brought in Bob Ruttenberg as president for a six-month trial period early in 1988. Oil and water mix better than Gale and Ruttenberg, who bowed out when his six months were up. Ruttenberg was as bitter about working with Gale as Weiss had been. Gale, cavalierly saying, "If it isn't broken, why fix it?" decided she didn't need a president to help her run the company. Instead, she hired Randy Harrel, a thirty-five-year-old finance and operations executive from Merle Norman. He lasted a year before quitting, which left the company with fifteen employees, including one of the "girls" who had worked with Gale on the sales floor at Giorgio, Claudette Calzada. Gwen Lavery, the other former Giorgio sales associate who switched ranks, remained with Gale for about a year.

Reportedly, the response to Gale's first catalogue had been around .6 percent, a decent mail-order result, generating around $500,000 in business. The second major catalogue was mailed in September 1988. Without a Fred Hayman, a Jim Roth, or even a Red Weiss to temper her, Gale went wild. There were more leopard spots in her line than on the plains of the Serengeti or in the San Diego Zoo. The line now included leopard raincoats, pens, headbands, jeweled headscarves to double as bandeau tops, leopard "movie star" sunglasses, umbrellas, silk suspenders, watches, and traveling alarm clocks. Gale was featured on the cover in a black sleeveless Chanel dress in front of a palatial Beverly Hills estate with the quote, "I gave the world GIORGIO perfume. . . . But that was only the beginning! Now—I bring you Beverly Hills GLAMOUR GUARANTEED!" By November, for the cover of the Christmas catalogue, she was decked out in leopard knee-high boots and gloves, sporting a green faux gorilla mini-coat. Posed next to Santa Claus in a red Porsche convertible overflowing with leopard-wrapped packages, Gale proclaimed "Now, do all your Christmas shopping in Beverly Hills without ever leaving your home—from the woman who brought you Giorgio."

Glamour Guaranteed was the title of the thirty-minute video explaining Gale's philosophy of makeup. Director William Friedkin (*The Exorcist, The French Connection*, and husband of her friend, anchorwoman Kelly Lange) produced and directed the video, filming Gale at several L.A. status landmarks. The video debuted on cable television stations in the fall of 1988.

Gale made her return to retailing on September 25, 1988, when her line was introduced at Nordstrom's West Los Angeles store. Nordstrom South Coast Plaza and San Francisco also carried the line in time for the 1988 Christmas season. It was off to a good start, averaging $1,000 a day per door in the first few weeks and settling in at $25,000 per door per month in early 1989. The mail orders had slowed to a trickle by March 1989. Gale had invested over $7 million in the business but had generated less than $2 million in sales. The New York launch of Gale Hayman cosmetics was scheduled for October 1989.

Giorgio, under Avon, operated similarly to other major fragrance companies. Richard Recker, an industry pro, was in charge of building a sales force. He deployed visual display and training people across the country. Gould, with his cadre of former Robinson's executives, was still thinking retail and planned to open a Giorgio boutique in 1990 on Rodeo Drive directly across from Fred's store.

The original Giorgio women's fragrance business failed to regain its momentum, but with domestic distribution going over a thousand doors and stepped-up international distribution, the company's volume remained over $100 million in 1988. Profitability (as a percentage of sales), however, was well below the 1985 levels set when Fred, Gale, Roth, and Horner were running the business.

The second Giorgio fragrance, which the company needed in 1986, finally was launched at Robinson's and Saks Fifth Avenue in January 1989. Called Red, the scent was chosen by Gould after many months of agonizing. Avon acquired the name, originally given to an unsuccessful Geoffrey Beene fragrance in 1976, from Sanofi Beauty Products for $85,000. Gould said choosing the scent was the toughest decision he had ever made in his business career because the company's future was riding on it. Avon invested millions of advertising dollars in Red, using between ten and fifteen million ScentStrips in fourteen magazines during the two-month launch period, far more than were used in any two-month period for Giorgio. Gould's marketing team used an innovative though expensive vehicle to get Red into the hands of consumers. Their mailing of thousands of oversize sample vials to a list of credit-card customers and socialites brought women into the stores to buy the softer-smelling Red.

Gould set a first-year sales goal of $25 million in only six hundred doors, but when the fragrance hit $6.5 million in two months in three hundred seventy-two doors, he revised the projections upward and called Red the most successful launch in the industry's history. Gould claimed in a Giorgio press release that Red made Giorgio, Inc., the first company in fragrance history to launch back-to-back phenomenons.

Now competitors, Gould and Hayman were not on speaking terms. Gould was furious when Fred started a national magazine advertising campaign in March, 1988, depicting the Giorgio yellow-and-white striped shopping bag alongside the new all-yellow Fred Hayman bag with the headline, AFTER 27 YEARS WE'VE CHANGED FROM STRIPES TO SOLIDS.

Giorgio filed a trademark-infringement/false-advertising suit against Fred in federal court on March 13, 1989, trying to prevent Fred from continuing to run the ad. Giorgio's attorney asserted the ad made it appear as if Giorgio were out of business, creating confusion among consumers. A federal judge forced Fred to change the ad's headline to read, FRED HAYMAN HAS SOLD GIORGIO AND HAS CHANGED FROM STRIPES TO SOL-IDS.

Fred was shocked by the lawsuit and said in part, "To intimate that I or any member of my company would in any way consciously or otherwise, attempt to create confusion, denigrate or undermine a company which I built and operated with the utmost love and devotion for twenty-seven years, is both shocking and hurtful." Fred added that 273 was doing triple the volume that Giorgio did in the Rodeo Drive boutique when it launched in December 1981.

Giorgio planned to return to Rodeo Drive in September 1989 with a boutique at, ironically, 327 Rodeo Drive; but the store would not have a pool table, bar, or celebrity photos.

Roth and Horner, under contract to Caesars World Merchandising, Inc., a division of the publicly owned resort-and-casino company, introduced their Caesars fragrances with all the fanfare of a Roman bacchanal. After a Las Vegas launch party at Caesars Palace in December 1987, toga-clad models were carried in sedan chairs by bulging centurions through shopping malls in Los Angeles and into Macy's Herald Square during the fall 1988 launch season. The fragrances failed to equal Giorgio's launch figures, but at some smaller stores, such as Renberg's, the fragrances were among the top five.

Roth was concerned about maintaining a friendship with Fred and feared possible litigation over comments he and Horner had been making in the press. The issue of who was responsible for the Giorgio success still dogs them. Roth believes the success of Giorgio was achieved because of the combined talents of all four, and he is right. If Fred or Gale had embarked on his or her own in 1981, it is doubtful Giorgio would have reached such heights. They needed a third party with cosmetics expertise. Roth and Horner, on the other hand, so desperately needed the Haymans' concept and capital they made an effort most cosmetics executives never would have considered.

David Horner gave Jim Roth a commemorative gift. Placed on Roth's desk between photos of his new multimillion-dollar home in Sherman Oaks and his fifty-three-foot yacht is a small plaque that Roth reads every time he thinks about the Giorgio days and why things went right and then wrong. The little sign puts the saga into perspective: THERE IS NO LIMIT TO WHAT A MAN CAN DO OR WHERE HE CAN GO, IF HE DOESN'T MIND WHO GETS THE CREDIT.